Human Information Processing in Accounting

Robert H. Ashton
New York University

AMERICAN ACCOUNTING ASSOCIATION

The By-Laws of the American Accounting Association state that the first purpose of the Association shall be "To initiate, encourage, and sponsor research in accounting and to publish or aid in the publication of the results of research." In harmony with this objective, the publication of the Studies in Accounting Research is aimed at encouraging and publishing research. This series is an outgrowth of the research program initiated by the Association in 1965. Under this program, research projects and authors are selected by the Director of Research, who is assisted by a Research Advisory Committee.

When the project is commissioned, the author is allowed maximum freedom in conducting research. The author is solely responsible for the procedures followed and the research conclusions. An Editorial Consulting Committee is appointed for each project. Members of this Committee are expected to suggest ideas and offer comments on the scope of the project, the methodology, and the researcher's findings. They are not empowered to block publication, nor may they insert dissents in the final report; they are advisory only. The Editorial Consulting Committee for this project was:

G. Richard Chesley	Dalhousie University
Hillel Einhorn	University of Chicago
Thomas Hofstedt	Southern Methodist University
Michael J. Barrett	The University of Illinois-Chicago Circle
Thomas H. Williams	University of Wisconsin-Madison
Gerald A. Feltham	University of British Columbia

This project was commissioned by Thomas R. Dyckman (Cornell University) when he was Director of Research. The Research Advisory Committee at that time consisted of Russell M. Barefield (University of Arizona), Robert E. Jensen (Florida State University) and Robert S. Kaplan (Carnegie-Mellon University).

Library of Congress Catalog Number: 81-70856
ISBN 0-86539-038-X
Printed in the United States of America

American Accounting Association
5717 Bessie Drive
Sarasota, Florida 33583

Contents

Part 2. The SEU Paradigm

Part 3. Relation to Accounting

Preface

The relationship between accounting and decision making has led to much interest in understanding the decision activities of accountants, auditors and users of accounting information. A body of research that focuses on such activities, known as human information processing research, has grown rapidly in accounting over the past ten years. The ultimate goal of human information processing research in accounting is to improve decision making. Before decision making can be improved, however, it is useful to evaluate the current quality of decision making, and before decision quality can be evaluated, decision making must be understood. Human information processing research in accounting focuses on the understanding, evaluation and improvement of decision making as it relates to accounting.

This book is devoted to the human information processing research conducted to date in accounting. It describes the history of, and the rationale for, human information processing research, and the relationship of this research to other perspectives within which accounting research is conducted. The book describes in detail the two major paradigms that have guided this type of research, and it reviews the existing studies through the middle of 1981.

The book provides substantial background in the research methods used, and the results generated, by cognitive psychologists in their efforts to understand human decision making. This emphasis reflects my belief that producers and, to some extent, consumers of human information processing research in accounting must be exposed to the research methods and content that comprise this more "basic" discipline before the research in accounting can be fully appreciated.

As a result of its emphasis on research issues, methods and results, this book is appropriate for readers who currently are doing, or who anticipate doing, research in human information processing, and for readers who want an in-depth review of this research. Readers seeking a broader overview of accounting applications of the research will find a recent book by Libby [1981] very useful. Two books by psychologists — Hogarth [1980] and Nisbett and Ross [1980] — may also be of interest to some readers.

After an introductory chapter, the book is divided into three parts. The first two parts present the two major paradigms of human information processing research in accounting — the lens and subjectively expected utility (SEU) paradigms. Part 3 discusses the use of these paradigms in accounting and auditing contexts. Part 1 is devoted to the lens paradigm: A framework and some related methodologies for judgment modeling research are discussed in Chapter 2; the two principal topics of judgment modeling research, judgment accuracy and judgment agreement, are covered in Chapter 3. Part 2 concerns the SEU paradigm: Chapter 4 discusses several models of risky decision making, while Chapter 5 focuses on the narrower area of probability assessment and revision. Part 3 consists of a general discussion of the role of human information processing research in accounting and its relationship to other types of accounting research (Chapter 6), a review of lens and SEU studies in accounting (Chapters 7 and 8), and some observations on recent trends, generalizations and other issues in human information processing research in accounting (Chapter 9). Further comments on the organization of the book and the topics covered in each chapter are provided at the end of the first chapter.

Acknowledgments

Without implicating him in any way, I wish to acknowledge the influence of Carl Devine, Professor Emeritus at Florida State University, on my appreciation for academic pursuits. I am often reminded of the scholarly example he has set and the gentle encouragement he gave me during my brief association with him when I was an MBA student.

I am indebted to several people for specific contributions to this project. Tom Dyckman commissioned the project, and Rashad Abdel-khalik coordinated the review process and made useful comments on the manuscript. The first draft of the manuscript was completed while I was an Audit Research Fellow in the executive office of Peat, Marwick, Mitchell & Co. Peat's Audit Research Group — under the leadership of Cliff Graese, Bob Elliott, and John Willingham — provided a supportive environment for this and other research projects, and I am grateful for that support. I am also grateful to the members of my Project Consulting Committee. Mike Barrett, Dick Chesley, Hilly Einhorn and Tom Williams reviewed the manuscript and responded with many comments and criticisms. The substantive and detailed comments provided by Tom Williams were particularly helpful to me.

My greatest debt is to Alison Hubbard Ashton, who has shared the intellectual and personal strain of this project for more than four years and has made major contributions to the resolution of both. Her critical academic contributions were complemented by encouragement and support which enabled me to take advantage of her ideas. Because of her contributions, I dedicate this book to her.

CHAPTER ONE

Introduction

The relationship between accounting and decision making dominates contemporary accounting research. This relationship takes many forms. Accountants supply information to decision makers within organizations for use in operating, financing, and performance-evaluation decisions. They supply information to external parties for use in investment portfolio, credit granting and other types of decisions. Accountants themselves make decisions about which information to produce and supply via their choices among alternative information systems. Independent auditors make a broad range of judgments and decisions when performing an audit and reporting its results.

A substantial amount of research on judgment and decision making in accounting contexts has been conducted. The most extensive and important part of this work is known as human information processing research. The goals of this research involve understanding, evaluating, and improving decision making as it relates to accounting.

Human information processing research in accounting is introduced in this chapter by providing some historical perspective on the broader area of behavioral accounting research. The emergence of behavioral accounting research, the predominance of studies relating to decision making and budgeting/control systems, and two significant problems of "early" behavioral accounting research are considered. Then, two important paradigms of human information processing research, which overcome these two problems to a great extent, are briefly described. Finally, the scope and organization of this book are explained.

1.1 HISTORICAL PERSPECTIVE

Knowing the history of a discipline can be very useful in terms of understanding and interpreting the current status of that discipline. One problem in attempting to communicate history is that the account is influenced by the particular viewpoint adopted by the reporter. Another problem is that historical reports tend to make the events and trends of the past appear more orderly and purposeful than was actually the case when those events and trends unfolded. Subject to these problems, however, historical information can be instructive. Therefore, this section offers a brief historical perspective on the subject matter of this book.

1.1.1 Behavioral Accounting Research

Human information processing research in accounting is a subset of behavioral accounting research. While the origins of behavioral accounting research can be traced at least to the early 1950s, few empirical or experimental studies appeared before the middle 1960s. Two monographs on budgeting and management control systems, both written by nonaccountants, were published in the 1950s [Argyris, 1952; Simon, Guetzkow, Kozmetsky, and Tyndall, 1954]. Within a few years, these works were considered major contributions to the "human side" of accounting, although some dissenters to this view existed (see, e.g., Anthony's [1960] critique of Argyris' work).

Carl Devine is recognized as the first accounting researcher to emphasize behavioral aspects of accounting. In one of his published papers, Devine [1960] introduced his concern for behavioral issues in this way (p. 394):

> Let us now turn to that part of accounting which is related directly to the psychological reactions of those who consume accounting output or are caught in its threads of control. On balance it seems fair to conclude that accountants seem to have waded through their relationships to the intricate psychological network of human activity with a heavy-handed crudity that is beyond belief. Some degree of crudity may be excused in a new discipline, but failure to recognize that much of what passes as accounting theory is hopelessly entwined with unsupported behavior assumptions is unforgiveable.

Devine mentioned several behavioral issues that typically were ignored by accountants, as well as some research methods that might be useful for investigating behavioral aspects of accounting. In addition, Devine's concern for behavioral issues is evident throughout many of his privately-distributed essays. For example, in "Some Behavioral Aspects of Accounting" [1962], he recognized some potential implications for accounting of the work of the psychologist Egon Brunswik. At that time, Brunswik's work was just beginning to be appreciated in psychology, and several years later it would serve as a paradigm for human information processing research in accounting.

The popularity of behavioral accounting research increased from the middle 1960s to the early 1970s, and the area seemed to include a potpourri of research topics. The two major topics were the impact of budgets and management control systems on the attitudes and performance of individuals who were subject to their control, and the impact of accounting information on the decision-making behavior of internal and external users. Two other topics that often were considered part of behavioral accounting were human resource accounting and social responsibility accounting. Some of the research in these two areas concerned the impact of human resource or social responsibility information on decision making, and might be considered a subset of the decision-making studies mentioned above. Still other topics that were considered by some to constitute behavioral accounting research were sociological and socio-psychological aspects of working in public accounting firms, turnover in public accounting firms, personality characteristics of accountants and users of accounting information, and almost any accounting-related issue for which individuals' attitudes or opinions were sought.

During the late 1960s and early 1970s, some accounting researchers wanted to "provide direction" and "establish boundaries" for behavioral accounting research. This desire is typified by a 1970 article by Hofstedt and Kinard, who advocated "an overall strategy for approaching future research and a means whereby topics and methods may be selected . . . ." (p. 39). While some observers found this to be a "galling" suggestion [Green, 1973, p. 103], it was not without some supporters because of the proliferation of research topics and methods that were considered part of behavioral accounting research. A related impetus for providing direction for behavioral accounting research was the "real world" orientation of such research. Many observers wanted to see this orientation strengthened further by increasing the external validity of behavioral accounting studies. They were especially concerned that behavioral accounting research have practical implications, and the way to insure this was thought to be to emphasize "realistic" research issues and situations. This emphasis was accompanied by a disdain for laboratory experiments and for using student subjects as decision makers.

An integral part of the concern for establishing boundaries was the effort to define behavioral accounting research. The AAA Committee on Behavioral Science Content of the Accounting Curriculum [1971] approached this task by first attempting to define behavioral science. The Committee argued that research had to satisfy two criteria to be part of behavioral science: "First, it must ultimately deal with human behavior . . . . Second, the research must be accomplished in a 'scientific manner' " (p. 248). The importance of *science* in behavioral science was elaborated by the Committee (p. 248):

> The differences between the deliberate research activities of the behavioral scientist and the casual observations and conclusions of the sophisticated layman are mainly matters of procedure or method. They have to do with how clearly and precisely a person formulates his concepts, how carefully and systematically he makes and records observations, and how rigorously he reasons from data to conclusions.
>
> The objective of behavioral science is to understand, explain and predict human behavior; that is, to establish generalizations about human behavior that are supported by empirical evidence collected in an impersonal way by procedures that are completely open to review and replication and capable of verification by other interested scholars.

Hofstedt and Kinard [1970] approached the definition issue more directly. They defined behavioral accounting research as " . . . the study of the behavior of accountants or the behavior of nonaccountants as they are influenced by accounting functions and reports" (p. 43). According to this definition, behavioral accounting research encompassed three areas — the behavior of accountants, the influence of the accounting function on behavior, and the influence of accounting information on those receiving that information. While Hofstedt and Kinard discussed all three areas, most of their attention was devoted to the third.

In contrast to Hofstedt and Kinard and the 1971 Committee, later writers contended that trying to define behavioral accounting research was not likely to be productive. For example, Bruns [1973, p. 124] maintained that "the question of how broadly behavioral accounting should be defined will have to be solved on an ad hoc basis by each researcher." Similarly, the AAA Committee on the Relationship of Behavioral Science to Accounting [1974, p. 127] argued that "it seems improper to worry very much about the 'correct' boundaries; they will evolve and be refined without help from writers of editorials or committee reports."

The extent to which editorials influenced behavioral accounting research is difficult to determine. However, the discipline did begin to assume certain characteristics. Hofstedt's 1975 survey found that the great majority of behavioral accounting studies that appeared in three "academic" journals over the period 1964 to 1975 was devoted to two areas: decision making and budgeting/control systems. More than half the 90 articles he identified concerned the impact of accounting information on decision making. Hofstedt's "crude definition" (p. 28) of behavioral accounting research excluded "nominally behavioral topics which bear only a tenuous link with a more fundamental social science — e.g., human resource accounting and social cost accounting; and . . . behavioral studies of accountants *qua* accountants — e.g., studies of the causes of turnover in CPA firms." It also excluded attitude and opinion surveys. The predominance in the literature of studies concerning the use of accounting information in decision making continued throughout the 1970s.

While research activity in behavioral accounting increased substantially during the time period covered by Hofstedt's survey, several observers began to voice reservations about this type of research. Two related problems became apparent. One was what the 1974 Committee called the quality control problem: " . . . as behavioral accounting has evolved, anything behavioral has been considered 'good.' Empirical behaviorism, however theory-free or ill-conceived, has been an almost sure ticket to success in accounting circles" (p. 130). The Committee argued that

> . . . we can no longer justify slipshod work by "relevance" or "applicability to *real* problems." The word slipshod is used advisedly. Our behavioral research is simply not conducted in accordance with the standards required of *applied* behavioral research in other areas. (p. 130)

The quality control problem arose, in part, because of insufficient knowledge of behavioral research methodologies — by those who attempted to do behavioral accounting research and those who evaluated it. The 1971 Committee's emphasis on the *science* in behavioral science had not been heeded by many academic accountants.

Insufficient knowledge of the *content* of behavioral science — in addition to the methodologies — also contributed to the quality control problem. A definitional rule-of-thumb appeared to be: If it's not "quantitative," then it must be "behavioral." While few researchers would have attempted quantitative research in accounting without thorough preparation, lack of preparation was seldom considered an obstacle for doing behavioral research. Knowledge of statistics and experimental design often was mistaken for knowledge of behavioral science. Inadequate preparation in the methodologies and content of behavioral science was detrimental to the development and acceptance of behavioral accounting research.

The other problem that plagued behavioral accounting research during the 1960s and early 1970s was the lack of theoretical frameworks to guide the research efforts. Some have referred to this problem as the lack of formal models. Without some type(s) of theory(ies) or model(s), each behavioral accounting study stood alone. Hypothesis formulation was precarious. It was difficult to anticipate the effects of independent variables or to know which variables to control in a particular study. The results of different studies were difficult to integrate.

Several observers commented on the lack of theoretical frameworks in behavioral accounting research. The 1974 Committee observed that " . . . too much of behavioral accounting research has consisted of hunting and tracking something without knowing what it was . . . [B]ehavioral accounting research has too much empirical data and too few formal models. Adding further empirical data to the existing, unrelated mountain of bits of information will not help progress toward a science of behavioral accounting, and may in fact actually hinder such progress" (p. 135). Hofstedt [1975] was particularly adamant: "[Behavioral accounting research] still suffers from a dearth of experimental controls, lack of replication and, most vital, from a near-complete detachment from any theory which would enable one to generalize beyond the immediate experiment" (p. 40). "[Behavioral accounting research] did not seem to do much to exploit the vast and rich intellectual heritage of the underlying social sciences . . . ." (p. 30).

These criticisms were directed toward the entire area of behavioral accounting research. Other observers offered similar critiques of the subset of studies dealing with the use of accounting information in decision making. The lack of a theory of users' information processing behavior was emphasized by Birnberg [1973]: " . . . we lack at least a tentative theory of how accounting information is processed by users. Such a theory once developed would permit the generation of new studies. These studies could explore the implications of the theory and investigate inconsistencies between the model and isolated studies" (p. 130). Dyckman, Gibbins, and Swieringa [1978] made a similar point in 1975:[1] "First and foremost, some theory, some model of the decision process is needed to support the empirical results found and to suggest reasonable and useful research projects . . . . Whether such a theory is developed from psychology (information-processing models, conflict and dissonance theory, attitude formation and change models) or from economics (information economics, market choice and marginal analysis, capital asset pricing) is not the critical issue. Indeed, separate theories may all prove productive" (p. 89).

Probably the harshest critique of decision-making studies at the individual level was that of Gonedes and Dopuch:

> . . . we would argue that if a researcher has no conceptual framework or perspective (however tentative) bearing on what he is investigating and if he has no ideas (however tentative) on the linkage(s) between his specific project and his ultimate object(s) of analysis, then he ought not to be doing his "research" until those issues have been attacked. Otherwise, he can hardly claim that he is dealing with a simplified model because he has no perspective on what it is that he is simplifying. Indeed, if he is in this position it is not clear that he can even design an experiment [1974b, p. 167].

Writers who wanted more theory in behavioral accounting research seemed to be calling for "middle-range" theories instead of one all-encompassing theory of

---

[1] This paper was widely available in 1975, although a publication lag delayed its publication until 1978.

behavior.[2] In addition, they seemed to recognize that relevant behavioral theories were beginning to emerge. Gonedes and Dopuch referred optimistically to emerging theories of human judgment:

> . . . with specific reference to the lab/field studies, it is important to note that substantial theoretical building blocks can be found in the behavioral literature. This is especially the case in the area of human judgment and human information usage [1974b, pp. 167-68].

1.1.2 Human Information Processing Research

The "substantial theoretical building blocks . . . in the area of human judgment and human information usage" referred to by Gonedes and Dopuch had been discovered by a small number of accounting researchers in the early 1970s. Much of the research in this area had been guided by two paradigms — the lens paradigm and the subjectively expected utility (SEU) paradigm.

Briefly, the lens paradigm emphasizes the construction of linear models as representations of the information-processing activities of decision makers. It further emphasizes the accuracy of intuitive decisions relative to those prescribed by formal models, the extent to which the intuitive decisions of expert decision makers agree, and several means of improving both accuracy and agreement. The SEU paradigm, like the lens paradigm, also entails decision modeling and it, too, emphasizes the relationship between intuitive decisions and those prescribed by formal models. In addition, the SEU paradigm explicitly focuses on the assessment, revision, and use of probabilities in decision making.

The lens paradigm is a product of the Brunswikian tradition in psychology (see, e.g., Brunswik [1943, 1952, 1955, 1956]). Brunswik's work was made more accessible to researchers through the efforts of Hammond [1955, 1966], and significant methodological contributions were made by Hammond, Hursch, and Todd [1964] and Hursch, Hammond, and Hursch [1964].[3] The roots of the SEU paradigm are in economics and statistics as well as psychology (e.g., Ramsey [1931], Savage [1954], Simon [1955], Edwards, Lindman, and Savage [1963]). An excellent historical account of the SEU paradigm has been provided by Edwards [1954c]. Comprehensive reviews and analyses of the research conducted within both the lens and SEU paradigms have been written by Edwards [1961], Becker and McClintock [1967], Slovic and Lichtenstein [1971], Rapoport and Wallsten [1972], Nickerson and Feehrer [1975], Slovic, Fischhoff, and Lichtenstein [1977], and Einhorn and Hogarth [1981].

The lens and SEU approaches to the study of human information processing may be considered paradigms in the sense that they " . . . define the legitimate problems and methods of a research field . . . , [have] attract[ed] an enduring group of adherents away from competing modes of scientific activity [and are]

---

[2] For elaboration on middle-range theories, see Merton [1967] in sociology, Weick [1974] in organization theory, and Becker [1969] and Caplan [1972] in accounting.

[3] The lens paradigm was introduced in accounting by the AAA Committee on Accounting Valuation Bases [1972].

sufficiently open-ended to leave all sorts of problems for the redefined group of practitioners to resolve'' [Kuhn, 1962, p. 10]. If, like Reynolds [1971, Chapter 2], one makes distinctions among Kuhn paradigms, paradigms, and paradigm variations, then the lens and SEU approaches would likely occupy one of the latter two categories. According to Reynolds, Kuhn paradigms entail radically new conceptualizations, or "world views," of phenomena associated with the paradigm, as well as dramatic new research methodologies or strategies; paradigms represent definite shifts in orientation, but less than "scientific revolutions"; paradigm variations involve refinements of details or variations in emphasis within a Kuhn paradigm or paradigm. Reynolds maintains that most theories or orientations in the social sciences can be considered paradigms, and he offers utility theory and information-processing models of cognition as examples. Another view would hold that these two examples (and, similarly, the lens and SEU approaches) are variations on a single paradigm.

Relying on well-developed paradigms for conceptual and methodological guidance offers substantial advantages for behavioral decision making research in accounting. The two major problems of earlier behavioral accounting research — the lack of theoretical frameworks and inadequate quality control — have been alleviated to a significant extent, in the area of human information processing research, by the introduction of the lens and SEU paradigms. In addition, two important corollaries to the introduction of these paradigms are (1) a retreat from the overriding devotion to external validity and an increased emphasis on the internal validity of behavioral decision making research in accounting,[4] and (2) a recognition that some form of training in the methodologies and content of behavioral science is essential for high-quality behavioral decision making research in accounting.

1.2 SCOPE OF THIS BOOK

Both the lens and SEU paradigms of human information processing research are covered in this book. These paradigms have several desirable features that make them useful for research in accounting and auditing. Both paradigms involve rigorous methodologies that can be applied to a broad range of accounting- and auditing-related research questions. These methodologies enable the researcher to investigate *how* information is used in decision making. In many cases, they also enable the researcher to evaluate *how well* information is used. Moreover, each of the paradigms entails prescriptions for improving decision making, and they provide criteria for evaluating decision improvement. The lens and SEU paradigms underlie a vast empirical literature in psychology. Finally, a "critical mass" of research results based on these paradigms is beginning to form in accounting and auditing contexts. A critical mass of findings is important for drawing conclusions or generalizations about human information processing in accounting and auditing.

[4] Campbell and Stanley [1963] provide an excellent discussion of internal and external validity.

Other perspectives on decision making in psychology and accounting are excluded from this book. In psychology, for example, some research has been conducted in multistage, or dynamic, decision making. Rapoport [1975] describes multistage decision settings as those in which " . . . decisions are made sequentially in time; the task specifications may change over time, either independently or as a result of previous decisions; information available for later decisions may be contingent upon the outcomes of earlier decisions; and implications of any decision may reach into the future" (p. 345). Obviously, many decisions in accounting and auditing fit this description. Rapoport and Wallsten [1972] and Slovic, Fischhoff, and Lichtenstein [1977] review multistage decision research, and the latter discuss some possible reasons for the paucity of recent work in this area. Hogarth [1979] provides additional discussion. Only the more typical single-stage applications of the lens and SEU paradigms are discussed here.

Another omitted area is that of information search, which involves the gathering of information to be used in decision making. One type of information-search research concerns the intuitive sampling behavior of individuals and its relationship to optimal sampling. This literature appears to be relevant for certain accounting and auditing applications. Slovic and Lichtenstein [1971] and Slovic, Fischhoff, and Lichtenstein [1977] provide several references in this area. Another type of information-search study, which often relies on a research technique known as "verbal protocol analysis," is discussed in the final chapter.

Research on multistage decision making and information search has seldom appeared in the accounting literature. As noted earlier, however, several accounting-related studies of decision making that do not rely on the lens or SEU paradigm have been reported. This work was initiated by Dyckman [1964a, 1964b, 1966], Bruns [1965, 1966], and Jensen [1966], and it continues today. Summaries and reviews of various portions of this literature are available (e.g., Becker [1969], Gonedes and Dopuch [1974a], Hofstedt [1975]). The omission of this research from the present book does not imply that it produced no benefits. To a great extent this "early" research sparked the interest of other accounting researchers in the behavioral aspects of decision making. Moreover, some of the early contributors were later good critics of the earlier research (including, in some cases, their own studies), and some of these researchers have made significant contributions to human information processing research in accounting. In these ways, the early behavioral decision-making researchers made, and continue to make, substantial contributions to the decision-making branch of behavioral accounting research.

Finally, studies that have examined the relationship between human information processing or decision making and personality characteristics of individuals are excluded from this book. One area affected by this exclusion is that of cognitive styles and cognitive complexity, which emerged from the work of Schroder, Driver, and Streufert [1967].[5] The general approach of studies in this

[5] Experimental studies have been published in accounting by Dermer [1973], Driver and Mock [1975], McGhee, Shields, and Birnberg [1978], Mock, Estrin, and Vasarhelyi [1972], San Miguel [1977], Savich [1977] and Vasarhelyi [1977]. Several nonempirical discussions (e.g., Revsine [1970a, 1970b], Miller [1972], Wilson [1973]) have also appeared.

area is to classify decision makers according to cognitive differences of some type, and to investigate the relationships between these differences and several decision-oriented variables. The ultimate goal of this research is designing information systems that are consistent with cognitive characteristics of decision makers or, alternatively, selecting decision makers who possess the cognitive characteristics best suited to a given information system. The former is emphasized.

This research has been criticized on several grounds, including the nature, measurement, and generality of the underlying constructs, the frequent failure to establish a link between the variables studied and measures of decision performance, and the absence of adequate criteria for evaluating decision quality. The AAA Committee on Human Information Processing [1977] elaborates on these and other problems. Libby and Lewis [1977, 1981] discuss the conflicting results generated by such studies; a critical mass of findings does not appear to be emerging in this area. Other observers (e.g., Hofstedt and Kinard [1970], McGhee, Shields, and Birnberg [1978]) have questioned the implementation potential of personality research in accounting, and McGhee, Shields, and Birnberg [1978] reached a pessimistic conclusion about the relationship between personality variables and human information processing. Based on a review of some literature in psychology and their own lens-paradigm study that investigated decision styles and tolerance for ambiguity, these researchers concluded that ". . . personality variables do not appear to be useful in describing, understanding, or predicting human information processing" (pp. 695-96).

1.3 ORGANIZATION OF THIS BOOK

The remainder of this book is divided into eight chapters. Chapters Two through Five explain the use of the lens and SEU paradigms in human information processing research generally, and do not address accounting issues *per se*. Chapters Six through Nine are devoted to human information processing research in accounting.

The material in Chapters Two through Five is presented first because accounting research in the human information processing area is guided by perspectives from the field of cognitive psychology at least as strongly as it is guided by perspectives from the field of accounting. Accounting researchers in this area, as well as readers wanting a thorough appreciation of the research in accounting, need substantial familiarity with the relevant psychological research perspectives in order to understand fully human information processing research in accounting. Thus, Chapters Two through Five focus on the perspectives, research methods, and representative results from human information processing research in psychology.

Chapters Two and Three are devoted to the lens paradigm. The use of the lens paradigm in studies of judgment and prediction, along with alternative ways of operationalizing the paradigm for the purposes of judgment modeling, are considered in Chapter Two. The two principal topics of judgment modeling research — judgment accuracy and judgment agreement — are discussed in Chapter Three.

The SEU paradigm is the topic of Chapters Four and Five. Several approaches to modeling choices among alternatives are described in Chapter Four. These include approaches that rely on the normative SEU model, as well as descriptive models that do not assume expected utility maximization. Chapter Five focuses on the narrower area of assessing and revising probabilities, and the use of probabilistic information in choice.

After the research perspectives associated with the lens and SEU paradigms are described, Chapters Six through Nine focus on the accounting research that has been guided by these paradigms. Chapter Six consists of a general discussion of the role of human information processing research in accounting and its relationship to some other perspectives within which accounting research is conducted, including the information economics and aggregate market perspectives. Chapters Seven and Eight review lens and SEU studies in accounting and auditing, and some summary comments on these studies are offered. The final chapter provides more general commentary on human information processing research in accounting, including remarks on recent research trends and the relationship of human information processing research to real-world decision making.

Part I

The Lens Paradigm

CHAPTER TWO

Judgment Modeling

Judgment modeling is concerned with individuals' utilization of information when they make judgments about the current state, or predictions about some future state, of a variable of interest. The research that has addressed this issue has been concerned with the questions of how individuals utilize information, how well they utilize it, and how such utilization might be improved. The techniques for studying these issues, as well as the related research findings, come primarily from the literature of cognitive psychology, although a growing amount of research is now being conducted in more applied fields such as accounting and auditing, management, medical diagnosis, and judicial decision making.

One of the primary concerns of information utilization research is that of "capturing" the judgment or prediction policy (or strategy) of the individual. This typically is done in an experimental setting that provides the individual with various combinations of values on each of several variables that are to be used for judgment or prediction purposes. The individual makes a judgment based on each combination of values presented, and various mathematical and statistical techniques are used to infer the individuals' judgment policy from the relationships among the variables and the resulting judgments. This approach has been referred to as a "black box" research strategy (e.g., Hayes [1968]).

It is important to recognize that judgment policies captured in this way are intended to *represent* the relationships among inputs and outputs. They are not intended to explain the "actual" mode of information processing used to form judgments. Hoffman [1960] refers to such modeling as "paramorphic" representation.[1] An example (from Hoffman [1960]) many clarify this point. The mathematical expressions $X+Y$ and $+\sqrt{X^2 + Y^2 + 2XY}$ are equivalent representations of an individual's judgment policy; i.e., the two expressions would simulate the individual's judgments equally well. However, paramorphic judgment modeling provides no basis for claiming that the individual is "using" one expression to formulate judgments rather than the other. Of course, the individual might not be "using" either expression.

---

[1] Hoffman borrowed the term paramorphic from mineralogy, where it is used to describe a substance having crystalline structural properties that differ from those of another substance with the identical chemical composition. Just as a chemical description of a mineral "explains" many, but not all, properties of the substance, a mathematical description of judgment is an incomplete representation which nevertheless may be extremely useful for certain purposes.

The paramorphic nature of judgment modeling is not necessarily troublesome, particularly in applications-oriented research. The major focus of judgment modeling is to produce representations that are "useful enough" for some specific purpose (e.g., as an initial step toward improving the accuracy of human judgments) as opposed to understanding cognitive processes. This latter function of judgment modeling is important in more theoretical research efforts. However, representation of judgment policies is not irrelevant to theoretical understanding. Hoffman [1960, p. 124] addressed this issue as follows:

> Mathematical models are designed to provide a scheme whereby one set of events may be satisfactorily predicted from another, and whereby testable derivations may lead to more complete theoretical understanding of the phenomena. Such models therefore constitute a level of description and explanation which suffices for scientific purposes. It is not required of models that they bear any semblance of some "actual" state of affairs, either within the organism or elsewhere, nor would this necessarily lead to a better understanding of nature.

Throughout this chapter, the representational nature of policy-capturing research should be kept in mind.

Organizationally, this chapter is divided into two main sections. First, Brunswik's lens model is described. This model provides the conceptual and methodological framework for all the topics discussed in this chapter and the succeeding chapter. Second, the major alternative approaches to capturing (i.e., representing) the judgment policies of individuals are reviewed, along with some of their advantages and disadvantages.

2.1 BRUNSWIK'S LENS MODEL

The work of Egon Brunswik resulted in the development of an important framework for conceptualizing and investigating human judgment. The development of Brunswik's position is described in many of his works (e.g., Brunswik [1940, 1943, 1952, 1955a, 1955b, 1956]) and is summarized and evaluated by Hammond [1955, 1966]. One of Brunswik's most basic positions was that individuals frequently must rely on probabilistic information in making judgments about some relevant part of an uncertain environment. Brunswik's framework is represented most often as a "lens" model, as shown in Figure 2.1.

2.1.1 Modeling the Environment and the Individual

The lens model has been described by Ashton [1973, 1974c], Beach [1967] and Dudycha and Naylor [1966], and their descriptions are relied on here. Castellan [1972, 1973], Stenson [1974] and Stewart [1976] provide further development of the model. For lens model purposes the world is divided into two parts: (1) the environment, represented by the left side of the lens; (2) the individual's judgment system, represented by the right side of the lens. The three basic elements of the model are: (1) the criterion, or distal, variable (Y_e) about which the individual is concerned; the individual may wish to judge the current value or to predict some future value of the criterion variable; (2) the cues, or items of information (X_i), that may be used to judge or predict the criterion; (3) the individual's judgment or

Figure 2.1
Brunswik's Lens Model

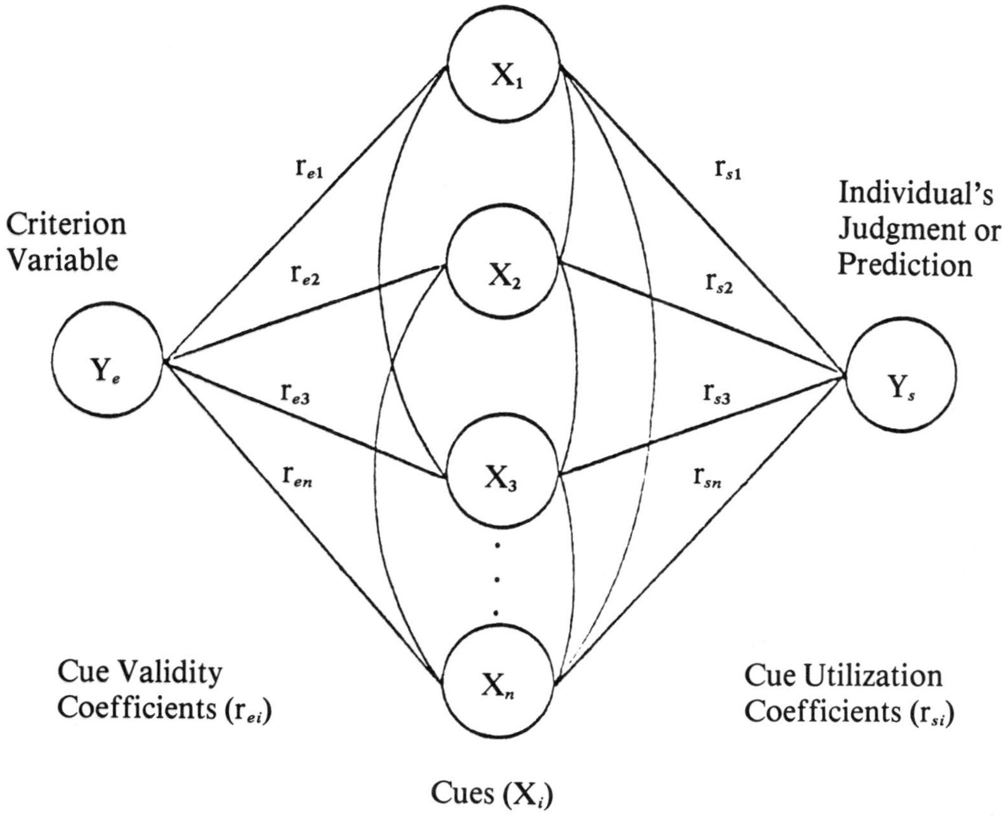

prediction (Y_s). The Y_s and Y_e values will differ if the statistical relationship between Y_e and the cue set is less than perfect and/or the individual's use of the cue set is nonoptimal relative to the environment.

The relationship between Y_e and each X_i variable (r_{ei}) is expressed most often via correlation coefficients, and r_{ei} values are called validity coefficients. Similarly, the relationship between Y_s and each X_i variable (r_{si}) often is expressed in correlational terms, and r_{si} values are called utilization coefficients. Such values are considered representations of the extent to which an individual utilizes X_i to formulate judgments concerning Y_e. The lines connecting the cues with each other in Figure 2.1 indicate that the cues may be intercorrelated.

The multivariate relationships existing on each side of the lens typically are represented via linear multiple regression equations.[2] The left, or environmental, side of the model may be represented as

$$\hat{Y}_e = b_{e1}X_1 + b_{e2}X_2 + \ . \ . \ . \ + b_{en}X_n, \tag{2.1}$$

where $\hat{Y}_e$ is the optimal prediction, in a least squares sense, of Y_e, each b_{ei} is a regression weight, and the X_i are in standardized form. Likewise, the right side of the model may be represented as

$$\hat{Y}_s = b_{s1}X_1 + b_{s2}X_2 + \ . \ . \ . + b_{sn}X_n, \tag{2.2}$$

where $\hat{Y}_s$ is the optimal linear regression prediction of the individual's judgment, and b_{si} and X_i are defined as above.

2.1.2 Indices of Judgment

Values of Y_e, Y_s, $\hat{Y}_e$ and $\hat{Y}_s$ can be used to evaluate the quality of an individual's judgments or predictions. Six judgment indices can be computed by correlating every pair of these four sets of values, as shown in Figure 2.2. R_e is the multiple correlation coefficient, or the correlation between observed and predicted values, in the environment. It indicates the degree to which the X_i variables can be used to predict Y_e, and often is referred to as a measure of environmental (or task) predictability. Similarly, R_s is the multiple correlation coefficient for the individual. It is considered a measure of the individual's consistency, or the degree to which the individual consistently utilizes his or her judgment policy as represented by a multiple regression equation. The squares of these multiple correlations (R_e^2 and R_s^2) indicate the degree to which the linear regression models of Equations 2.1 and 2.2 account for the variance in Y_e and Y_s, respectively.

The index r_a $(=r_{y_e y_s})$ denotes the individual's achievement, or accuracy, in judging or predicting the criterion values, and is an extremely popular index of the individual's performance. However, r_a does not consider the fact that Y_e generally is not perfectly predictable from any set of X_i values, i.e., $R_e < 1.00$. For this reason two additional indices are of substantial importance. First, r_o $(=r_{\hat{y}_e y_s})$, or the optimality index, represents the relationship between the individual's responses and the optimal multiple-regression prediction of the criterion. Second, the matching index, or G $(=r_{\hat{y}_e \hat{y}_s})$, represents the degree to which the regression equation of the individual "matches" the optimal regression equation of the environment. The matching index is a measure of the similarity of the equations that generate $\hat{Y}_e$ and $\hat{Y}_s$, and is an important index of the individual's performance.[3]

---

[2] Discriminant analysis is used frequently when Y_e and Y_s involve a small number (e.g., two) of discrete levels.

[3] More precisely, G denotes the degree of isomorphism between Equations 2.1 and 2.2. Isomorphism does not necessarily imply identity; the value of G will be 1.00 when the b_{si} of Equation 2.2 are proportional to the b_{ei} of Equation 2.1 (see, for example, Castellan [1973]).

Figure 2.2
Indices of Human Judgment

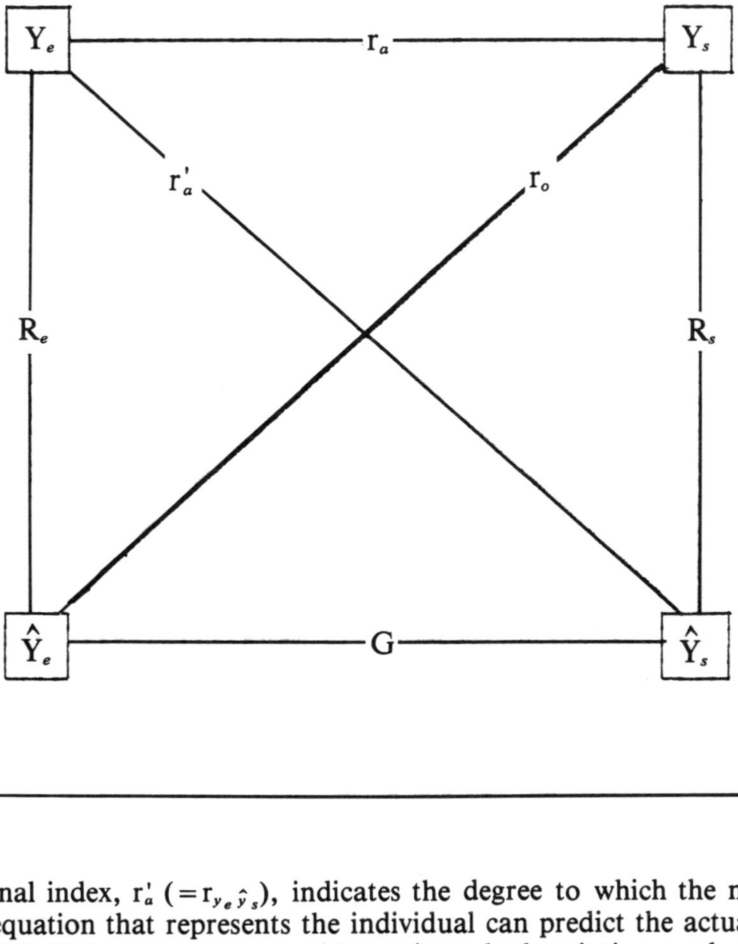

The final index, r'_a ($= r_{y_e \hat{y}_s}$), indicates the degree to which the multiple regression equation that represents the individual can predict the actual criterion values. While little attention was paid to r'_a in early descriptions and applications of the lens model (e.g., Beach, [1967], Dudycha and Naylor [1966]), it has assumed increased importance in recent years in the "man versus model" literature, i.e., studies that compare man's judgment performance with that of man's model (e.g., Goldberg [1970]). The importance of r'_a is discussed in Chapter 3.

2.1.3 The Lens Model Equation

The individual's judgment achievement, or accuracy, was defined earlier as the correlation between actual criterion values and the individual's judgment or prediction of those values, i.e., $r_a = r_{y_e y_s}$. Hursch, Hammond, and Hursch [1964] and Hammond, Hursch, and Todd [1964] proved that r_a can be decomposed into components that encompass some of the other judgment indices in Figure 2.2. Their formulation has been restated by Tucker [1964] as

$$r_a = G R_e R_s + C \sqrt{1 - R_e^2} \sqrt{1 - R_s^2}, \qquad (2.3)$$

where G, R_e and R_s are defined as above, and C is the correlation between the residual variance unexplained by Equations 2.1 and 2.2. The C index may be regarded as a partial correlation coefficient between Y_e and Y_s when the effects of the cues (X_i) are removed. Equation 2.3 is called the lens model equation [Slovic and Lichtenstein, 1971], and is important because it quantifies both linear (GR_eR_s) and nonlinear ($C \sqrt{1-R_e^2} \sqrt{1-R_s^2}$) components of the individual's achievement.

The C index can be large and positive only if systematic nonlinear variance exists in the environment and this variance is detected and utilized appropriately by the individual [Hammond, Hursch, and Todd, 1964]. Appropriate utilization entails that the individual's dependence on the cues follows the same nonlinear form present in the environment. Such detection and utilization of nonlinear relationships will increase the individual's achievement. Large negative values of C indicate that the individual is using a negative function of the nonlinear relationships among Y_e and X_i, and decreased achievement will result. A C value of zero implies that the individual is using a nonlinear function that differs from that existing in the environment, or that the residual variance in the environment and/or the individual's response system is random. Thus, while the value of C may provide some useful information concerning the nonlinear component of the individual's achievement, it does not define any specific mode of nonlinear utilization [Hursch, Hammond and Hursch, 1964]. Hammond, Hursch, and Todd [1964, p. 445] summarize the importance of C by noting that "the magnitude of C specifies the extent to which the [individual] effectively uses those special properties which distinguish him from [his] multiple regression equation." Therefore, C can play an important role in evaluating the judgment or prediction performance of an individual.

In addition to distinguishing between linear and nonlinear components of achievement, the lens model equation demonstrates that achievement is a function of (1) certain properties of the environment (R_e), (2) certain properties of the individual's judgment policy (R_s), and (3) the extent to which the equations representing the environment and the individual are similar (G). For example, given a certain level of environmental predictability (R_e), an individual can improve his or her achievement by increasing G, R_s, or both. Similarly, unsatisfactory achievement can be traced to the effects of G and R_s.

2.2 POLICY CAPTURING

The central issue in the use of the matching index (G) as a performance measure is the extent to which the b_{si} values from the individual's regression equation are similar to the b_{ei} values from the optimal environmental regression equation. The evaluation of matching requires that a "full" lens model analysis be conducted; that is, both the left and right sides of the model must be evaluated. However, analyses of individual judgment often involve only the right side of the model. Such analyses may be useful, for example, when criterion values are unavailable or when agreement among the judgment policies of different individuals is of major concern. In such cases the lens model serves as a framework for policy capturing.

Several statistical approaches are available for policy capturing, and each has certain characteristics, advantages, and disadvantages that make it more or less useful in specific situations. Three approaches that are particularly important are those based on multiple regression, analysis of variance, and conjoint measurement.

2.2.1 Multiple Regression Models

Multiple regression analysis is the most common technique used for capturing and representing an individual's judgment policy. Two issues are of paramount importance in any attempt to represent judgment policies via multiple regression analysis: (1) the functional form of the relationship between cues (X_i) and judgments (Y_s); (2) the weighting parameters for the cues.

2.2.1.1 Linear and Nonlinear Models

The judgment policy represented in Equation 2.2 implies a linear additive combination rule. Individuals often maintain, however, that such a simplified representation of their judgment strategies is inappropriate, and that a model that incorporates curvilinear or configural terms is needed. An early study by Meehl [1954] found that clinical psychologists often claimed to process information in a configural manner, in which their interpretation of one cue was dependent on the value of another cue. Configural judgment strategies may seem apparent in other areas also. A physician, for example, may believe that body temperature is related to the probability that a patient has a particular disease if the patient also has symptom S, but that body temperature is irrelevant to the diagnosis if the patient does not have symptom S [Goldberg, 1968]. The judgment strategy of Equation 2.2 could be amended to incorporate configurality by the inclusion of cross-product terms (e.g., $b_{sij}X_iX_j$).

Curvilinear relationships between cues and judgments are also possible. For example, a personnel officer who evaluates applicants for the position of salesperson may feel that those applicants who score in the middle range of an intelligence test are more likely to be successful than those who score at either extreme [Goldberg, 1968]. Such relationships could be incorporated into the modeled judgment strategy by adding exponential terms (e.g., $b_{si}X_i^2$, $b_{si}X_i^3$, etc.) to Equation 2.2.

The linear, curvilinear and configural models are compensatory; that is, a high value on one cue tends to offset a low value on another cue. Einhorn [1970, 1971] has investigated two nonlinear, noncompensatory models: (1) a conjunctive model, in which the individual requires some minimum value for each cue (in the selection of new faculty members, for example, one may require some minimum level of potential on all three attributes of research, teaching and service abilities); (2) a disjunctive model, in which a judgment is made solely on the basis of the "best" cue (for example, in recruiting a football player, one may examine the ability to run *or* pass *or* kick with a high level of skill).

Despite experts' claims that their judgment policies should be represented by complex nonlinear models, the research evidence has shown consistently that such models provide little, if any, increase in predictive power over that provided by simple linear models. Studies comparing the relationship between an individual's actual judgments (Y_s) and the predicted judgments generated by linear and nonlinear models ($\hat{Y}_s$) have found only minimal increases in $R_s(=r_{y_s\hat{y}_s})$ as a result of adding exponential and/or configural terms.[4] Wiggins and Hoffman [1968] investigated a nonlinear model that included 77 terms (11 cues, as used in the linear model, plus the 11 squared and 55 cross-product terms based on these cues). Even for the "most nonlinear" individual in that study, the R_s of the nonlinear model was only .04 greater than that for the corresponding linear model.

Such results are supported by other studies (e.g., Hammond, Hursch, and Todd [1964], Hursch, Hammond, and Hursch [1964], Newton [1965]) that have assessed nonlinearity via the C index of the lens model equation (Equation 2.3). The value of C generally does not differ significantly from zero, indicating a virtual absence of a nonlinear judgment component. Slovic and Lichtenstein [1971, p. 681] concluded their review of the linearity issue in multiple regression studies by stating: "The linear model accounts for all but a small fraction of predictable variance in judgments across a remarkably diverse spectrum of tasks."

Goldberg [1968, p. 488] identified three possible reasons for the finding that linear models effectively represent judgment policies:

> (a) human judges behave in fact remarkably like linear data processors, but somehow they believe that they are more complex than they really are; (b) human judges behave in fact in a rather configural fashion, but the power of the linear regression model is so great that it serves to obscure the real configural processes in judgment; (c) human judges behave in fact in a decidely linear fashion on most judgmental tasks (their reports notwithstanding), but for some kinds of tasks they use more complex judgmental processes.

Goldberg believed (p. 491) that (b) is the most likely explanation, and Hoffman [1968, p. 63] reached a similar conclusion. Dawes and Corrigan [1974] investigated this issue more rigorously and found that linear models are robust over deviations from linearity for two primary reasons. First, linear models are good approximations to all multivariate models in which each cue has, or can be rescaled to have, a monotone relationship with the criterion, i.e., where higher values on each cue are positively related to higher values on the criterion, independently of the values of the remaining variables. Second, error in the measurement of cues tends to make conditionally monotone functions more linear. Dawes and Corrigan [1974, p. 99] concluded that linear models represent judgment policies well "because the contexts in which they are evaluated tend to be conditionally mono-

---

[4] See, for example, Goldberg [1971], Huber, Sahney, and Ford [1969], Kort [1968], Summers and Stewart [1968], and Wiggins and Hoffman [1968].

tone contexts in which there is much error." This conclusion implies that characteristics of the judgment *task* are very important in the representation of judgment policies via linear regression models. Since the task characteristics investigated by Dawes and Corrigan seem pervasive, linear regression models almost certainly will continue to be found to effectively represent human judgment policies.

2.2.1.2 Measures of Cue Importance

When interpreting Equation 2.2 as a representation of an individual's judgment policy, standardized regression weights (b_{si}) are considered measures of the individual's utilization of cues. In other words, a b_{si} value is interpreted as an importance measure that reveals the extent to which the individual relies on cue X_i in making a judgment or prediction, Y_s. In many cases, however, the interpretation of b_{si} as a measure of cue importance is less than straightforward. In fact, determining the most appropriate measure of cue importance is a problem that human information processing researchers have considered for years.

In an important article, Darlington [1968] identified five possible measures of cue importance: (1) r, the zero-order correlation coefficient (or its square); (2) b, the standarized regression weight (or its square); (3) br; (4) r_p, the part correlation coefficient (or its square); (5) a measure proposed by Englehart [1936]. Englehart's measure assigned a "contribution to variance" to each cue and to the joint effect of each pair of cues; the sum of the independent and joint effects was Englehart's measure of importance. While this and similar measures have been discussed and debated in the literature,[5] such measures generally have not been advocated by human information processing researchers, and Englehart's measure will not be considered here. The other four measures discussed by Darlington, as well as variations of some of these measures, have been advocated and used in human information processing research.

If all cue intercorrelations are zero, then br, as well as the squares of b, r, and r_p will (1) provide identical indications of the relative importance of each cue and (2) sum to R_s^2. If all cue intercorrelations are not zero, however, these four measures will differ and may not rank cues in the same order of importance. This has been demonstrated by Green and Tull [1975], Schmitt and Levine [1977] and Ward [1962]. Further, r^2, b^2, and $r_p{}^2$ will not sum to R_s^2 when some cue intercorrelations are nonzero.

Perhaps the most debated measure of importance is br. This measure was proposed by Hoffman [1960], criticized by Ward [1962] and Darlington [1968], and defended by Hoffman [1962]. A great deal of human information processing research has used br as the measure of cue importance. One advantage claimed for br is that it sums to R_s^2 even when cue intercorrelations are nonzero, and thus allows the total predictable variance to be "successfully partitioned into a simple sum of ingredients, each referring to a specific predictor and each being independent of any joint effect or interaction" [Hoffman, 1962, p. 79]. Further, Hoff-

[5] See, for example, Chase [1960], Mood [1969, 1971], Pugh [1968], Ward [1969], and Werts [1968, 1970].

man [1960] suggested that br be divided by R_s^2, producing measures of importance, called relative weights, which sum to 1.00.

When cue intercorrelations are nonzero, however, the importance of a cue as measured by br or br/R_s^2 may be zero, or negative, resulting in a severe problem of interpretation. However, heuristic solutions to such a problem exist. For example, Oskamp [1967] avoided negative importance measures by computing the weight for each cue as the absolute value of its relative weight divided by the sum of the absolute values of the relative weights for all cues. However, the interpretation of relative weights when cue intercorrelations are nonzero continues to be problematic.

Another measure of cue importance is r_p, or the part correlation coefficient. This measure is called a semipartial coefficient by Nunnally [1967], and the square of r_p is called "usefulness" by Darlington [1968]. The measure defined by r_p^2 is the amount by which R_s^2 would decrease if the cue of interest were removed from the regression equation and the equation were recalculated based on the remaining cues. A related regression statistic, the squared partial correlation coefficient, may be obtained by dividing r_p^2 by 1-R_s^2. Thus, the values of the part coefficient and the partial coefficient are proportional for a given multiple regression equation. Part correlation coefficients are considered more appropriate than partial correlation coefficients for the purposes discussed here because the former partials out variance from the cues only, whereas the latter partials out variance from the cues and from the criterion. Nunnally [1967], for example, maintains that the criterion should be left "intact" for multiple regression analysis.

The relative merits of r, b, r_p (and their squares) and br (and br/R_s^2) as measures of cue importance seem to depend, at least in part, on the goal of the particular policy-capturing analysis. Darlington [1968, p. 168] argues that "When the focus is on prediction . . . rather than causal analysis, usefulness [r_p^2] is clearly the measure of greatest interest," and human information processing researchers appear to accept this view (cf. Schmitt and Levine [1977, p. 17]). A more significant problem is the selection of an importance measure when the research goal is descriptive rather than predictive. On this point Darlington seems to argue that b is the preferred measure when certain assumptions (p. 167) are met. However, since these assumptions are not likely to be met fully in many applications, the use of b as a cue importance measure in descriptive research should be tempered with a great deal of caution.

Very little systematic research has been conducted on the sensitivity of results to the use of different importance measures. Demonstrations that different measures will rank cues in different orders of importance (e.g., Ward, 1962) typically are based upon data sets chosen for the purpose of showing that this *can* happen.[6] Studies that have shown different rankings generally have employed data sets in which intercorrelations were high, although Schmitt and Levine

---

[6] Similarly, arguments against correlation coefficients as meaningful indices in human judgment research typically are based upon carefully-selected counterexamples. See, for example, Birnbaum [1973]. Obviously, interpretational problems can arise with any of the measures discussed here, and such measures cannot be used "blindly" to judge the importance of cues.

[1977] found some differences in rankings based on r and b when intercorrelations were between .09 and .32. Most studies, however, simply ignore such problems when cue intercorrelations are "low," and proceed to measure cue importance via *one* of the measures discussed above.

Finally, it should be noted that interpretation problems caused by cue importance measures are likely to be more significant when one attempts to generalize across studies that used different importance measures than when one attempts to interpret the results of any particular study. Human information processing experiments typically represent "closed" systems of variables; that is, the variance in judgments or predictions must be accounted for by either the known quantitative data presented to the subjects or by chance. As Linn and Werts [1969] point out, however, in using any measure of cue importance one must be careful about unwarranted generalizations to other sets of variables or other judgment contexts.

2.2.2 Analysis-of-Variance Models

The inclusion of various nonlinear (e.g., exponential or configural) terms in the linear judgment model of Equation 2.2 is one way to make that model sensitive to nonlinear information utilization by the individual. Studies that take this approach, however, often are criticized as being "fishing expeditions." As noted earlier, for example, one model in the Wiggins and Hoffman [1968] study included 66 nonlinear terms. It has been suggested that a better modeling approach, especially when a particular type of nonlinear utilization can be hypothesized, is to use a technique that restricts the proliferation of nonlinear terms and, at the same time, is conducive to "uncovering" the hypothesized nonlinear utilization.

Since several types of experts have claimed that configural processing is important and is practiced in their fields, an analysis-of-variance approach to policy capturing seems a reasonable alternative to multiple regression analyses. Configural information processing should be represented by significant interactions in the analysis of variance. This approach was suggested by Hoffman, Slovic, and Rorer [1968], and is described in more detail by Slovic, Fleissner, and Bauman [1972] and Ashton [1973]. Those descriptions are relied on here. Applications of analysis of variance have been concerned solely with the right side of the lens model; that is, the concern has been that of modeling the individual's judgment process, instead of evaluating judgment accuracy or any of the other judgment indices discussed earlier.

For purposes of experimental expediency, analysis-of-variance studies typically employ a small number of discrete levels of each cue. In fact, many such studies have employed only two cue levels, e.g., "high" and "low." Within this approach a significant main effect for a particular cue implies that the individual's responses varied systematically with the levels of that cue. Similarly, a significant two-factor interaction implies that the individual responded to patterns of cue levels, i.e., that the effect on judgments of one cue differed as a function of the level of the other cue.

An indication of the extent to which the individual relies upon the cues, both individually and in combination with one or more other cues, can be obtained by computing significance statistics (e.g., F ratios) and related strength-of-association statistics (e.g., ω^2) for each main effect and interaction. In policy-capturing studies, ω^2 [Hays, 1973] is an estimate of the proportion of variation in the individual's judgments that is accounted for by the specific main effect or interaction. As such, its interpretation is analogous to the interpretation of a squared correlation coefficient.[7]

2.2.2.1 Factorial and Fractional Factorial Designs

Factorial designs [Cochran and Cox, 1957; Cox, 1958; Kempthorne, 1952] typically are used in the analysis-of-variance approach to policy capturing. Such designs enable one to assess the effects of a cue in conjunction with various combinations of other cues [Federer, 1955] and, therefore, are extremely useful when one wishes to study simultaneously the impact on judgments of several cues. Factorial designs become unmanageable, however, when the number of cues is large and, especially, when the number of discrete levels of the cues is large. For example, if one wishes to model judgment as a function of six cues, each of which is quantified at two levels, then $2^6 = 64$ combinations of cue levels exist. If the number of cues is increased to ten, then the number of possible combinations increases to $2^{10} = 1{,}024$. If each cue could assume three levels instead of two (say, "low," "medium," and "high" instead of simply "low" and "high"), then 729 and 59,049 combinations of cue levels exist for the 3^6 and 3^{10} designs, respectively. Considerations such as these often restrict the researcher's attention to judgment or prediction tasks involving a relatively small number of cues and cue levels.

Such considerations also make *fractional* factorial designs (see Cochran and Cox [1957]) attractive. A one-eighth fractional replication of the 2^{10} factorial design involves only 128 combinations of cue levels instead of 1,024 as in the complete design. The popularity of fractional factorial designs stems from the fact that they permit judgment policies to be captured within realistic experimental constraints.

A disadvantage of such efficient designs is the inability to evaluate higher-order interactions. Judgment variance explained by higher-order interactions is not separable from that explained by main effects and lower-order interactions. Additionally, when the individual makes only one judgment for each combination of cue levels, as is usually the case, some higher-order interactions must be used to form the experimental error term for the estimation of main effects and lower-order interactions. In a one-half fractional replication of the 2^6 design, for example, the effects due to five-cue interactions are not separable from those due

---

[7] It should be noted that the quantification of cue values as a small number of discrete levels restricts somewhat the interpretation of ω^2; that is, ω^2 must be interpreted as the proportion of variation in judgments accounted for by a particular cue or combination of cues *given* the quantification of the cues in the experiment [Glass and Hakstian, 1969]. Of course, such considerations apply to the interpretation of all association statistics (e.g., correlation coefficients). Moreover, it is possible for ω^2 to be negative. This is not a serious problem, however, since negative ω^2 values can occur only when the corresponding F ratio is less than 1.00, and F ratios of this size are nonsignificant. When negative ω^2 values occur, they are set equal to zero [Hays, 1973; Kempthorne and Folks, 1971].

to main effects, the effects due to four-cue interactions are not separable from those due to two-cue interactions, and the three-cue interactions must be used to form the error term.

While these characteristics of fractional designs should be recognized, they are not likely to constitute serious problems. Significant higher-order interactions that account for even a moderate amount of judgment variance rarely have been found (e.g., Hoffman, Slovic, and Rorer [1968]). The most important fractional designs are those in which main effects and two-cue interactions (and perhaps three-cue interactions) can be separately estimated. Such designs enable judgment policies, including configural cue utilization, to be captured in an efficient manner.

2.2.2.2 Main Effects and Interactions

Full or fractional factorial designs have been used by several researchers in psychology.[8] So far as configural cue utilization is concerned, the results of these studies can be summarized very succinctly: While statistically significant two-cue and higher-order interaction terms often are found, they account for an extremely small amount of judgment variance. In the initial application of the analysis-of-variance approach, Hoffman, Slovic, and Rorer [1968, pp. 343-44] found, in a medical diagnosis context, that "the largest main effect usually accounted for 10 to 40 times as much of the total variance in judgments as the largest interaction. On the average, roughly 90 percent of a judge's reliable variation of response could be predicted by a simple formula combining only individual symptoms in an additive fashion and completely ignoring interactions." Hoffman, Slovic, and Rorer used a full factorial design, and thus were able to estimate all higher-order interactions (involving as many as six cues). Moreover, since their subjects evaluated each combination of cue levels twice, no higher-order interactions had to be used to form the experimental error term. Finally, the Hoffman, Slovic, and Rorer [1968] results have held up remarkably well when the analysis-of-variance approach has been applied to different judges in different contexts.

Perhaps it should not be surprising that large configural effects are not found in analysis-of-variance studies. For such effects to be found, different patterns of cue levels would have to reverse the implications of certain cues [Hoffman, Slovic, and Rorer, 1968]. Because of the nature of most judgment tasks, however, it is more likely that the finding of small interaction effects in several studies simply represents attenuation or augmentation, instead of reversal, of the implications of some cues.[9] This is consistent with Dawes and Corrigan's [1974] argument that characteristics of typical judgment tasks are instrumental in the ability of linear models to capture individuals' judgment policies.

---

[8] See, for example, Hoffman, Slovic, and Rorer [1968], Rorer, Hoffman, Dickman, and Slovic [1967], Slovic [1969], and Slovic, Fleissner, and Bauman [1972]. Factorial designs also have been very popular in accounting-related studies; see Chapter 7.

[9] For elaboration of this issue, see Digman [1966].

Further evidence for the ability of linear models, specifically the main effects in analysis-of-variance models, to represent configural processes comes from simulation studies. Using a computer programmed to make predictions according to the "purely configural" rule J = XY (where J is the prediction and X and Y are independent variables), Rorer [1973] found that 78 percent of the variance in predictions was accounted for by the two main effects (representing linearity) in an analysis-of-variance. Only 22 percent of the variance was attributed to the interaction term, XY. Similarly, Yntema and Torgerson [1961] constructed a hypothetical data set involving three variables. The formula W = IJ + JK + IK was used to compute values of the dependent variable, W. Analysis-of-variance attributed 94 percent of the variance to main effects and only 6 percent to interactions.

2.2.3 Conjoint Measurement Analysis

Both the analysis-of-variance and multiple regression approaches to policy capturing implicitly assume that cues and judgmental responses can be measured objectively, and that the validity of a particular function form, or composition rule, can be tested directly. As Krantz and Tversky [1971] point out, however, these may be questionable assumptions in much research. An approach to the representation of judgment policies that attempts to overcome such problems is conjoint measurement analysis [Luce and Tukey, 1964]. While this approach has not been as popular as multiple regression and analysis of variance, it possesses certain characteristics that make it potentially useful for judgment research. Coombs, Dawes, and Tversky [1970] and Krantz and Tversky [1971] provide introductory explanations of conjoint measurement, while Krantz, Luce, Suppes, and Tversky [1971] and Tversky [1967a] provide more advanced treatments.

Conjoint measurement analysis addresses the measurement issue and the composition issue simultaneously by constructing measurement scales for the cues and responses so that a *proposed* composition rule, or function form, is satisfied. "The problem investigated in this approach, therefore, is not whether a specified functional relation holds among several (independently measured) variables, but rather whether there *exist* scales of measurement (for both the dependent and the independent variables) that satisfy the proposed composition rule" [Krantz and Tversky, 1971, p. 152]. Moreover, only ordinal properties of the data must be compatible with a proposed composition rule. This, in turn, requires only ordinal responses, or rankings based on the various combinations of cue levels, by the individual whose judgment policy is to be modeled.

Conjoint measurement analysis consists of two complementary approaches, axiomatic and numerical. The axiomatic approach addresses the composition rule issue by determining if there exist interval scales for the cues and judgments that satisfy a hypothesized function form. Krantz and Tversky [1971] are concerned primarily with the axiomatic approach. In addition, Barron [1977] has written a tutorial on the axiomatic approach. The numerical approach *assumes* a particular function form and then searches for the best-fitting scales. In the case of the additive composition rule, "best-fitting" is defined as minimization of Kruskal's [1965] "stress" measure. The numerical approach also produces "part-worth functions" for the cues, which are analogous to weighting parameters in more conventional approaches; that is, they represent the contribution of each cue to the judgments. Green and Rao [1971] provide a tutorial on the numerical approach. Ideally, the axiomatic and numerical approaches should be employed in conjunction with one another: The numerical approach would locate the best-fitting scales and part-worth functions for the composition rule isolated by the axiomatic approach.

2.2.3.1 Axiomatic Conjoint Measurement

Axiomatic conjoint measurement permits the routine analysis of a class of composition rules known as simple polynomials in three variables. There are four such composition rules: (1) additive, A + B + C; (2) multiplicative, ABC; (3) distributive, (A + B)C; (4) dual-distributive, AB + C. If the judgment task can be represented by three cues, and if the hypothesized function form relating cues to judgments is one (or more) of these four composition rules, then axiomatic conjoint measurement analysis can evaluate ordinal properties of the data set to determine which, if any, of the above four rules applies.

Krantz and Tversky [1971] present five ordinal properties that can be tested to determine which of the four composition rules, if any, holds. Mathematically, these properties represent necessary conditions for deducing the composition rule. However, Krantz and Tversky [1971, pp. 164-65] argue that, as a practical matter, they are also sufficient conditions. Tests for these five properties are described by Krantz and Tversky [1971], and computer programs to implement the tests have been provided by Holt and Wallsten [1974] and Ullrich and Cummins [1973]. Thus, the analysis of simple polynomials in three variables can be as routine as the application of multiple regression analysis or analysis of variance.

Krantz, Luce, Suppes, and Tversky [1971] show that it is possible, though not routine, to apply axiomatic conjoint measurement analysis to tasks involving more than three independent variables. As a practical matter, however, the use of axiomatic conjoint measurement is restricted to the three-variable case. The importance of this restriction is debatable. Krantz and Tversky [1971] and Tversky [1967a] give several examples of testable psychological theories based on simple polynomials in three variables, e.g., the theory of achievement motivation, and certain applications of expected-utility theory. Further, Slovic and Lichtenstein [1971, p. 684] observe: "Across a number of studies, varying in the number of cues that were available, three cues usually sufficed to account for more than 80 percent of the predictable variance in the judge's responses." Thus, with judicious cue selection there may exist a sizable number of judgment tasks amenable to analysis by axiomatic conjoint measurement procedures.

An important problem with ordinal analyses, including axiomatic conjoint measurement, is the presence of error in the data set. If the data are errorless, then the testing procedures developed by Krantz and Tversky [1971] yield an unequivocal conclusion concerning which, if any, of the four composition rules holds. In this case, the failure of a single necessary condition calls for rejection of the corresponding composition rule. If, however, the data contain error, then a hypothesized composition rule may be rejected erroneously. The testing procedures cannot distinguish between noisy data and an incorrect composition rule. Errors in rankings may be revealed, for example, by imperfect test-retest reliability when the individual is required to make more than one response to each combination of cue levels, or by intransitivities in certain applications (e.g., Ullrich and Painter [1974]). While there is no universally accepted method for handling this problem, a "reasonable" number of failures typically is tolerated before rejecting a composition rule, where reasonable is defined on an *ad hoc* basis within a particular study (e.g., Coombs and Bowen [1971], Moriarity and Barron [1976], Ullrich and Painter [1974]). However, some recent work [Person, 1977, 1979] has been devoted to a stochastic method of handling noisy data.

In the few applications of axiomatic conjoint measurement analysis that have appeared in the literature, the additive composition rule has been found to predominate.[10] In fact, Ullrich and Painter [1974] point out that only Coombs and Huang [1970] have produced unequivocal evidence for any nonadditive composition rule. For some purposes, however, it seems important to determine empirically the composition rule employed, instead of simply assuming the additive rule. For example, a study by Fischer [1976] argued for the use of axiomatic conjoint measurement in theoretical research efforts. Fischer hypothesized an additive composition rule in a decision task involving both risky and riskless choices and tested this hypothesis via axiomatic conjoint measurement and linear multiple regression analysis. While the regression models provided excellent fits to the judgments of all subjects (the worst fit being $R_s^2 = .84$), several subjects violated the conjoint measurement axioms for the additive model. Fischer concluded (p. 144): "To the applied decision theorist who simply wants a numerical representation of a decision maker's preferences, goodness-of-fit is an appropriate criterion. Our results suggest that the models studied here are adequate for this purpose. But to the theoretical psychologist, concerned with explaining the judgment process, goodness-of-fit is not enough."

2.2.3.2 Numerical Conjoint Measurement

Numerical conjoint measurement analysis finds the best-fitting component scales for a particular function form. For the additive composition rule, this approach transforms monotonically any joint effects of cues such that the rescaled joint effects can be represented by the sum of the scaled cues, while maintaining the same rank ordering of the dependent variable. Such rescaling procedures produce numerical estimates of the scale values regardless of whether the proposed composition rule is appropriate. Thus, in applying the numerical approach it is desirable to have performed the axiomatic analysis first to determine the appropriate composition rule. Some studies have performed both types of analyses (e.g., Moriarity and Barron [1976]), while others have simply assumed an additive composition rule and applied only the numerical approach (e.g., Green, Carmone, and Wind [1972]). Several rescaling procedures are available if the compo-

---

[10] See, for example, Coombs and Bowen [1971], Coombs and Huang [1970], Fischer [1976], Moriarity and Barron [1976], Person [1979], Tversky [1967b] and Ullrich and Painter [1974].

sition rule is found (or assumed) to be additive (e.g., Kruskal [1965], Lingoes [1967], Tversky and Zivian [1966]). Recently, scaling algorithms have become available for the distributive rule [Emery, 1977a] and the dual-distributive rule [Emery, 1977b]).[11]

Neither axiomatic nor numerical conjoint measurement is without problems, however. For example, Emery and Barron [1979] used computer simulation to generate error-free data sets from simple polynomials in three variables. Krantz and Tversky's [1971] axiomatic testing procedures made several errors in diagnosing the composition rules that had actually generated the data sets. Briefly, the procedures seemed to be biased toward the diagnosis of nonadditive rules as additive, and none of the data sets generated by the dual-distributive rule was diagnosed correctly. These problems could have occurred because, as Krantz and Tversky [1971] pointed out, the diagnostic procedures represent necessary, not sufficient, conditions for deducing the correct composition rule. Problems were also encountered when numerical rescaling algorithms were applied to the data sets. Earlier, Green [1975] had found similar problems with numerical conjoint measurement. Thus, conjoint measurement analysis, like multiple regression analysis and analysis of variance, does not provide a panacea for policy capturing. The strengths, weaknesses, and other characteristics of all three approaches must be given consideration by judgment researchers.

---

[11] An approach to policy capturing that is not discussed in this book is functional measurement. This approach is similar to axiomatic conjoint measurement in that it tests theories about specific, hypothesized composition rules, generally involving adding, averaging, subtracting or multiplying cue values. It is similar to multiple regression and analysis-of-variance approaches in that it uses numerical, instead of ordinal, response measures. In some empirical applications, monotonic transformations (e.g., Bogartz and Wackwitz [1971], are applied to the numerical responses to achieve interval scaling; this causes functional measurement to resemble numerical conjoint measurement. In fact, Schönemann, Cafferty, and Rotton [1973] argue that functional measurement is a special case of additive conjoint measurement. The rationale for functional measurement and a review of its applications are provided by Anderson [1970, 1971, 1974], and a critical evaluation of certain aspects of the approach is contained in Hodges [1973].

CHAPTER THREE

Judgment Accuracy and Agreement

This chapter considers two focal areas of judgment modeling research: (1) the accuracy of individual judgments and (2) agreement among the judgments of different individuals.

Judgment accuracy may be partitioned into several independent components so that the determinants of an individual's level of accuracy can be specified. The methodology used for partitioning judgment accuracy is the lens model equation, introduced in Chapter 2 and elaborated in Section 3.1. That section also discusses several ways of improving the accuracy of individual judgments.

A modified form of the lens model equation may be used for partitioning judgment agreement into its components, thus allowing certain reasons for judgment agreement (or disagreement) to be specified. This form of the lens model equation is emphasized in Section 3.2, along with a multi-person lens model (the cognitive conflict paradigm) that enables investigation of the structure and dynamics of judgment agreement.

3.1 JUDGMENT ACCURACY

The judgment performance measure to receive the greatest research attention is judgment accuracy or achievement, r_a. Recall that accuracy is defined as the correlation between actual criterion values and the individual's judgments or predictions of those values over a series of trials, i.e., $r_a = r_{Y_e Y_s}$. Goldberg's [1968] comprehensive review of the clinical judgment literature revealed that judgment accuracy generally is quite low, is largely unaffected by the amount of information available to the individual or the amount of professional training and experience, and is unrelated to the degree of confidence that the individual has in his or her judgments. Later reviews by Slovic and Lichtenstein [1971] and Slovic, Fischhoff, and Lichtenstein [1977] reveal the same picture. Furthermore, low accuracy has been demonstrated across a wide variety of judgment tasks, ranging from predicting the length of straight lines to predicting psychosis and neurosis.

Of course, some variability in the level of judgment accuracy is found in different studies. This variability seems to relate to certain characteristics of the judgment tasks studied rather than to the subjects themselves. For example, accuracy increases with increases in task predictability (R_e) and cue validities (r_{ei}), and accuracy is higher when cues are linearly related to the criterion than when they are nonlinearly related. Slovic and Lichtenstein [1971] and Snowball [1976] review the effects of task characteristics on judgment accuracy. For present purposes, however, the important point is that, across a wide spectrum of judgment tasks and experimental conditions, the accuracy of human judgment often is low.

3.1.1 Components of Judgment Accuracy

Judgment researchers have been concerned with the related questions of why human judgments are relatively inaccurate and how judgment accuracy can be improved. With regard to the first question, an important development was the use of the lens model equation (Equation 2.3) to determine the relative importance of the components of accuracy. Ignoring the contribution of nonlinear information utilization to accuracy, the lens model equation becomes

$$r_a = G\, R_e R_s, \qquad (3.1)$$

where accuracy is seen to be a function of three terms. Each of these terms is discussed below (see Hammond and Summers [1972]).

First, R_e denotes the extent to which the criterion can be predicted with the available cues. It sets an upper limit on judgment accuracy, even if the other two components are perfect. In experimental studies of human judgment, R_e is specified by the researcher.

Second, G (the matching index) measures the extent to which the individual detects essential properties of the judgment task. As described earlier, G is the correlation between the optimal prediction of the criterion ($\hat{Y}_e$; see Equation 2.1) and the optimal prediction of the individual's judgments ($\hat{Y}_s$; see Equation 2.2), based on the same set of cues. As such, G represents the extent to which the b_{si} values of Equation 2.2 "match" (are proportional to) the b_{ei} values of Equation 2.1. Hammond and Summers [1972] refer to G as a measure of the knowledge the individual has acquired in the judgment task.

Finally, R_s (response consistency) measures the extent to which the individual consistently applies the judgment policy represented by Equation 2.2. Hammond and Summers [1972] call R_s a measure of cognitive control, i.e., a measure of the extent to which the individual controls the execution of knowledge.

The lens model equation has important implications for research on judgment accuracy because it reveals that accuracy is a function of both the acquisition of knowledge (G) and the application of the knowledge acquired (R_s). Even if perfect knowledge were acquired (i.e., $G = 1.00$), r_a would be less than the limit of achievement (R_e) permits unless the individual also applied the knowledge perfectly consistently (i.e., $R_s = 1.00$). Conversely, the limit of achievement would not be reached with a perfectly controlled judgment strategy unless that strategy were appropriate to the environment. In short, high levels of both knowledge and cognitive control are needed for high levels of judgment accuracy.

An interesting empirical question is the relative importance of acquisition and application of knowledge in explaining low judgment accuracy: Are human judgments inaccurate because individuals fail to acquire appropriate knowledge of the data relationships inherent in judgment tasks, or because individuals find it difficult to consistently apply the knowledge they have acquired? The latter possibility is generally supported by the evidence (see, for example, Brehmer [1976a], Hammond and Summers [1972]). Individuals tend to acquire appropriate task-related knowledge concerning relative cue weighting (high G), but fail to apply this knowledge consistently (low R_s). The evidence suggests that cognitive skills bear some resemblance to motor skills: "[W]ith both, we can know what we want to do without necessarily being able to do it" [Slovic, Fischhoff, and Lichtenstein, 1977, p. 13].

3.1.2 Improving Judgment Accuracy

Four approaches to improving judgment accuracy have been suggested and two have attracted substantial research effort. The first major approach focuses on providing the individual with various forms of feedback information concerning the judgment task and/or the individual's past performance in the task. This approach relies on the belief that detailed information about task properties, past performance, and the individual's own judgment policy can and will be assimilated by the individual and applied to subsequent judgments. The other major approach focuses on the relative accuracy of the individual versus that of his or her judgment policy as represented by a multiple regression equation. Specifically, this approach entails the replacement of the individual by the individual's model. The third approach involves using the individual and the individual's model in tandem with one another. Finally, the fourth approach involves combining the judgments of several individuals into a composite judgment. The primary distinguishing feature of each approach is the manner in which it deals with the inconsistency of human judgment.

3.1.2.1 Feedback

The effects of feedback on judgment accuracy have been studied extensively in multiple-cue probability learning tasks. Such studies rely on the lens model for conceptual and analytical guidance. The cues are typically numerical, bear varying degrees of relationship to the criterion, and may be linearly or nonlinearly related to the criterion. Further, the criterion generally is not perfectly predictable from the cues. According to Hammond and Summers [1972, p. 59], "A major reason for the emphasis on multiple-cue probability learning tasks is the fact that such tasks have essential features in common with a broad range of inference tasks human subjects routinely encountered outside the laboratory." This position is echoed by Castellan [1974, p. 44]: "The importance of these tasks derives from their close similarity to diagnostic judgments in fields such as clinical psychology, medicine, and business."

Types of Feedback. A large number of multiple-cue probability learning studies has focused on the effectiveness of some particular type of feedback, or on the relative effectiveness of several types of feedback.[1] Various subsets of

---

[1] These studies include Castellan [1974], Deane, Hammond, and Summers [1972], Dudycha and Naylor [1966], Goldberg [1968], Hammond [1971], Hammond and Summers [1965, 1972], Hammond, Summers, and Deane [1973], Lee and Tucker [1962], Lindell [1976], Naylor and Schenck [1968], Newton [1965], Nystedt and Magnusson [1973], Peterson, Hammond, and Summers [1965a, 1965b], Schmitt, Coyle, and King [1976], Schmitt, Coyle, and Saari [1977], Steinmann [1974, 1976], D. Summers [1967, 1969], S. Summers [1962], Summers and Hammond [1966], Summers, Summers, and Karkau [1969], Summers, Taliaferro, and Fletcher [1970a], Todd and Hammond [1965], and Uhl [1963].

these studies are reviewed by Kessler [1977], Slovic and Lichtenstein [1971] and Steinmann [1976]. These studies involve metric tasks, in which cues and criteria are intervally scaled. Multiple-cue probability learning in nonmetric tasks has been investigated far less frequently and is omitted from the following discussion (see Bjorkman [1973], Castellan [1974]).

Three basic types of feedback have been employed in multiple-cue probability learning studies: (1) *outcome* feedback, in which the correct response is revealed to the individual immediately after each prediction; (2) *task properties* feedback (also known as "feedforward" [Bjorkman, 1972]), in which the individual is given statistical information about the task — including, perhaps, cue validities, cue intercorrelations, and the form of the function relating the cues to the criterion; (3) *cognitive* feedback, in which the individual is given statistical information about his or her judgment policy (e.g., cue-utilization coefficients and the form of the function relating cues to judgments) and perhaps a measure of past achievement.

In addition, various combinations of these three types of feedback have been used. The combination used most frequently is task properties feedback plus cognitive feedback (called "lens model" feedback by Todd and Hammond [1965]). This combination allows the individual to compare his or her judgment policy with the optimal (environmental) model. Other combinations often involve the provision of outcome feedback along with task properties, cognitive, or lens model feedback. The criterion used for evaluating the effectiveness of feedback in such studies is the increase in achievement, r_a, over a large number of predictions based on varying sets of cue values.

Effectiveness of Feedback. Two major findings have emerged from this body of research. First, the most effective type of feedback is task properties feedback. In fact, task properties feedback is typically as effective as lens model feedback, indicating that providing individuals with information about what they should be doing is as effective as providing an opportunity to compare what they should be doing with what they are doing. Providing the individual with only cognitive feedback typically is relatively ineffective. Second, the least effective type of feedback is outcome feedback. Learning occurs at a much slower rate with outcome feedback vis-a-vis other types of feedback in simple, straightforward laboratory tasks, and may not occur at all in more complex tasks. For example, Goldberg [1968] studied the effect of outcome feedback on subjects' abilities to improve the accuracy of their predictions of psychosis and neurosis based on Minnesota Multiphasic Personality Inventory (MMPI) profiles. (The MMPI consists of 550 statements concerning such things as attitudes, fears, sex roles, and vocational interests. The instrument is scored on several clinical scales, and an individual's combination of scores on these scales constitutes a profile.) His subjects, some of whom were "MMPI experts," went through a daily program of training and testing for 17 weeks. Goldberg [1968, p. 492] concluded that "there was virtually no cross-sample generalization of learning as a result of intensive training on over 4,000 MMPI profiles."

Moreover, it has been found that outcome feedback may impede learning when provided in conjunction with task properties feedback or lens model feedback. The reason appears to be that outcome feedback contains "noise" as a result of the probabilistic relationships between the cues and the criterion [Hammond, Summers and Deane, 1973]. Because of this noise element, outcome feedback reduces the consistency with which individuals apply whatever knowledge they have acquired about the judgment task — even the knowledge acquired in the form of task properties or lens model feedback.

In summary, it appears that information about statistical properties of the judgment task is necessary for substantial improvement in judgment accuracy. Such information would be difficult to infer from outcome feedback alone, because of the trial-and-error nature of such learning and because of the noise component of outcome feedback. Task properties feedback, and in some cases lens model feedback, facilitates performance by enabling individuals to improve the matching and/or consistency components of accuracy.

3.1.2.2 Man Versus Model of Man

Another frequently researched approach to improving accuracy is to replace the individual with the multiple regression equation that represents his or her judgment policy. Ashton [1975a, 1976c, 1979a, 1980b] has discussed this approach in accounting/business contexts, and those discussions are relied on here. Much of the early research in this area compared the individual's accuracy ($r_a = r_{Y_eY_s}$) with the accuracy of the individual's multiple regression model ($r'_a = r_{Y_e\hat{Y}_s}$) in the prediction of criterion values. Application of the regression approach to the "man versus model" issue was suggested by Goldberg [1970]. Working with the lens model equation (Equation 2.3), Goldberg showed that linear multiple regression models will outperform their human counterparts when $GR_e(1 - R_s) > C\sqrt{1 - R_e^2}\sqrt{1 - R_s^2}$. Goldberg [1970, p. 425] noted that when $R_e = 1.0$, i.e., the criterion is perfectly predictable from a linear model of cue-criterion relationships, and the individual has any validity, the model will always outperform the individual. Also, as R_s approaches 1.0, i.e., the individual's predictions become more linearly predictable, these predictions become less distinguishable from those of the model, and the differences between the individual and the model begin to disappear. Since in natural prediction situations neither the individual nor the environment is perfectly predictable, it becomes an empirical question whether the conditions favoring the model over the individual generally hold.

Goldberg [1970] conducted an extensive study of this issue. His data were those originally collected by Meehl [1959], involving 29 clinical psychologists making diagnostic predictions based on 861 MMPI profiles. The psychologists rated each profile on an 11-step scale from least psychotic to most psychotic. Goldberg constructed a linear multiple regression equation for each psychologist. Since criterion information was available (hospital staff diagnoses), both r_a and r'_a could be computed for each subject.

The models almost always outperformed their human counterparts. When r_a and r'_a were based on the total sample, the most accurate model ($r'_a = .43$) outperformed the most accurate individual ($r_a = .39$), the "typical" model ($r'_a = .31$) outperformed the "typical" individual ($r_a = .28$), and the least accurate model

(r_a' = .16) outperformed the least accurate individual (r_a = .14). Goldberg [1970, p. 428] observed ". . . if one accepts as 'essentially identical' those cases where the differences between man and model were zero when rounded to two decimal places, then for 28 of the 29 judges (97 %), the models were at least as valid as were the judges themselves." In addition, Goldberg [1970, p. 429] found that even when the models were derived from only a fraction of the cases, and cross-validated on the remainder, models still outperformed individuals in the vast majority of instances. For example, when half the cases were used to derive the models, the models were superior 86 percent of the time; when one-fourth were used, 79 percent of the time; when one-seventh were used, 79 percent of the time; and when only one-tenth were used, 72 percent of the time.

Goldberg's results were replicated in a grade-point prediction task by Wiggins and Kohen [1971] and in a graduate-admissions task by Dawes [1971]. The Wiggins and Kohen study found that "for *every 1* of the 98 judges in the present study, the model of the judge was more valid than the judgments themselves" (p. 102). In addition, the differences between models and individuals were considerably larger than those in Goldberg's study; the incremental validity of models over individuals ranged from 0.03 to 0.37, with an average of 0.17. The Wiggins and Kohen results have been replicated at another university [Dawes and Corrigan, 1974].

Similar results have been found in business contexts. For example, in a study concerning production-scheduling and work-force-scheduling decisions in four companies, Bowman [1963] constructed multiple regression models based on management's past scheduling behavior. He found that in three of the four companies the managers' models would have resulted in lower costs that did the managers' actual behavior [Bowman, 1963, p. 315]. In a similar study, Moskowitz and Miller [1972] found that "in no individual case was a manager's performance better than his LRM [linear regression model]" (p. 854). Bowman's results were also supported by Kunreuther [1969].

These studies showed that individuals were outperformed by their own models. Moreover, this result is supported by a large body of research on "clinical versus statistical prediction". Meehl [1954] analyzed 20 studies and Sawyer [1966] analyzed 45 studies that compared the accuracy of individuals, principally clinical psychologists, with the accuracy of various statistical or actuarial prediction formulas. They found that the models were more accurate than clinicians.[2]

Systematic Bias and Random Error. Why do multiple regression models outperform their human counterparts? Note that the studies discussed above concern *linear* models. The ability of a linear model to simulate an individual's predictions is reflected in the model's residuals, i.e., the differences between the individual's predictions and the model's predictions. Linear model residuals may encompass random error and/or some type of nonlinear information utilization.

[2] Some clinical psychologists (e.g., Holt [1958, 1970]) have criticized such studies and have argued against their practical significance. In addition, Korman [1968] has found that "clinical prediction . . . *does work* in some instances" (p. 312) better than statistical prediction. However, the evidence favoring model over man is overwhelming.

Therefore, to understand why linear models of individuals work so well, it is useful to distinguish between two important components of human predictions, systematic bias and random error, and between two representations of information utilization, linear and nonlinear.

Concerning the first distinction, predictions made by individuals often encompass, in addition to valid information utilization, systematic bias and random error [Campbell, 1958; Ruesch, 1967; Webb, 1969]. Systematic bias occurs, for example, when the individual consistently overestimates or underestimates the validities of particular cues for predicting a criterion. Random error occurs when the individual is inconsistent in the extent to which he or she relies upon particular cues. To the extent that an individual's predictions include systematic bias, such bias will be captured in the individual's model. However, use of the model to make predictions will eliminate the random error component. The other issue concerns linear versus nonlinear representation of individuals' judgment policies. As Chapter 2 indicated, linear representations account for all but a small fraction of predictable judgment variance, despite individuals' claims of nonlinear information processing.

The importance of distinguishing between systematic bias and random error, and between linear and nonlinear representations, was considered by Goldberg [1970, p. 424]: "To the extent that the [linear] model fails to capture valid nonlinear variance in the judge's decision processes, it should perform less creditably than the judge. To the extent that it eliminates the random error component in human judgments, it should perform more validly than the judge." The evidence suggests that elimination of random error adds more to the validity of predictions than is lost by failure to capture nonlinear information utilization. Different researchers using different approaches have reached the same conclusions about the detrimental effect on accuracy of random error (e.g., Bowman [1963], Dudycha and Naylor [1966], Goldberg [1970]).

Robustness of Cue Weights. The distinctions between systematic bias and random error, and between linear and nonlinear representations, relate primarily to characteristics of human information processing. Certain characteristics of the *models* used to represent human information processing are perhaps equally important to the "man versus model" issue. As noted in Chapter 2, Dawes and Corrigan [1974] showed that linear models are robust with respect to deviations from linearity. These researchers also found that linear models are robust with respect to weighting parameters. For example, Dawes and Corrigan demonstrated that linear models with weights chosen *at random* outperformed human beings. Ten thousand models were constructed for each of five prediction situations by selecting normal deviates at random from a normal distribution with unit variance and using the absolute values of the deviates as weights for predictor variables. Average validities indicated that these random linear models outperformed individuals in four of the five situations (the other was a tie). Random models outperformed individuals' models in three of the five situations.

Dawes and Corrigan's results represent more than an interesting curiosity. Subsequent analytical research, most notably by Einhorn and Hogarth [1975] and Srinivasan [1977], has revealed the conditions under which linear models are robust over deviations from optimal (least-squares regression) weighting. In fact, such robustness had been recognized in the psychometric theory literature several decades earlier and had been formalized by Wilks [1938], whose work showed very clearly the conditions under which the outputs of linear models are robust with respect to the weighting parameters employed. Some implications of Wilks' work for human information processing research, discussed by Ashton [1979a, 1980b], are briefly summarized here.

Wilks [1938] derived, under some very innocuous conditions, an expression for the correlation between two additive composites formed by combining a common set of independent variables by the application of different sets of weighting coefficients. If we let $\hat{y}_v = v_1x_1 + v_2x_2 + \ldots + v_nx_n$ and $\hat{y}_w = w_1x_1 + w_2x_2 + \ldots + w_nx_n$ be two linear composites (or predictions) based upon the weighting coefficients $v_1, v_2 \ldots v_n$ and $w_1, w_2 \ldots w_n$, respectively, and if $x_1, x_2 \ldots x_n$ are in standardized form, then Wilks' formula is:

$$\bar{r}_{\hat{y}_v \hat{y}_w} = 1 - \frac{\left[\left(\frac{\sigma_v}{\bar{V}}\right)^2 + \left(\frac{\sigma_w}{\bar{W}}\right)^2\right]}{2nr}, \tag{3.2}$$

where

$\bar{r}_{\hat{y}_v \hat{y}_w}$ is the expected value of the correlation between $\hat{y}_v$ and $\hat{y}_w$,

$\frac{\sigma_v}{\bar{V}}$ and $\frac{\sigma_w}{\bar{W}}$ are the coefficients of variation of the sets of v-weights and w-weights, respectively,

n is the number of x_i variables combined, and

r is the mean correlaton among the x_i's.

This equation indicates that the correlation between predictions produced by applying alternative sets of weights to the same set of independent variables is an increasing function of the number of independent variables and the average intercorrelation among those variables, and a decreasing function of the coefficients of variation of the sets of weights. Working through the equation with representative sets of values for n, r, $\frac{\sigma_v}{\bar{V}}$ and $\frac{\sigma_w}{\bar{W}}$ (see Ashton [1980b]) suggests that "a combination of (1) few independent variables, (2) low intercorrelations among those variables and (3) highly variable sets of weighting coefficients must exist in order for composites produced from linear additive models *not* to correlate highly with each other" [Ashton, 1980b, p. 346].

These results involve potentially important implications for three types of weighting coefficients that are used in human information processing research: regression weighting, equal (including unit) weighting, and subjective weighting. Several studies have examined the simplest possible weighting scheme — one in which all variables are assigned equal weights. An equal weighting model has obvious practical advantages: Modeling of people is unnecessary; it is necessary to know only which variables to include and the sign of the zero-order correlation between each variable and the criterion of interest. *Unit* weighting models, in which all variables are assigned a weight of ± 1.0, are a special case of equal weighting models, and any results that can be derived for equal weighting schemes are applicable to unit weighting schemes since outputs from a unit weighting model will correlate + 1.0 with outputs from any other equal weighting model [Einhorn and Hogarth, 1975, p. 177].

The conditions under which the outputs of equal (and unit) weighting models should correlate highly with the outputs of other linear models (including multiple regression models of individuals) are those implied by Equation 3.2, i.e., large n, large r and small $\frac{\sigma_v}{\bar{\bar{V}}}$ or $\frac{\sigma_w}{\bar{\bar{W}}}$.[3] Several analytical, simulation and empirical studies,[4] dating back to 1920, have shown that (1) predictions from equal (and unit) weighting models often correlate very highly with predictions from other linear models (including multiple regression models) and (2) equal (and unit) weighting models often predict a criterion at least as well as do multiple regression models.

The weighting scheme used most frequently in human information processing research is regression weighting. Of particular significance in multiple regression modeling is the decrease in predictive power that occurs when regression weights derived from one sample of data are used for predicting a criterion from a different sample of data.[5] It is well known that a decrease, or "shrinkage," in R^2 will occur because of overfitting the original sample (i.e., fitting some of the "noise") and/or the presence of outliers in the original sample [Wainer, 1976, p. 215]. The use of equal (or unit) weights avoids these problems since such weights are not estimated from the data [Einhorn and Hogarth, 1975, p. 183]. This constitutes another practical advantage of equal (or unit) weighting models.

The amount of shrinkage that will obtain on a different sample can be determined by cross-validating the multiple regression equation on that sample.

---

[3] Note that the coefficient of variation of the weights in an equal-weighting model will be zero.

[4] Analytical studies include Einhorn and Hogarth [1975], Ghiselli [1964], Gulliksen [1950], Newman [1977], Srinivasan [1977], Wainer [1976] and Wainer and Thissen [1976]. Simulation studies include Claudy [1972] and Schmidt [1971]. Empirical studies include Beckwith and Lehmann [1973], Blood [1971], Charters [1920], Dawes and Corrigan [1974], Douglass and Spencer [1923], Ewen [1967], Grant and Bray [1970], Lawshe and Schucker [1959], Ryans [1954], Stalnaker [1938], Trattner [1963], Wesman and Bennett [1959], West [1924], and Yerkes [1921].

[5] Shrinkage of R^2 upon cross-validation is sometimes thought to reflect an advantage that an individual has over multiple regression models. For example, Sawyer [1966, p. 196] stated that: "Predicting in a population different from the one in which experience was derived offers a possible relative advantage to [man because man, unlike model] can adjust to the altered situation. How successfully [man] adjusts depends, of course, upon his ability to recognize the differences in the two samples and to anticipate their effect on the relation between predictors and criterion." This suggestion was contradicted by the results of Moskowitz [1974], who found that 15 of 21 subjects were outperformed by their respective linear regression models even when the models were used in an environment different from that in which they were derived. The regression weights of the subjects' models were robust with respect to the change in the environment. Even if these regression weights had not been so robust, however, equal (or unit) weights would have been perfectly robust since they are not estimated from the data and, therefore, are not sample-specific (see Einhorn and Hogarth [1975]). Thus, robustness to changed environments constitutes another important advantage of equal (and unit) weights relative to regression weights.

Alternatively, the amount of shrinkage can be estimated via several available formulas (e.g., Cattin [1978], Darlington [1968]). Still another way to evaluate the sensitivity of a regression equation developed on a specific sample is to use certain parameters of that sample to estimate the true R^2 in the *population* (e.g., Wherry [1931], [1975]). The following formula, developed by Wherry [1931], can be used for this purpose.

$$\hat{R}_a^2 = 1 - \{(1 - R^2)\,[(N - 1)/(N - n - 1)]\} \tag{3.3}$$

where

$\hat{R}_a^2$ is an estimate of the "adjusted" R^2, i.e., the true value of R^2 in the population,
R^2 is the value of the coefficient of multiple determination computed from the sample,
N is the number of observations on which the multiple regression equation is estimated, and
n is the number of independent (x_i) variables in the equation.

It is clear from Equation 3.3 that the amount of shrinkage of R^2 is a decreasing function of N and R^2, and an increasing function of n. Working through Equation 3.3 with representative sets of values for N, n and R^2 (see Ashton [1980b]) shows that the decrease in R^2 is quite sizable for low to moderate values of R^2 unless a combination of large N and small n is present. Only at a N:n ratio of 20:1 is the (percentage) decrease in R^2 small. Therefore, Equation 3.3 suggests that a simple equal (or unit) weighting model may perform well relative to a multiple regression model applied to a different sample of data unless the combination of a relatively high R^2 value and N:n ratio obtains (cf. Dawes and Corrigan [1974], Schmidt [1972]).

Einhorn and Hogarth's [1975] analytical comparison of regression weighting and unit weighting is consistent with these results. They found that sample size is an important determinant of the relative efficacy of regression weighting and unit weighting. Deriving results for the case of four independent variables, Einhorn and Hogarth found that only in the case of large samples (defined by the researchers as $N > 200$) will regression weighting consistently outperform unit weighting. With moderate sample sizes ($50 < N < 200$), the results were mixed but generally supported the use of unit weighting. With small sample sizes ($N < 50$), unit weighting was found to be superior because regression weights were estimated with too much error. Further, a sample could be so small that regression analysis cannot be performed.

Einhorn and Hogarth [1975] found that a second important factor in the comparison of regression weighting and unit weighting is the degree to which the criterion variable is defined. They considered three possibilities: (1) a *well-defined* criterion is one which is (a) available, (b) measured with a moderate degree of reliability, and (c) related to an "ultimate" criterion (in the sense, for example, that the criterion of grade point average is related to the ultimate criterion of success in graduate school); (2) a *vague* criterion is one which is available and measurable, but whose relationship to an ultimate criterion is questionable (in the sense, for example, that the criterion of salary is questionable as a measure of success); (3) the *absence* of a criterion because of conceptual or measurement problems. Working with four independent variables, Einhorn and Hogarth found that for well-defined criteria regression weighting was superior to unit weighting under two conditions: (1) large sample sizes ($N > 200$), and (2) moderate sample sizes ($50 < N < 200$) if $R^2 > 0.50$; when $R^2 < 0.50$, as is frequently the case in applied settings, unit weighting was preferable to regression weighting. The relative efficiency of regression weighting and unit weighting in decision situations with vague criteria depends on the degree of reliability and ultimate relevance of the criterion. Finally, in situations where criteria are absent, regression analysis cannot be performed.

Another type of weighting coefficient that has been used in human information processing research is a subjective weight. A common technique for eliciting subjective weights is to have the individual allocate 100 points across the cues to indicate the relative importance the individual feels he or she has placed on each cue. This simple elicitation method has been shown to yield cue weights that reproduce actual predictions as well as those obtained by more complex elicitation methods [Cook and Stewart, 1975].

Subjective weights are compared with the weights obtained from a statistical analysis of the individuals' judgments, i.e., standardized regression coefficients (or ω^2 when analysis of variance is used). The result of such a comparison is considered a measure of the degree of self-insight that an individual has into his or her judgment policy as represented by the particular policy-capturing technique used.

One method of comparing subjective weights and statistical weights is to compute correlations between the two sets of weights. The evidence[6] indicates that (1) the degree of association between subjective weights and statistical weights generally is very low, (2) individuals typically overweight relatively unimportant cues, and (3) individuals typically think they utilize more cues than is revealed by the statistical weighting technique employed.

Another method of comparing subjective and statistical weights, suggested by Equation 3.2, is to compute the correlation between the outputs of models using both types of weights, instead of the correlation between the weights themselves. Equation 3.2 suggests that sizable discrepancies between statistical and subjective weights may result in very little difference between the outputs of statistical-weight models and the outputs of subjective-weight models. Apparently, no research that correlates the outputs of these two types of models has been published (cf. Schmitt and Levine [1977]). However, several studies using subjective-weight models to reproduce actual judgments have appeared.[7] Generally, these studies

---

[6] See, for example, Ashton [1974b], Blevins [1975], Hoepfl and Huber [1970], Hoffman [1960], Hofstedt and Hughes [1977], Joyce [1976], Permut [1973], Slovic [1969], Slovic, Fleissner, and Bauman [1972], and Summers, Taliaferro and Fletcher [1970b].

[7] See, for example, Chandler [1970], Cook and Stewart [1975], Green, Carmone, and Wind [1972], Hoepfl and Huber [1970], Nystedt and Magnusson [1975], Summers, Taliaferro, and Fletcher [1970a], and Wright [1977b].

have found that subjective-weight models are very effective, vis-a-vis multiple regression models, in reproducing actual judgments. Moreover, subjective-weight models have been shown to reproduce actual judgments better than multiple regression models when both types of models are cross-validated on a different sample (e.g., Nystedt and Magnusson [1975]).

In summary, the presence of certain task characteristics insures that the outputs of linear (including regression) models will be robust with respect to weighting coefficients. In many cases equal (or unit) weights, as well as subjective weights, will produce outputs that correlate very highly with criterion values. Such robustness is important in explaining the consistent finding that linear models typically outperform their human counterparts in terms of judgment accuracy.

3.1.2.3 Combining Man and Model

An alternative to replacing the individual with a model of his or her judgment policy is to combine the individual and the model in some fashion. A similar alternative is to combine the individual and the (optimal) environmental model. Holt [1958, p. 12] maintains that combination is extremely important: "The real issue is not to find the proper sphere of activity for clinical predictive methods and for statistical ones, conceived in ideal-type terms as antithetical. Rather, we should try to find the optimal combination of actuarially controlled methods and sensitive clinical judgment for any particular predictive enterprises." Many of the issues involved in this approach are discussed by Pankoff and Roberts [1968] and by Sawyer [1966].

Two types of combinations, or syntheses, are possible: (1) *clinical synthesis*, in which the individual uses the output of a model as an additional input to his or her intuitive judgment process; (2) *statistical synthesis*, in which the individual's judgment is treated as an additional variable in a statistical model. Clinical synthesis may be more appealing than statistical synthesis because the former allows the individual to make the ultimate prediction. This position was favored by Bowman [1963, p. 317], who suggested a type of clinical synthesis in a managerial context: "Let the manager look at the decision rule with his regression coefficients and then decide what his decision will be . . . ."

Evidence concerning the effectiveness of such syntheses comes from several studies of "clinical versus statistical prediction," where "statistical prediction" is not restricted to models of individuals but may include other types of optimal, or "actuarial," models as well. In an unusually thorough analysis of 45 such studies, Sawyer [1966] found that while statistical synthesis was superior to clinical synthesis, neither was as effective as simply using the statistical model. Since Sawyer's review, Goldberg [1968] has reported similar results for clinical synthesis. In a study involving the MMPI, Goldberg [1968, p. 493] found that "giving judges the actual values of the optimal formula for each profile . . . did result in a stable increase in diagnostic accuracy, though the accuracy of these judges' diagnoses was not as high as would have been achieved by simply using the formula itself." A statistical synthesis study by Einhorn [1972] produced mixed results: For two of his four subjects (physicians), the linear model that excluded the subject's judgments was more accurate than the linear model that included these judgments; for the other two subjects, the opposite was true.[8]

3.1.2.4 Composite Judgments

Modeling, statistical syntheses, and the use of certain types of feedback are effective for improving judgment accuracy because they reduce, or eliminate, the inconsistency inherent in human judgment. Another way to reduce inconsistency is the mathematical aggregation of individual judgments into composite judgments. One way to form composite judgments is to weight all the individuals' judgments equally [Einhorn, Hogarth, and Klempner, 1977], i.e., to compute the mean judgment across several individuals for each combination of cue levels. This simple aggregation technique avoids the behavioral problem of specifying differential weights to be applied to the judgments of different individuals.

It can be shown analytically that the accuracy of such mean judgments will be greater than or equal to the mean accuracy of the individuals' judgments. Thus, the mean accuracy of the individuals' judgments is a lower limit for the accuracy of composite judgments. However, empirical research conducted within the lens model framework has shown composite judgments to be substantially more accurate than this lower limit. For example, Wiggins and Kohen [1971] found the accuracy of composite judgments in a grade-point prediction task to be .47, compared to a mean individual-judgment accuracy of .33; moreover, their most accurate judge (of 98 subjects) had an accuracy index of only .48. Goldberg [1970] reported in an MMPI prediction task that the accuracy of the composite (.35) was closer to that of the most accurate judge (.39) than to the accuracy of the "average" judge (.28). Similarly, Cooke [1967a, 1967b] found that the temporal stability of composite judgments was higher than that of any individual judge. In addition, Goldberg [1970] found that composite judgments were slightly more accurate than were judgments generated by the multiple regression model based on the composite judgments, but this finding was not replicated by Wiggins and Kohen [1971].

The principal problem involved with substituting composite judgments for individual judgments is the relatively high cost of the composite procedure. Having all individuals in a group respond to all combinations of cue levels as a basis for

---

[8] Given the relatively low accuracy of individual judgments and the increased accuracy gained by modeling, one role that often is discussed for the individual is that of specifying or measuring the inputs that will be combined by a mathematical model (e.g., Einhorn [1972, 1974]). Most judgment situations involve the specification and measurement of independent variables by individuals. There are some judgment situations, however, in which mechanical data collection, as well as mechanical integration of that data into a final judgment, is possible. In the areas of clinical psychology and personnel selection, for example, mechanical data collection includes self-report procedures, psychometric tests, biographical data, and personnel records, i.e., situations in which rules can be prespecified so that human judgment is not directly involved in the data collection process. Clinical methods of data collection involve interviews and observations. Sawyer's [1966] analysis revealed that judgments and predictions were more accurate when the data underlying them were collected mechanically than when the data were collected clinically. This finding held regardless of the mode of data integration (i.e., clinical or statistical). Thus, it appears that the pitfalls of human inconsistency are manifested in data collection as well as in the use of that data in judgment.

forming composite judgments is likely to be considerably more expensive than simply modeling some particular individual. Further, in many applied settings the composite approach may be impossible because of a large number of judges and other uses for their time. In response to this problem, various time-saving schemes have been suggested. Goldberg, for example, suggested using the individual whose judgments have the highest correlation with the composite judgments. He recognized, however, that this individual will not necessarily be the most accurate of all individuals in the group, and this possibility was confirmed by Wiggins and Kohen. Goldberg also suggested that the multiple regression model of the composite judgments could be used, and Wiggins and Kohen's data supported this possibility.

Libby and Blashfield [1978] suggested a different way of reducing the inefficiency of the composite-judgment procedure — by forming composites based on small subsets of the individuals in the group. Libby and Blashfield found that the majority of the incremental accuracy to be gained by forming composites of all individuals in a group could be achieved by forming composites of only three individuals. This result held across three contexts (MMPI; graduate admissions; business failure) involving as many as 43 individuals in the composite. Libby and Blashfield also found that the amount of improvement achieved by three-person composites was greater for the least accurate individuals in the group, although such composites reached asymptote more slowly than did composites based on highly accurate individuals. As a practical matter, then, composites may need to be based on more than three individuals when accuracy is low. The principal importance of Libby and Blashfield's results is not that three-person composites are emphasized; they recognized that larger composites may be desirable for important real-life decisions. This study is important primarily because it suggests that very simple inconsistency-reducing procedures can be effective.

3.2 JUDGMENT AGREEMENT

While much of the research guided by the lens paradigm has investigated judgment accuracy, a great deal of effort has also been devoted to judgment agreement. Several types of judgment agreement have been studied, and suggestions for improving judgment agreement have appeared.

3.2.1 The Importance of Judgment Agreement

The question of why one should be concerned with judgment agreement, in addition to (or instead of) judgment accuracy, sometimes arises. There are two reasons for studying judgment agreement. One involves the relationship between judgment agreement and judgment accuracy. The other reflects the fact that agreement is considered important in many practical judgment contexts.

Concerning the first reason, note that criterion values must be available in order to study judgment accuracy, and they must be measured with some acceptable degree of reliability and validity. In many judgment situations, adequate criterion specification and measurement involve significant problems.[9] However, the four approaches to improving judgment accuracy discussed earlier can be used when criterion values cannot be measured and, therefore, accuracy cannot be assessed directly. Of course, in the feedback approach to improving accuracy, task properties feedback (the most effective type) could not be used since knowledge of criterion values is necessary to specify certain statistical properties of the task. Cognitive feedback could be used in the absence of criterion information.

More important, however, is the replacement (or synthesis) of the individual with his or her model and the use of composite judgments. These techniques should be effective even when criterion values are absent or cannot be measured adequately. For example, Bowman [1963, p. 317] conjectured that "if the theory [that models can outperform individuals] can be verified where it is felt that the system criteria can be measured . . . then some assurance might exist for using it where the criteria can't be measured." This speculation is supported by the notion of attenuation, which concerns the limit placed on accuracy as a result of unreliability. One type of unreliability is instability over time, a major component of which is random error. Goldberg's [1970, p. 423] argument for replacing the individual with his or her model was based, in part, on attenuation:

> . . . if the judge's reliability is less than unity, there must be error in his judgments — error which can serve no other purpose than to attenuate his accuracy. If we could remove some of this human unreliability by eliminating the random error in his judgments, we should thereby increase the validity of the resulting predictions.

A similar rationale, which applies both to replacing the individual by a model and to the use of composite judgments, is given by Ward and Davis [1965, p. 164]:

> Computer judgments will be more consistent and therefore somewhat more valid than human judgments from the same information; in effect, the validity is raised by correcting for "attenuation" arising from fluctuations in the judge's standards and attentiveness, and, if several judges are used in establishing weights, for attenuation due to idiosyncracies of the judge.

In other words, the principal rationale underlying modeling and composite judgments, i.e., that accuracy is increased by eliminating judgment inconsistencies, is applicable when criterion values are absent. In fact, some researchers (e.g., Goldberg [1970], Wiggins and Kohen [1971]) who have investigated these two judgment-improvement approaches have been concerned primarily with judgment tasks in which criterion information is absent. Of course, it was necessary to investigate tasks containing criterion information in order to demonstrate empirically the effectiveness of modeling and composite judgments relative to unaided individual judgment.

---

[9] In addition to criterion specification and measurement problems, several criteria may be relevant in a particular judgment context, and the choice among them may influence the level of judgment accuracy (see Ashton (1976b]). One possible way to handle multiple criteria is to combine them into a composite criterion, but no agreed-upon method for forming such a composite exists (Blum and Naylor [1968]). Also, there are numerous real-life judgment situations in which criterion values will not be known until long after a judgment must be made.

In addition, judgment agreement often is considered desirable in real-life situations when accuracy is not a major concern. For example, it may be considered desirable that different representatives from the same firm or profession (e.g., physicians, attorneys, auditors) agree in their judgments on a particular issue, or make consistent judgments across time when presented with identical information, even if an ultimate appeal to criterion values never will be made. In many judgment situations disagreement is more visible than inaccuracy and may assume greater prominence.

Of course, placing too much emphasis on judgment agreement would be a mistake. As Einhorn [1974, p. 570] notes, "the history of science is replete with oddballs who did not agree with anyone, yet, were proved to be correct by subsequent events." However, he further observes that (p. 571) "from a practical point of view, we cannot afford to wait long periods of time to see who may be correct. Actions and decisions have to be taken within a limited time perspective. Therefore, although agreement is by no means the only criterion, it is one that seems relevant to the discussion of expertise."

3.2.2 Agreement in Fact and in Principle

Judgment agreement may be viewed in two different, yet complementary, ways: (1) agreement in fact; (2) agreement in principle. The former concerns agreement with respect to overall judgments, while the latter concerns agreement with respect to the policies generating the overall judgments. Research concerning agreement in fact often emphasizes the relationship between judgment agreement and judgment accuracy. Research concerning agreement in principle emphasizes potential *reasons* for agreement (or disagreement) in fact.

Much of the early research on judgment agreement was concerned simply with agreement in fact. Goldberg and Werts [1966] identify three types of agreement in fact that have been studied: (1) *stability*, or agreement over time for the same individual using the same data, (2) *consensus*, or agreement across individuals using the same data at one point in time; (3) *convergence*, or agreement across data sources for the same individual at one point in time. Consensus has received most of the research attention, followed by stability, while convergence has been investigated infrequently.[10]

Stability generally is found to be higher than consensus or convergence. Convergence generally is found to be quite low. The research on consensus has produced mixed results. Goldberg [1968] and Nystedt [1974] reference 25 studies, primarily in clinical psychology, in which consensus had a very wide range. More recent research dealing with several different types of experts (e.g., radiologists [Hoffman, Slovic, and Rorer, 1968] and stockbrokers [Slovic, Fleissner, and Bauman, 1972]), has found consensus to be quite low.

---

[10] A more complex experiment is needed to study convergence than to study consensus or stability. However, the use of Campbell and Fiske's [1959] multitrait-multimethod matrix (or, in the case of judgment studies, multidata-multijudge matrix) enables all three types of agreement to be studied simultaneously. Einhorn [1974], Goldberg and Werts [1966] and Nystedt, Magnusson, and Aronowitsch [1975] have employed this approach. The approach has also been suggested for studying the objectivity of accounting measures (R. Ashton [1977]).

While agreement in fact concerns the similarity of overall judgments, agreement in principle concerns the similarity of *judgment policies*. By investigating similarities (or differences) in judgment policies, it is possible to determine some reasons for agreement (or disagreement) in fact.

One way of studying agreement in principle is via the weighting coefficients of individuals' judgment policies, i.e., standardized regression weights when multiple regression is the policy-capturing tool, and ω^2 when analysis of variance is used. Most such comparisons reveal tremendous differences in cue weights across individuals and, to some extent, for the same individual over time. It sometimes is found that each of the available cues is weighted most heavily by some subjects and least heavily by others. Of course, differential cue weighting is one important reason for less than perfect agreement in fact. Subjects whose cue weights are most disparate often show the least agreement in their overall judgments, while those whose cue weights are more similar show higher levels of agreement in fact.

3.2.2.1 The Modified Lens Model Equation

A more precise way of studying agreement in principle, and of comparing agreement in principle with agreement in fact, is to use a modified form of the lens model equation (Equation 3.1). Recall that the lens model equation allows one to measure judgment accuracy (r_a) as a function of task predictability (R_e), judgment consistency (R_s) and the similarity between the environmental and the individual equations, i.e., the matching index (G). Brehmer [1971] suggested that the lens model equation be reformulated to measure the consensus between the judgments of two individuals (r_A), as a function of the matching of their individual equations (G) and their judgment consistency (R_{S1} and R_{S2}), as follows:

$$r_A = G\,R_{S1}R_{S2} \tag{3.4}$$

In this case r_A represents agreement in fact, i.e., the correlation between the Y_s values for the two individuals. The G index represents agreement in principle, or the correlation between the $\hat{Y}_s$ values of the two individuals; as such, G measures the extent to which the systematic features of their judgment policies agree.

Equation 3.4 reveals two possible sources of disagreement in fact ($r_A < 1.00$): (1) the systematic differences between the judgment policies of the individuals (G); (2) the consistency with which the individuals apply their respective policies (R_{S1} and R_{S2}). It is clear from this formulation that disagreement in fact does not necessarily imply disagreement in principle; because of inconsistency (i.e., $R_{S1} < 1.00$ and/or $R_{S2} < 1.00$), disagreement in fact may exist despite perfect agreement in principle ($G = 1.00$). Consistent with the results for judgment accuracy, research reviewed by Brehmer [1976b] indicates that inconsistency is more detrimental to agreement in fact than is disagreement in principle.[11]

---

[11] A slightly different reformulation of the lens model equation would allow a similar analysis for judgment stability. In that case G would represent the systematic features of one individual's judgment policy at two points in time, and R_{S1} and R_{S2} the individual's judgment consistency at two points in time.

3.2.2.2 The Cognitive Conflict Paradigm

The modified lens model equation (Equation 3.4) provides a systematic means for examining reasons for disagreement in fact. In recent years a growing body of research has addressed the structure, determinants, and dynamics of judgment disagreement. This research extends the basic lens model to include two or more individuals. The extended model is called the cognitive conflict paradigm and/or the social judgment theory paradigm [Hammond, Stewart, Brehmer, and Steinmann, 1975].

The type of situation studied via the cognitive conflict paradigm is described by Hammond, Todd, Wilkins and Mitchell [1966, pp. 343-344]:

> The paradigm produces the following situation: two persons who (1) attempt to solve problems which concern both of them, (2) have mutual utilities (their gain [or loss] derives from their approximations to the solution of the problem), (3) receive different training in the solution of a problem involving uncertain inference, (4) are then brought together and find themselves dealing with a familiar problem which their experience apparently prepared them for, but (5) find that their answers differ, and that neither answer is as good as it has been, although each answer is logically defensible and, (6) who must provide a joint decision as to the correct solution and, therefore, (7) must adapt to one another as well as to the task if they are to solve their problems. These conditions were chosen so that the research paradigm would include those circumstances in which men find themselves when attempting to deal with problems to which they bring different and inadequate cognitive systems.

It is important to recognize that this paradigm is concerned with conflict caused by *cognitive* factors, not motivational or conflict-of-interests factors. That is, the paradigm is concerned with conflicts (disagreements) caused by differences in the judgment policies of two or more individuals. Since human judgment is based on a mixture of analysis and experience, instead of analysis alone (called "quasi-rationality" by Hammond and Brehmer[1973]), and since judgment situations involve uncertainty, legitimate differences of opinion concerning the preferred solution to particular problems may exist, and these differences of opinion may lead to disagreement on the part of individuals who must reach joint solutions [Brehmer, 1976b]. Moreover, since an individual may not be fully able to explain how his or her judgments are made, speculations about why particular judgments were made by others may involve assumptions about the motives of the other individual(s) involved. "As a consequence, suspicion and distrust develop, and what started as a purely cognitive disagreement turns into a full-scale emotional and motivational conflict" [Brehmer, 1976b, p. 986].

Note that this formulation presumes an absence of criterion values in real-world settings.[12] That is, the individuals cannot appeal to "the truth" as a means of settling their disagreements. A large number of judgment situations fall into this category, including peace negotiations between warring countries, labor-management negotiations, auditor-client conflicts, inter-auditor disagreements, and the setting of accounting and auditing standards by professional groups. Of

---

[12] In *experimental* settings, however, criterion values are often employed (see Figure 3.1).

course, human judgment is most indispensable when objective criterion values are absent, or are themselves a subject of disagreement.

One of the primary notions underlying the cognitive conflict paradigm is that such conflicts could be at least partially alleviated, and agreement increased, by making an individual aware of his or her judgment policy as well as the policy(ies) of the individual(s) with whom a joint solution must be reached. This is sometimes called "inter-personal understanding" (e.g., Miller [1973]). Most of the research conducted within the cognitive conflict paradigm has focused on the structure of disagreement (via Equation 3.4) and has relied upon simplified laboratory tasks. However, a few studies[13] have applied the paradigm to real-life conflict situations, with results consistent with those found in the laboratory.

Application of the Paradigm to Two Persons. Application of the cognitive conflict paradigm to two individuals is described below, based on Hammond (1965, 1973).[14] The paradigm involves two stages: (1) a training stage, in which the individuals are trained to think differently about the same problem; (2) a conflict stage, in which the individuals are brought together for the purpose of making joint decisions concerning the problem.

The purpose of the training stage is to develop different judgment policies on the part of each individual. In a three-cue task, for example, one individual may be taught to depend most heavily on Cue X_1, less heavily on Cue X_2, and least on Cue X_3, while the second individual learns the reverse pattern of dependencies. Of course, it may be possible to select individuals whose judgment policies will differ as a function of pre-experimental experience, instead of training individuals to think differently about a particular issue. An important advantage of the experimental training method, however, is that it brings cognitive differences under experimental control; as such, it is very useful for initial, basic studies of the nature and structure of disagreements. For more applied work, however, the researcher may choose to investigate cognitive differences generated outside the experiment itself. Such studies have been conducted, and Hammond and Brehmer. [1973] report that essentially the same results were obtained as with laboratory training.

In the conflict stage, the individuals are brought together to apply what they have learned in the training stage. Typically, each individual will make an initial judgment based on each combination of cue values presented, and will communicate this judgment to the other individual. The individuals are then required to reach a joint judgment with respect to that set of cue values, after which each individual makes a second judgment that remains private. In other words, the individual may reconsider his or her initial individual judgment in light of the discussion leading to the joint judgment, but does not communicate this latter judgment to the other individual. Either the criterion value or an estimate of this value typically is provided at this point.

---

[13] See, for example, Adelman, Stewart, and Hammond [1975], Balke, Hammond,and Meyer [1973], Miller [1973].

[14] While the paradigm is applied most often to only two individuals, it has also been applied to three-person (Moscovici, Lage, and Naffrechoux [1973]) and five-person (Cvetkovich [1973]) groups.

An important variable under experimental control is the conflict task. For example, if the two individuals were trained to weight cues differentially and oppositely from each other, the conflict task might require that they weight cues uniformly in order for their joint judgments to agree with the criterion. This situation is depicted in Figure 3.1, where Individual 1 is trained to weight Cues X_1, X_2 and X_3 by r = .75, .50 and .25, respectively, Individual 2 is taught the reverse pattern of weights, and the conflict task sets the optimal weighting at .50 for each cue.

Figure 3.1
The Lens Model in the
Cognitive Conflict Paradigm.

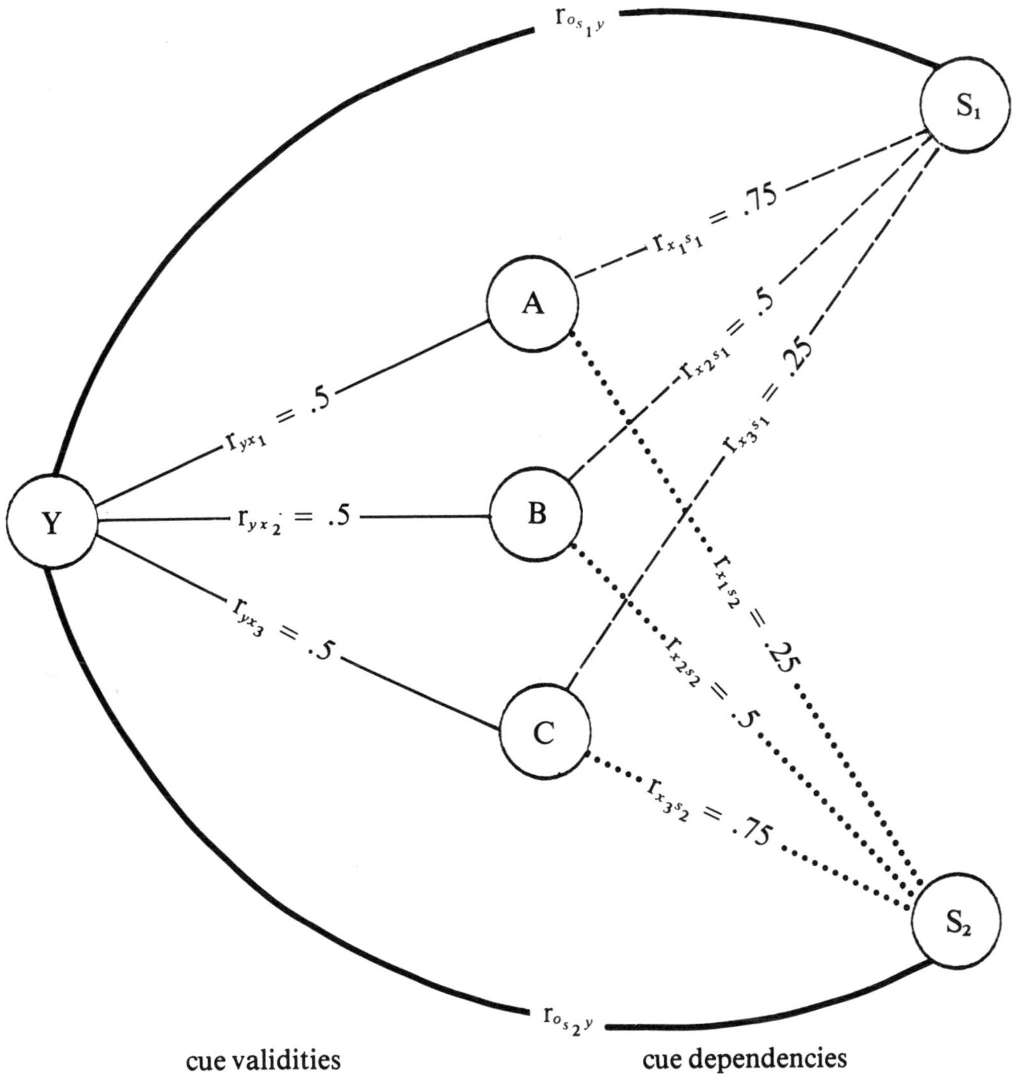

The cognitive conflict paradigm involves the collection of several data for each trial, i.e., for each combination of cue values for which individual and joint judgments must be made. As shown in Figure 3.2, these data are: (1) T_1, the judgment that Individual 1 would make if the individual followed his or her training exactly; (2) T_2, the same for Individual 2; (3) S_1, the "overt" judgment made by Individual 1 and announced to the other individual; (4) S_2, the same for Individual 2; (5) J, the joint judgment made by the two individuals; (6) S_1', the "covert" judgment made privately by Individual 1 after hearing the other individual's initial judgment, listening to the rationale for that judgment, and concurring in a joint judgment with the other individual; (7) S_2', the same for Individual 2. In Figure 3.2, Y is the criterion value and $\hat{Y}$ is an estimate of the criterion value. Either may be given to the individuals as feedback. The $\hat{Y}$ value is sometimes provided instead of Y to make it more difficult for the individuals to reach correct judgments.

Figure 3.2
Basic Data for Each Trial
in the Cognitive Conflict Paradigm.

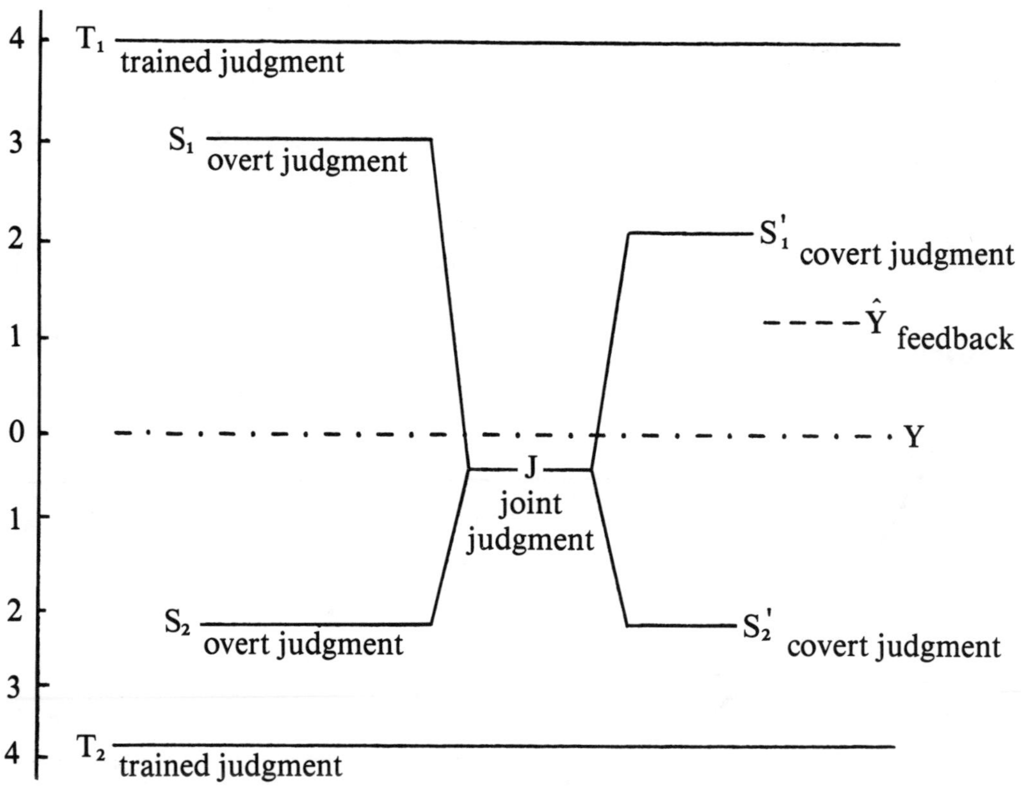

This is a rich paradigm for studying the structure and determinants of disagreements, as well as the dynamics of disagreements over several trials. For example, $T_1 - T_2$ is a measure of the potential disagreement that could arise as a result of differential training, $S_1 - S_2$ is a measure of overt disagreement arising from $T_1 - T_2$, and $S_1' - S_2'$ is a measure of covert disagreement that remains after negotiation has occurred. Similarly, $S_1 - J$ and $S_2 - J$ are measures of compromise on an overt level, while $S_1' - J$ and $S_2' - J$ are measures of compromise on a covert level. Several other intra-trial measures may also be of interest in particular applications. In addition to providing information about the intra-trial structure of disagreement, the paradigm allows inter-trial changes in these measures to be computed as a way of evaluating changes in disagreement or compromise over time. Finally, various attributes of conflict situations that lie outside the paradigm itself (e.g., status differences, or differential threat or power) could be studied via the paradigm.

Structure and Dynamics of Disagreement. Brehmer [1976b] provides an excellent review of studies conducted via the cognitive conflict paradigm. Two of the principal findings concern the importance of consistency (R_s) relative to that of matching (G), and the importance of task variables, to the extent and structure of disagreement.

A large number of studies show that individuals reduce the systematic differences between their judgment policies (increase G) as they interact with each other, but are prevented from reaching high agreement in fact (r_A) because of the inconsistent application of their respective policies (low R_s). In the early trials of a 20-trial sequence, for example, lack of agreement is largely attributable to the use of different judgment policies, presumably as a result of differential training. By the end of the sequence, however, agreement in principle has improved, but this is largely offset by decreased consistency on the part of one or both individuals. Thus, while the *extent* of agreement in fact may change little over trials, its *structure* may change substantially. Individuals apparently decrease their dependency on the cues they were initially trained to use at a faster rate than they learn to use the other cues present in the task, and such an "imbalance" results in decreased judgment consistency.[15] Further, when increased agreement does occur, it apparently results from the individuals' attempts to improve accuracy, relative to $\hat{Y}$, rather than from their attempts to reach compromise. Brehmer [1976b, p. 991] points out that these results concerning the structure of disagreement have been generated across a wide range of subjects and task conditions, including both laboratory and real-life tasks.

The second major result from cognitive conflict studies is the finding that both the extent and structure of agreement are affected by the formal characteristics of the task. While the results of such studies generally do not differ as a function of substantive (content) task characteristics, they do differ with respect to formal (statistical) task characteristics. "The formal characteristics are a set of dimensions by which it is possible to characterize all policy tasks regardless of

---

[15] This finding is consistent with the results of multiple-cue probability learning experiments, i.e., the learning of probabilistic relationships is extremely difficult — especially when outcome feedback is provided.

their content" [Brehmer, 1976b, p. 995]. Brehmer lists seven formal task characteristics: (1) the number of cues; (2) the metric level of the cues; (3) cue intercorrelations; (4) the distribution of cue validities; (5) the form of the function relating cues to the criterion (linear or nonlinear); (6) the organizing principle for information integration (additive or configural); (7) environmental (task) predictability. Three of these dimensions have received substantial attention from researchers (task predictability, function form and cue intercorrelations).

Brehmer reviews several studies which indicate that agreement in fact is lower when task predictability is low and/or the function form is nonlinear. While neither of these dimensions affects the level of policy similarity (agreement in principle), both affect the consistency with which the individuals apply their respective policies. Of course, agreement in fact is directly related to consistency. The level of cue intercorrelation is important because high positive cue intercorrelations can result in similar judgments by two individuals, even if they rely on different cues. In other words, high positive cue intercorrelations can result in high agreement in fact, despite low agreement in principle. Thus, high positive cue intercorrelations may mask the underlying nature of the individuals' agreement. A high level of agreement in fact is much more difficult to achieve when cue intercorrelations are zero.

The cognitive conflict/social judgment theory paradigm is a promising approach to the study of judgment agreement. It and the modified lens model equation enable agreement in fact and agreement in principle to be studied simultaneously, and they provide a rigorous framework within which several determinants of judgment agreement can be studied.

3.2.3 Clustering of Judgment Policies

Some researchers have searched for subgroups of individuals whose judgment policies are similar. Such analyses may be useful for locating individuals who process information similarly — subject, of course, to the limitations of paramorphic representation. Within the cognitive conflict paradigm, such an effort may reveal factions within a group that are likely to disagree.

The mathematical tool used is cluster analysis. It can be applied to either the individuals' actual judgments or to their judgment policies — a distinction corresponding somewhat to that between agreement in fact and agreement in principle. Clustering based on actual judgments has the advantage that models of judgment are not needed, but has the disadvantage that the inconsistency in the individuals' judgments will affect the clustering; thus, two individuals having similar judgment policies but who apply those policies inconsistently, could be placed in different clusters [Hammond, Stewart, Brehmer, and Steinmann, 1975].[16] Clustering based on judgment policies eliminates the effects of judgment inconsistency, but is affected by the policy capturing technique used. This method often is preferred, however, unless there is reason to believe that some problem exists in the policy-capturing analysis that precedes clustering.

---

[16] Ashton [1975b] provides an example of a clustering scheme based on actual judgments.

Several algorithms are available for clustering individuals on the basis of their judgment policies.[17] The use of such algorithms may be illustrated by reference to the JAN (Judgment ANalysis) technique developed by Christal ([1968]; also see Naylor and Wherry [1965]). JAN, a modified hierarchical pairwise clustering scheme,[18] represents each individual's judgment policy in the form of a multiple regression equation. Thus, for a group of N individuals there initially will be N one-person "clusters." Each of the N individual judgment policies is compared with each of the N-1 other policies; N(N - 1)/2 such comparisons are made. JAN determines the multiple regression equation that represents the joint policy of each pair of individuals and computes the loss in predictive efficiency (R_s^2) that results when the original N equations are replaced by N-1 equations. The two equations that are combined are those for which the decrease in R_s^2 is minimized. This process is repeated with the remaining N-1 individuals and clusters until one cluster containing all N individuals emerges. Since the number of individuals, or clusters, is reduced by one at each stage of the grouping procedure, N-1 iterations are required to place all individuals' policies into one cluster. When to stop clustering is determined by the researcher's judgment of "large" versus "small" changes in R_s^2 values. For example, if a "small" amount of predictive efficiency is lost in going from 20 to five clusters, but a "large" amount of predictive efficiency is lost in going from five to four clusters, this is considered evidence for the existence of five "types" of judgment policies among the group of N individuals.

Very little evidence exists concerning the performance of the JAN technique, or the comparative features of JAN vis-à-vis the other clustering algorithms available. However, Dudycha [1970] has conducted an extensive simulation analysis of JAN, varying a large number of factors that may be important in actual judgment situations. Since simulation was used, Dudycha was able to assess the "correctness" with which JAN clustered judgment policies under a variety of experimental conditions. The principal findings were that the ability of JAN to correctly cluster individuals' judgment policies was directly related to the number of cues, the number of judgments, and the individuals' linear consistency (R_s), and was inversely related to the extent of cue intercorrelation. Linear consistency and cue intercorrelation are of particular interest. Judgment policies that are more predictable (high R_s) may be discriminated easily from policies that are less predictable. However, as cue intercorrelations increase it becomes more difficult to discriminate among judgment policies. Two individuals may produce equally high R_s values by relying on different subsets of the available cues if those cues are highly intercorrelated. More research is needed for a fuller assessment of the characteristics of clustering procedures. At this stage of their development, they provide a useful but rough heuristic for assessing the similarity among a large number of judgment policies.

---

[17] See, for example, Christal [1968], Maguire and Glass [1968], Wherry and Naylor [1966] and Williams, Harlow, Lindem, and Gab [1970]. Dudycha [1970] provides several references to additional clustering algorithms.

[18] See, for example, Johnson [1967], King [1967], Ward [1963] and Ward and Hook [1963].

Part II

The SEU Paradigm

CHAPTER FOUR

Models of Risky Choice

Descriptive models of risky choice attempt to explain how individuals make "risky" decisions, i.e., decisions in which the potential outcomes of alternative actions are not known with certainty. Risky decisions may be contrasted with "riskless" decisions in which the outcomes associated with particular actions are known [Fischer, 1976]. Several types of risky choice models have been proposed. Some were developed primarily from a normative perspective, while others were suggested by the results of descriptive research on information processing and decision making.

Risky choice models entail the notion that decisions are influenced by the (objective or subjective) probabilities of relevant events. However, the role and importance of probabilities differ substantially in the various risky choice models. For example, in some models, probabilities are thought to be combined with subjective or objective values of possible outcomes. In other models, probabilities are thought to affect choices independently of the values of outcomes. Chapter 5 is devoted to the assessment, revision, and utilization of probabilities.

The present chapter considers the major types of risky choice models that have received attention by human information processing researchers. Expectation models, primary the subjectively expected utility and expected value models, are discussed first. Then, several models that do not rely on expectation are described. These include models that emphasize higher moments of probability distributions and risk "dimensions," models that entail some type of lexicographic choice procedure, and models that involve trade-offs between expectation and other parameters of the choice situation.

4.1 EXPECTATION MODELS

Expectation models of risky choice are predicated on the assumption that individuals make choices that maximize mathematical expectation. The expectation of each alternative choice may be represented by the summation, over all outcomes that could result from the choice, of the product of some measure of the probability of each outcome and some measure of the value of that outcome. Each variable in the expectation equation — probability and value — can be treated as either a subjective or an objective factor, resulting in the four expectation models shown in Table 4.1.

The most general expectation model assumes the maximization of subjectively expected utility (SEU). Like the other three models in Table 4.1, SEU is an "as if" theory of risky choice, and not a process theory [Rapoport and Wallsten, 1972]. That is, the SEU model does not hold that individuals actually assess probabilities and utilities, calculate SEU's, and deliberately choose the alternative with the greatest SEU. It does assume, however, that the hypothesis of SEU maximization will enable prediction of the choices made by the individual. The model further assumes that individuals' choice behavior conforms to a set of relatively simple and intuitively plausible axioms of "rational" choice (e.g., Savage [1954]). This is an important behavioral assumption because conformity to the axioms implies SEU maximization. A decision maker who accepts all the axioms is logically compelled to accept SEU maximization as his or her choice criterion. If, however, the decision maker rejects one or more of the axioms, then SEU maximization does not necessarily follow [MacCrimmon and Larsson, 1975].

Table 4.1
Types of Expectation Models

Model	Probability Measure	Value Measure	Expectation of Outcome i	Expectation of a Choice Alternative Having n Possible Outcomes
Expected Value	Objective	Objective	P_iV_i	$\sum_{i=1}^{n} P_iV_i$
Expected Utility	Objective	Subjective	P_iU_i	$\sum_{i=1}^{n} P_iU_i$
Subjectively Expected Value	Subjective	Objective	Ψ_iV_i	$\sum_{i=1}^{n} \Psi_iV_i$
Subjectively Expected Utility	Subjective	Subjective	Ψ_iU_i	$\sum_{i=1}^{n} \Psi_iU_i$

Legend: P_i = an objective probability
Ψ_i = a subjective probability
V_i = an objective measure of value (e.g., money)
U_i = a subjective measure of value (utility)

Source: Adapted from Nickerson and Feehrer [1975, p. 8]

4.1.1 Perspectives

A great deal of human information processing research has been conducted within the general framework of the SEU model. This research typically has addressed the descriptive validity of the SEU model vis-à-vis the choices actually made by individuals. The research has been conducted at two levels of analysis: (1) The *global* level concerns whether the hypothesis of SEU maximization will predict the choices actually made by decision makers; (2) the *axiom* level concerns whether decision makers' choices reflect the basic structural characteristics necessary for SEU maximization. The relative importance of these two levels of analysis depends on the dominant perspective from which the SEU model is viewed. Three perspectives — prescription, description and prediction — have been taken in the literature.[1]

4.1.1.1 Prescription

The prescriptive perspective on SEU theory has been emphasized frequently. Becker and McClintock [1967, pp. 239-41] describe this perspective: "Some . . . models [are] designed to help people make 'better' decisions in the sense of aiding them to behave consistently with some *a priori* set of requirements or rules to which they want their choices to conform . . . . The models are not designed to describe how men ordinarily behave . . . . The models prescribe how to act if one is to be 'rational'." One implication of the prescriptive perspective is that the SEU model should be taught, and some decision theorists have shown concern for training decision makers in the tenets of this model:

> . . . no one claims that most people *do* behave as they *ought* to behave. Indeed, the primary reason for the adoption of a prescriptive or normative theory (that is, an "ought to do" theory) for choice behavior is the observation that when decision making is left solely to unguided judgment, choices are often made in an internally inconsistent fashion, and this indicates that perhaps the decision maker could do better than he is doing. If people always behaved as this prescriptive theory says they ought to, then there would be no reason to make a fuss about a prescriptive theory. We could then just tell people, "Do what comes naturally" [Raiffa, 1968, pp. 81-82].

> . . . certain formal norms of good decision making have been formulated. They do not, in general, coincide with the habits of decision making among ordinary people in our or any other civilization. These habits can be studied empirically. Moreover, there may be a social need to bring these habits closer to the norms. It is important that at least people whose decisions involve the welfare of many others should fulfill certain norms of consistency, should know, for example, how to 'make up their minds': business administrators, public servants, military leaders. If so, the question of what are and how to change decision habits becomes one of great practical importance [Marschak, 1974, p. 122].

Training that emphasizes SEU maximization at the global level must focus on the assessment of subjective probabilities and/or utilities, as well as the proper combination rule for these two components. Evidence reviewed in Chapter 5 suggests that individuals have a great deal of difficulty assessing and revising probabilities, and that training is, at best, only moderately helpful.

Training that relies on descriptive research at the axiom level is likely to be much more successful. As Krantz and Tversky [1971, p. 168] note,

---

[1] These three perspectives are elaborated in A. Ashton [1979].

> . . . the test of [axioms] is typically a more efficient method than an overall test of goodness of fit, in order to discover which aspects of a theory, if any, are at fault. An evaluation of goodness of fit of a numerical model can indicate that the theory is violated, but unlike the test of specific axioms, it is not very likely to locate the source of the discrepancy. The failure of . . . transitivity in choice behavior . . . or of the [irrelevance principle] in decision making under uncertainty are . . . examples of significant empirical findings that were revealed by the direct test of critical axioms, and that were practically impossible to detect from global analyses of goodness of fit of the corresponding numerical models.

Within the prescriptive perspective, human information processing research at the axiom level may be useful in several ways. For example, if unaided individual choices are consistent with those prescribed by the axioms, then training will not be necessary. Second, the research could show that deviations from the requirements of the axioms are so minor that the global SEU model is robust with respect to them. Third, if violations of the axioms reflect a failure to understand the axioms, then training in the requirements and implications of the axioms may be useful. Fourth, if violations are found to be situation-specific, then research could focus on determining the characteristics of decision situations in which unaided choices do, and do not, conform to the axioms. Such research could be used to augment training efforts. Finally, it could be found that violations of the axioms are substantial and persistent because SEU maximization requires behavior that individuals are incapable of performing, or are unwilling to perform. In that case, modifications of the theory that encompass processing costs (e.g., time and cognitive effort) could be explored.

4.1.1.2 Description

The prescriptive and descriptive perspectives on SEU theory are not totally distinct. However, while the prescriptive view of SEU theory tends to emphasize the requirements that choices must meet to be "rational," the descriptive view tends to emphasize the actual choice behavior of individuals. The SEU model plays an important role in this perspective by providing a "starting point" in the search for adequate descriptive models of choice (c.f. Barclay, Beach, and Braithwaite [1971]). Moreover, many descriptive choice models may be viewed as modifications of the normative SEU model, even if their development was not specifically motivated by observed departures from that model. Human information processing researchers in psychology typically take the descriptive perspective on the SEU model because of their interest in understanding the cognitive processes involved in risky decision making.

The axiom-level formulation of the SEU model appears to be more useful in this regard than the global-level formulation for two reasons: First, the global SEU model was never intended to describe risky decision making; instead, its proponents claim only that it will predict the resulting decisions. Second, the behavior required to follow the axioms is presumed to be more "fundamental" than that required for SEU maximization at the global level. Krantz and Tversky [1971, p. 167] commented on choice-behavior research at the axiom level:

> . . . the qualitative assumptions of [SEU] theory (e.g., transitivity, the extended sure-thing principle) provide a much more satisfactory formulation of decision making under uncertainty than the assertion that people behave as if they assign utilities and subjective probabilities to outcomes and events, respectively, multiply the utility of each outcome by its subjective probability of occurrence, and then choose the alternative for which the sum of these products is maximal. Although the axiomatic and numerical formulations of . . . the expected-utility rules are equivalent, the former suggests a more plausible (non-numerical) psychological mechanism. In this respect, it explicates the proposed numerical rule in terms of more fundamental, and often more transparent, principles.

The emphasis on "fundamental" behavior in the study of risky decision making has a counterpart in research on intuitive probability revision. Some researchers, e.g., Kahneman and Tversky [1972], have argued that reliance on a normative model (Bayes' theorem) as a starting point for understanding intuitive probability revision is likely to be less productive than focusing on more fundamental aspects or dimensions of probabilistic judgments. Chapter 5 elaborates on this issue.

4.1.1.3 Prediction

The predictive perspective emphasizes the predictive validity of the global SEU model. Proponents of this view typically regard the axioms as "plausible provisional assumptions" (Fama and Miller, 1972, p. 5) from which the SEU maximization hypothesis can be derived. In this view, the descriptive validity of the axioms is irrelevant. Friedman [1953] is perhaps the principal proponent of this viewpoint: " . . . the relevant question to ask about the 'assumptions' of a theory is not whether they are descriptively 'realistic,' for they never are, but whether they are sufficiently good approximations for the purpose in hand. And this question can be answered only by seeing whether the theory works, which means whether it yields sufficiently accurate predictions" (p. 15).

Critics of Friedman's viewpoint argue that, while predictive accuracy is important, it is not a sufficient basis for evaluating a theory. For example, in the context of the economic theory of the firm, Marschak [1965, pp. 447-48] argues that "Dissenters to the general view that realism of assumptions is unimportant in economic theory have recently grown in numbers . . . . With respect to the theory of the firm, the goodness of predictions from the traditional theory has been questioned, and increasing the realism of the theory has been defended on the traditional ground that improved predictions are a likely result, as well as on the ground that improved realism may be desirable in itself (e.g., in order to give better advice to firms)." Good discussions and critiques of Friedman's argument are provided by Koopmans [1957], Rotwein [1959], Nagel [1963], Simon [1963] and Samuelson [1963].

For the purposes of human information processing research, it can be concluded that when the axioms of the SEU model are not violated the predictive validity of the global SEU maximization hypothesis is assured. However, for those individuals and decision tasks for which the global hypothesis does not "work," the descriptive validity of the axioms can be important because of their potential role in training decision makers. In other words, one way to increase the predictive validity of the SEU model is to teach people to follow the axioms.

4.1.2 The Global Level

Studies at the global level typically investigate the extent to which the SEU maximization hypothesis can predict choices actually made by individuals. Other studies have focused on the expected value (EV) model. The remaining two models in Table 4.1 have received little attention from human information processing researchers. Representative examples of SEU and EV studies are reviewed in this section.

4.1.2.1 SEU Maximization

In order to determine the extent to which the SEU model can predict individuals' choices, subjective probability and utility functions must be established for individual decision makers. These functions may be established via direct elicitation methods, or they may be inferred from the decision maker's choices. In such studies, decision makers typically make choices among gambles, and these choices are compared to those predicted by the SEU model [Edwards, 1955].

Studies that infer subjective probability and utility functions from choices are subject to the criticism that they allow the SEU model to "explain too much" (see, e.g., Coombs and Pruitt [1960]). Edwards [1962, pp. 43-44] elaborated on this feature of global SEU studies:

> We usually suppose that choices among risky courses of action are determined by both utilities and subjective probabilities, and we then attempt to infer appropriate values of these quantities to account for observed sets of choices. Since we permit considerable arbitrariness in determining utility and subjective probability values, it takes some substantial set of observations, very carefully chosen, to obtain a contradiction of the SEU model . . . . I know of no experiment in the psychological literature which cannot be explained in terms of appropriate utility and subjective probability functions. Consequently I am compelled to argue that no evidence against the SEU model exists.
>
> I do not consider this fact to be in favor of the SEU model, however. What it means is that the SEU model, in the form in which it has usually been defined, is so vague that it is almost impossible to find a reasonable pattern of behavior which is inconsistent with it.

Studies that have inferred subjective probability and utility functions from individuals' choices include Coombs, Bezembinder, and Goode [1967], Tversky [1967b] and Wallsten [1970, 1971]. Tversky [1967b; also see 1967c] and Wallsten inferred simultaneously subjective probability and utility functions to account for individuals' choices among two-outcome gambles that involved small positive and zero payoffs. While the results of these studies were mixed, each found substantial support for SEU theory. Coombs, Bezembinder and Goode [1967] inferred subjective probability and utility functions from individuals' choices among pairs of gambles in which one outcome of each gamble was always zero, and they identified inconsistent preferences among the pairs of gambles. The

SEU model was rejected as an adequate representation of subjects' choice behavior for five to ten percent (depending on certain experimental conditions) of the subjects. In another study of two-outcome gambles involving one payoff of zero (and the second payoff ranging to ± $5.50), Edwards [1955] found that individuals' choices could be predicted by the SEU maximization hypothesis in 73 percent of the cases. Of the non-SEU choices, 64 percent were "transient errors," i.e., in which the subjects chose the non-SEU gambles in only some of the four experimental sessions. The other 36 percent represented consistent non-SEU choices in all four sessions.

The above studies found support for SEU theory. All the authors were careful to point out, however, that the experimental tasks were extremely simple. This point was presented most succinctly by Wallsten's [1970, p. 3] description of his own study: "The experiment and analysis were done in the simplest risky choice situation possible, that of choices between two gambles, each of which had one positive and one zero outcome, whose occurrences depended on simple probabilistic events. It was reasoned that this situation is the most likely to be satisfactorily described in terms of an SEU model . . . . If . . . the theory . . . fails here, it is hard to see how [it] could be extended to more complicated cases."

In a lengthy review of the literature in this area, Rapoport and Wallsten [1972] observed that studies that support SEU theory are based on experiments that are simpler than those that refute SEU theory. An example of a more complex experiment is that by Davenport and Middleton [1973]. These authors used the same methodology as Coombs, Bezembinder, and Goode [1967] but employed duplex gambles (described later in this chapter) instead of simple two-outcome gambles. SEU theory was not upheld for 23 percent to 33 percent of their subjects, as compared to five to ten percent in the Coombs, Bezembinder, and Goode [1967] study.

4.1.2.2 EV Maximization

Other studies have investigated the expected value model, a special case of the SEU model which employs objective measures of probabilities and values. Several of these studies have found that the EV model predicts choices among simple gambles very well (e.g., Miller and Lanzetta [1962], Mosteller and Nogee [1951], Myers, Reilly, and Taub [1961], Myers, Suydam, and Gambino [1965], Royden, Suppes, and Walsh [1959], Suydam [1965]).

Some studies, however, have not supported the EV model. For example, Lichtenstein, Slovic, and Zink [1969] found that expected value was hardly used, even when the concept was carefully explained and EV's were clearly displayed. Edwards [1956], Lee [1971b], Suydam [1965], and Taub and Myers [1961] found that expected regret ratio (see [Lee, 1971a]) often was a more important choice criterion than was expected value difference. In addition, Slovic [1967] and Slovic and Lichtenstein [1968a] found that explicitly-stated probabilities and payoffs had greater influence on choice behavior than did expected values.

Task complexity appears relevant to EV studies as well as SEU studies. For example, Herman and Bahrick [1966] found an inverse relationship between the complexity of experimental gambles and the appropriateness of the expected value model. Scodel, Ratoosh, and Minas [1959] found almost no relationship between expected values and choices among extremely complex gambles.

To summarize the evidence from studies conducted at the global level, it appears that the SEU model is a fairly good predictor of actual choice behavior in simple tasks. However, some evidence from both SEU studies and EV studies suggests that these expectation models become poorer predictors as the experimental tasks become more complex. Wallsten's [1970] analysis of the simplicity/complexity issue concluded that "the psychological changes from simple to progressively more complicated situations is qualitative, not quantitative" (p. 30). Based largely on this argument, Rapoport and Wallsten [1972] suggested that "the basic experimental question should not be whether to accept or reject SEU theory as a whole, but rather to systematically discover the conditions under which it is or is not valid" (p. 141).

While several alternative risky choice models have been proposed and investigated, none is as comprehensive or as carefully formulated as the SEU model. However, some of these alternative models can explain certain choice behaviors that are inconsistent with the SEU model,[2] and some can predict actual choices better than expectation models, at least in some types of choice situations. Alternative risky choice models are described in Section 4.2.

4.1.3 The Axiom Level

As noted earlier, SEU theory does not assume that individuals actually assess subjective probabilities and utilities and consciously calculate SEUs. Instead, it maintains that the hypothesis of SEU maximization will enable prediction of individuals' choices. SEU theory does assume, however, that individuals' choices conform to a set of axioms that entail consistent decision behavior at an elementary level. Several sets of axioms have been developed (e.g., Arrow [1971], Marschak and Radner [1972], Savage [1954], von Neumann and Morgenstern [1947]). Luce and Suppes [1965] and MacCrimmon and Larsson [1975] summarize and compare several axiom systems.

A typical system consisting of five axioms has been described informally by Becker and McClintock [1967]: (1) *Transitivity* — If A is preferred to B, and B is preferred to C, then A should be preferred to C; (2) *Comparability* — An individual should be willing to compare two outcomes and to decide either that he or she prefers one to the other or is indifferent between them; (3) *Dominance* — If, under every possible state of nature, action a leads to an outcome that is at least as desirable as the outcome that would result from a second action, b, and for at

---

[2] One type of choice behavior that cannot be explained by the SEU model is a response-mode effect. For example, Lichtenstein and Slovic [1971, 1973] and Lindman [1971] found, in some fairly complex experiments, that when subjects responded by *choosing* among alternative gambles, their responses were influenced most heavily by the probabilities of winning. However, when subjects responded by *bidding* for gambles, higher bids were made for gambles with the larger amounts to win. This response-mode bias often caused subjects to choose one gamble over another when the choice procedure was used, but to make the opposite choice when the bidding procedure was used. As Lichtenstein and Slovic [1971, p. 54] observed, "subjectively expected utility theory postulates both a subjective probability function and a subjective worth function, but does not allow either function to change its shape as the response mode changes."

least one possible state of nature, action a leads to a more desirable outcome than b, then action b should not be preferred to action a; (4) *Irrelevance* (of identical outcomes) — If, for some particular state of nature, two actions lead to the same outcome, the individual's preference between those actions should not be affected by the outcome associated with that state. In other words, a change in the outcome associated with that state should not affect the individual's preference, so long as both actions continue to have the same outcome for that state; (5) *Independence* (of utility and probability) — The individual's beliefs about the probability of the occurrence of a given outcome should not be affected by his or her desires for or against that outcome.

Several studies have investigated the extent to which individuals' actual choices correspond to the requirements of axioms. However, only three axioms — transitivity, irrelevance and independence — have received a significant amount of research attention.

4.1.3.1 Transitivity of Preferences

While experimental studies typically support the descriptive validity of the transitivity axiom, individuals' preferences have been found to violate this axiom in two types of settings.[3] One involves the intransitivity of indifference (e.g., being indifferent between one and two grains of sugar in your coffee and between two and three grains, but reaching a point, say 3000 grains, at which you are no longer indifferent). The second and more important setting involves multidimensional alternatives.

Tversky [1969] provides an example of the multidimensional alternative case. He designed two experiments specifically to demonstrate intransitivities among multidimensional alternatives. Tversky [1969, pp. 32-33] noted: "The purpose of the following studies was to create experimental situations in which individuals would reveal consistent patterns of intransitive choices. The experiments are not addressed to the question of whether human preferences are, in general, transitive; but rather to the question of whether reliable intransitivities can be produced, and under what conditions." Tversky preselected subjects for the main experiments by administering pilot tests to determine which subjects were likely to be intransitive. The pilot test for the first experiment employed simple gambles of the form (x, p, 0), where the subject received a payoff of $x if an event with probability p occurred and $0 if that event (with probability 1-p) did not occur. The probability p corresponded to the relative size of the black sector of a black and white circular disk. The exact numerical size of p was not displayed; thus, the subjects were unable to compute the gambles' expected values. The payoffs, however, were displayed numerically. The five gambles shown in Table 4.2 were used. It was hypothesized that some subjects would choose between adjacent gambles (a and b; b and c; etc.) on the basis of payoffs, but would choose between

---

[3] Tests and discussions that are relevant to transitivity include Armstrong [1939, 1948, 1950, 1951], Davidson and Marschak [1959], Davis [1958], Edwards [1953], Griswold and Luce [1962], Luce [1956], MacCrimmon and Larsson [1975], May [1954], Morrison [1963], Papandreou, Sauerlander, Brownlee, Hurwicz, and Franklin [1957], Quandt [1956], Rose [1963], Tullock [1964], Tversky [1969] and Weinstein [1968].

gambles lying far apart in the chain (e.g., a and e) on the basis of the probabilities of winning or the expected value. Such a preference pattern must violate transitivity at some point in the chain.

Table 4.2
Gambles Used by Tversky [1969]

Gamble	Probability of Winning	Payoff (in $)	Expected Value (in $)
a	7/24	5.00	1.46
b	8/24	4.75	1.58
c	9/24	4.50	1.69
d	10/24	4.25	1.77
e	11/24	4.00	1.83

Source: Tversky [1969, p. 33]

The following criterion was used to identify subjects who were likely to exhibit consistent intransitivities in Experiment 1: On at least three of the four pairs of adjacent gambles, the subject had to choose the alternative with the higher payoff (a > b; b > c; c > d; d > e), while on the most extreme pair the subject had to choose the gamble with the higher expected value (e > a). The subject had to exhibit this preference pattern on at least two of three replications of the pairs. Eight of 18 subjects met this criterion, and were chosen for Experiment 1, which was almost identical to the pilot study. Experiment 2 was structurally similar to Experiment 1. It involved the selection of hypothetical college applicants on the basis of three dimensions. A pilot test was used to select subjects for Experiment 2, and 15 of 36 subjects met a criterion similar to that employed in the pilot test for Experiment 1. In the two main experiments, six of the eight (and 11 of the 15) subjects consistently exhibited intransitive preferences.

Post-experimental debriefing revealed that most subjects believed that people (including themselves) are and should be transitive. The subjects were surprised to learn of their own intransitivities. Tversky [1969, p. 45] suggested four possible reasons why individuals are confident that their preferences are transitive: (1) Individuals may view transitivity as a logical principle whose violation represents an error of reasoning; thus, individuals are unlikely to admit making intransitive choices; (2) One can attribute intransitivities to changes in tastes that occur between choices; (3) Many important decisions are made sequentially; thus, an individal who has chosen y over x, and then z over y, may feel committed to z and may not even compare it to x, which has already been eliminated; (4) The eliminated alternative may no longer be available; therefore, it may be impossible to determine whether one's preferences are transitive.

4.1.3.2 Irrelevance of Identical Outcomes

The irrelevance axiom maintains that if alternatives have identical outcomes under a particular state of nature, then the ordering of those alternatives should be independent[4] of the value of that common outcome; in other words, "identical outcomes of alternative decisions should be disregarded, and a choice among alternatives should be made utilizing only the remaining information" [Moskowitz, 1974, p. 227].

Studies of the irrelevance axiom typically are based on a decision problem originally suggested by Allais [1953]. The problem presents an individual with two decision situations, each involving a pair of gambles, as shown in Table 4.3. An individual who chooses Gamble 1 over Gamble 2 in Situation A must choose Gamble 3 over Gamble 4 in Situation in order to conform to the axiom; that is, the identical outcomes in Gambles 1 and 2 (.89 probability of receiving $1,000,000) and the identical outcomes in Gambles 3 and 4 (.89 probability of receiving $0) should be disregarded. After the common outcomes have been eliminated, Gambles 1 and 3 are identical (as are Gambles 2 and 4); thus the choice of Gamble 1 (2) should be accompanied by the choice of Gamble 3 (4).

Table 4.3
The Allais Problem

	Probability of Winning	Amount to Win
Situation A		
Gamble 1	1.00	$1,000,000
Gamble 2	.10	$5,000,000
	.89	$1,000,000
	.01	$ 0
Situation B		
	Probability of Winning	Amount to Win
Gamble 3	.11	$1,000,000
	.89	$ 0
Gamble 4	.10	$5,000,000
	.90	$ 0

[4] The "irrelevance of identical outcomes" axiom often is referred to as the "independence from irrelevant outcomes" axiom. The experimental studies discussed in this section, and in Chapter 8, typically shorten this label and refer to the axiom simply as the independence axiom. In this book, however, the word independence is used for the "independence of utility and probability" axiom.

The choice of Gamble 1 in Situation A and Gamble 4 in Situation B violates the axiom. However, this pair of choices appeals to many individuals. In Situation A, one may wish to avoid even a small probability (.01) of not receiving $1,000,000. In Situation B, one may feel that because the probability of receiving any non-zero amount is small, and the probabilities of receiving $1,000,000 and $5,000,000 so nearly equivalent, one should choose the gamble that offers the larger payoff. This reasoning leads to a choice of Gambles 1 and 4 in violation of the axiom.[5]

The choice of Gambles 1 and 4 also violates the SEU maximization hypothesis directly. The choice of Gamble 1 over Gamble 2 implies U($1,000,000) > .10 U($5,000,000) + .89 U($1,000,000) + .01 U($0), or .11 U($1,000,000) > .10 U($5,000,000) + .01 U($0). The choice of Gamble 4 over Gamble 3 by the same individual implies .11 U($1,000,000) + .89 U($0) < .10 U($5,000,000) + .90 U($0), or .11 U($1,000,000) < .10 U($5,000,000) + .01 U($0).

MacCrimmon [1965, 1968] reported the first descriptive test of the irrelevance axiom. MacCrimmon presented 36 business executives with a hypothetical investment situation involving the same probabilities as the original Allais problem. The outcomes of "a 500 percent return," "a 5 percent return," and "bankruptcy" were substituted for $5,000,000, $1,000,000 and $0, respectively. After having made their choices, the subjects were presented with two prepared answers to the problem (one conforming to the axiom, the other violating it) and were asked to critique each answer and to select the one that seemed more logical. Forty percent of the subjects gave initial answers that violated the axiom. However, 80 percent selected the violating answer as more logical than the conforming answer. During a post-experimental interview, an additional 15 percent of the subjects accepted the conforming reasoning, and the remaining 25 percent *would have* accepted it, according to MacCrimmon [1968, pp. 10-11], had the probability of the identical outcomes not been so extreme. Slovic and Tversky [1974], Moskowitz [1974] and MacCrimmon and Larsson [1975] reported similar studies in which the proportion of subjects who violated the axiom ranged from 30 percent to 60 percent.[6]

---

[5] Normative decision theorists sometimes object to decision problems that are designed to elicit violations of the axioms. For example, Marschak [1968, p. 49] has referred to such problems as "brain twisters." Others complain that decision makers who violate the axioms have been tricked [Samuelson, 1952, p. 678], trapped and dazzled [Borch, 1968, p. 489]. Still others attribute such violations to carelessness, complexity, and vagueness [Winkler, 1972,p. 263], mistakes and misinterpretations [Roberts, 1963, p. 330], judgmental slips [Raiffa, 1968, p. 83], and logical lapses [MacCrimmon, 1968, p. 10]. One proponent of this view is Borch [1968], who has stated (p. 488): "It is well known that the question posed by Allais contains a trap, which the unsophisticated easily might fall into." One who accepts Borch's view might conclude that Savage was unsophisticated since Savage violated his own axiom when initially presented with the Allais problem. According to Savage [1954, p. 103]: "When the two situations were first presented, I immediately expressed preference for Gamble 1 as opposed to Gamble 2 and for Gamble 4 as opposed to Gamble 3, and I still feel an intuitive attraction to those preferences. But I have since accepted the following way of looking at the two situations . . . ."

[6] A closely related implication of this axiom concerns the risk/uncertainty distinction discussed by Ellsberg [1961], who has devised problems that often result in violations of the axiom. Ellsberg-type problems are discussed and debated by Becker and Brownson [1964], Ellsberg [1961, 1963], MacCrimmon [1965, 1968], MacCrimmon and Larsson [1975], Raiffa [1961], Roberts [1963], Slovic and Tversky [1974], and Smith [1969]. In addition, MacCrimmon and Larsson [1975] discuss other related implications of this axiom.

4.1.3.3 Independence of Utility and Probability

The independence axiom maintains that utilities are functions only of the possible outcomes and are not influenced by subjective probabilities, and that subjective probabilities are functions only of the individual's degree of belief that the outcomes will occur and are not influenced by the utilities for those outcomes. As Tversky [1967b, p. 178] explains, "The fundamental assumption of all psychological expectation models . . . is that utility and subjective probability contribute independently to the overall 'worth' of a gamble. That is, judgments of desirability of outcomes are independent of judgments of likelihoods of events. More specifically, utility and subjective probability are compensatory but noninteracting."

Experimental studies show that the independence axiom is violated in several ways. The most common forms of violation involve the dependence of subjective probability estimates on utilities or objective values. Slovic [1966, p. 23] has sketched several possible forms that this type of violation might take, and these are reproduced in Table 4.4. Graph (a) depicts the independence between utilities and subjective probabilities assumed by the axiom. Graphs (b) and (c) indicate that individuals may overestimate the probability of desirable events and underestimate the probability of undesirable events. If the level of assessed probability is a function of the sign, but not the magnitude, of the utilities, then the situation is referred to as one of "partial optimism." If the relationship between utilities and subjective probabilities is more or less continuous over the entire range of utilities, this is referred to as "complete optimism." Partial and complete pessimism (Graphs (e) and (f)) may be considered the converse of partial and complete optimism.

Graph (d), depicting what Slovic [1966] has called the "it can't happen to me" phenomenon, is based on the notion that the probability of events with extremely desirable or undesirable outcomes will be underestimated. Conversely, Graph (g), depicting the "it can happen to me" phenomenon, entails the notion that extremely desirable or undesirable events will trigger extreme hope or fear, which will cause an individual to assess a high probability that such an event will, in fact, occur.

Several studies of the independence axiom have appeared, and virtually all the interaction patterns shown in Table 4.4 have been demonstrated.[7] Slovic [1966] also found more complex interaction patterns than those depicted in Table 4.4, and he found these complex patterns to be highly idiosyncratic.

While the dependence of subjective probability estimates on utilities is the most common form of interaction, Edwards [1962a] has suggested that utilities may be dependent on subjective probabilities in some situations: "[A]n outcome which has a low probability will, by virtue of that low probability, have a higher value or utility than the same outcome would have if it had a high probability"

---

[7] Relevant studies include Atkinson [1957], Crandall, Solomon, and Kellaway [1955, 1958], Irwin [1944, 1953], Irwin and Graae [1968], Irwin and Metzger [1966, 1967], Irwin and Smith [1957], Irwin and Snodgrass [1966], Jessor and Readio [1957], MacCrimmon [1965, 1968], Marks [1951], Morlock and Hertz [1964], Pruitt and Hoge [1965], Scheibe [1964] and Worrell [1956].

Table 4.4

Possible Dependencies of subjective Probability on Utility

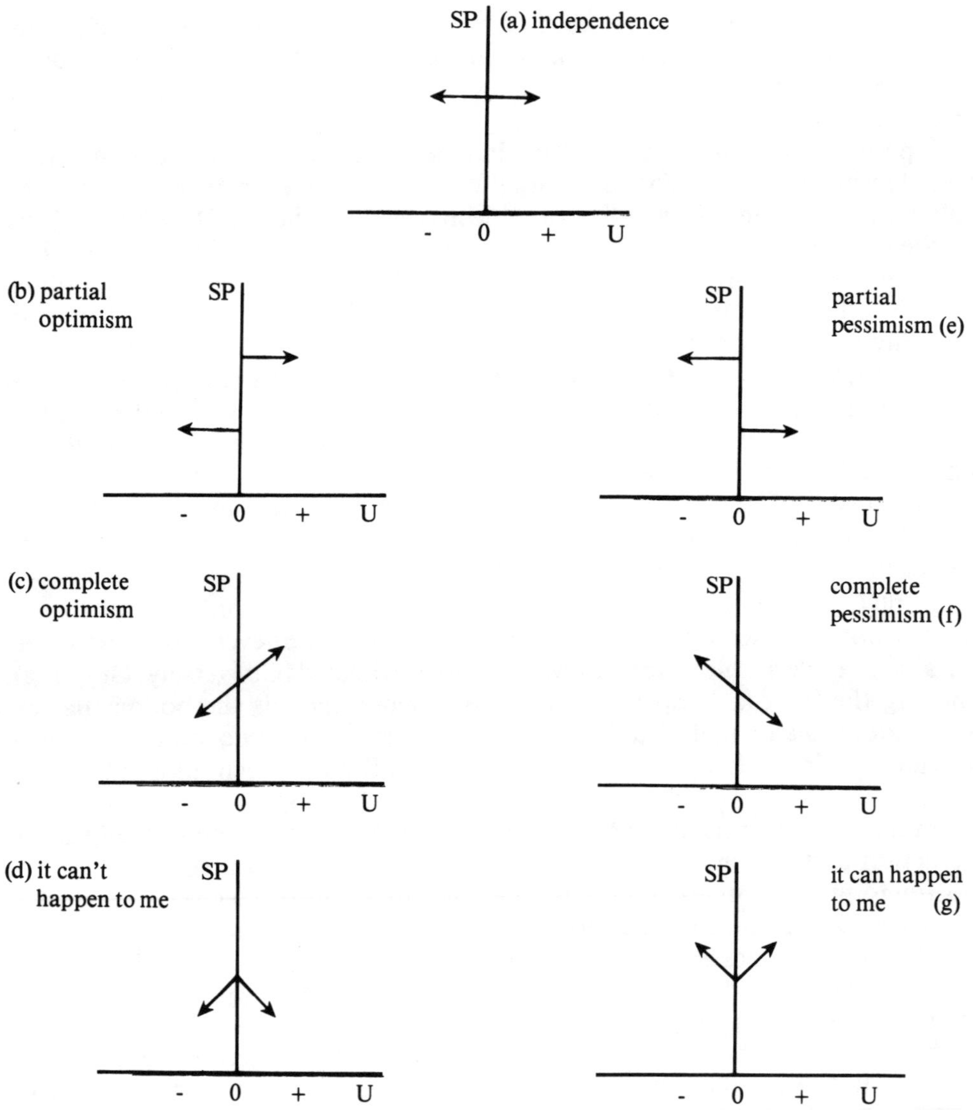

Source: adapted from Slovic [1966, p. 23]. Arrows indicate changes in the subjective probability of an event as the event becomes more desirable (+) or more undesirable (-).

(p. 43). Edwards referred to this as the "grass is greener on the other side of the fence" phenomenon. This hypothesized dependency maintains that utilities are inversely related to subjective probability estimates. In some cases, however, utilities may be positively related to probabilities. This type of dependency could serve as a partial explanation for violations of the irrelevance axiom. For example, in Allais-type problems the utility of $1,000,000 to be received with certainty may be considered greater than the utility of $1,000,000 which will not be received with certainty. According to SEU theory, however, the probability that an event will occur should not affect the utility of the outcome(s) associated with that event.

4.2 OTHER RISKY CHOICE MODELS

Evidence reviewed in the preceding section suggests that the basic behavioral assumptions (axioms) underlying SEU theory are descriptively invalid for at least some individuals in at least some choice contexts. Moreover, some studies indicate that the ability of SEU (and EV) models to predict individuals' actual choices varies inversely with the complexity of the choice situations. Related descriptive research has suggested alternative models of risky choice. Much of this work has been motivated by, or at least discussed in terms of, observed departures of actual choice behavior from the normative SEU model. Other work has reflected the efforts of cognitive psychologists to understand actual choice behavior, regardless of its relation (or lack of relation) to SEU theory.

4.2.1 Higher Moments Models

Expectation models of risky choice emphasize the first moment of the probability distributions over outcomes. Other types of models incorporate higher moments of the distribution. Most of the research on such models has concerned the second moment (variance), but some studies have examined third (skewness) and fourth (kurtosis) moments. Variance is a measure of dispersion around the expectation, while skewness and kurtosis relate to the probabilities of extreme outcomes and the "peakedness" of the distribution, respectively. Higher moments are sometimes considered important in conjunction with expectation. For example, mean-variance trade-off models are frequently proposed to account for risky choice behavior.

An early study of variance preferences by Edwards [1954d] concluded that variance preferences existed but were relatively unimportant in comparison with other types of preferences such as those for specific levels of probabilities (also see Edwards [1953, 1954a, 1954b]). Later, several authors claimed to find much stronger variance preferences, along with great individual differences in variance preferences [Coombs and Pruitt, 1960; Davidson and Marschak, 1959; Littig, 1962; Royden, Suppes and Walsh, 1959; Van der Meer, 1963]. Coombs and Pruitt, for example, concluded that one-third of their subjects preferred low variance, one-third intermediate variance, and one-third high variance. Coombs and Pruitt also claimed to find skewness preferences, again with large individual differences, and that variance and skewness preferences seemed to interact; for example, higher variance was preferred at a subject's preferred skewness level.

Slovic and Lichtenstein [1968b] warned that all prior studies purporting to find variance preferences should be interpreted with a great deal of caution. All these studies were based on choices between, or bids for, two-outcome gambles. For such gambles, expected value (EV), variance (V) and skewness (Sk) are defined as follows (Lee, 1971c):

$$EV = pa + (1\text{-}p)b \tag{4.1}$$

$$V = p(1\text{-}p)(a\text{-}b)^2 \tag{4.2}$$

$$Sk = \frac{1\text{-}2p}{\sqrt{p(1\text{-}p)}} \tag{4.3}$$

In these equations, a and b are payoffs and p is the probability of winning the gamble. It can be seen that skewness and probability are confounded. Thus, choice behavior interpreted as a preference for certain levels of skewness could also be interpreted as a preference for particular probability levels. Similarly, the variance of a two-outcome gamble is confounded with the gamble's probabilities and payoffs. Even when expected values and probabilities are held constant, variance is confounded with payoffs. Thus, effects interpreted as variance preferences could also be interpreted as probability and/or payoff preferences. Therefore, none of the early studies has anything definitive to say about variance preferences.

Lichtenstein [1965] overcame this type of confounding by using three-outcome gambles that permitted independent variation of expected value, variance and skewness. She also examined kurtosis preferences but kurtosis was confounded with other moments. Lichtenstein found preferences for expected value and variance, but not for skewness or kurtosis. This study showed that most subjects preferred low variance, as opposed to the Coombs and Pruitt [1960] study in which large individual differences in preferred variance level were found. Lichtenstein speculated that this difference between the two studies could have been caused by the fact that her subjects actually played some gambles for real money, whereas the Coombs and Pruitt subjects did not. Despite the fact that variance preferences were found, Lichtenstein suggested that the moments of probability distributions were an insufficient basis for building a model of risky choice. This contention was based on the failure to find skewness or kurtosis preferences and, more importantly, on the finding of large, consistent differences in the amounts bid for gambles whose expected value, variance and skewness were equivalent.

Slovic and Lichtenstein [1968b] avoided confounding variance with probabilities and payoffs via a clever device they called a duplex gamble. The duplex gamble methodology makes it possible to manipulate variance without changing the probability and payoff values explicitly displayed to subjects. A duplex gamble is composed of two separate chance situations. One is used to determine winnings; the other, to determine losses. In a duplex gamble, an individual can win and not lose, lose and not win, both win and lose, or neither win nor lose. A duplex gamble is displayed in the upper half of Table 4.5. In contrast, an individual simply wins or loses in a standard two-outcome gamble, as displayed in the lower half of Table 4.5.

Table 4.5

Parallel Duplex and Standard Gambles

Duplex Gamble

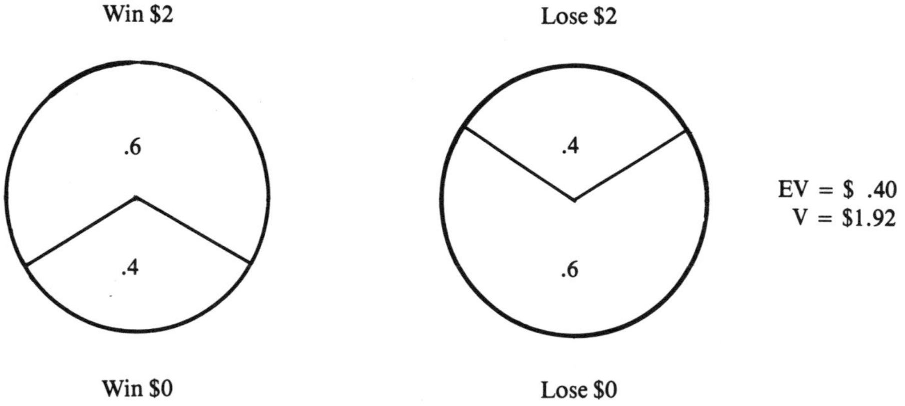

Standard Gamble

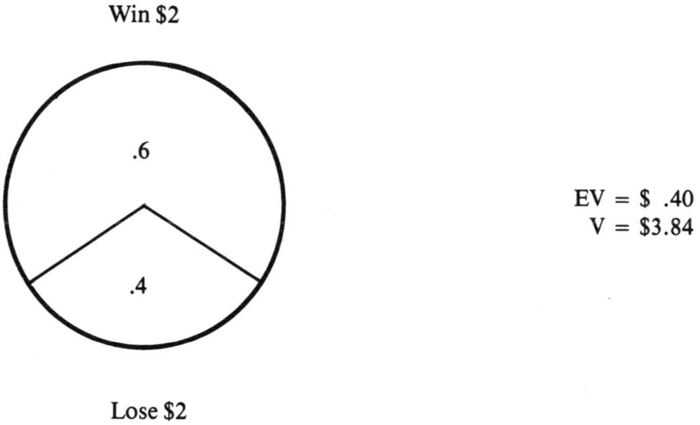

Source: Adapted from Slovic and Lichtenstein [1968b, p. 648]

The standard and duplex gambles in Table 4.5 are parallel in the sense that they have the same explicitly stated probabilities and payoffs. The variance of the duplex gamble, however, is smaller than that of the standard gamble. The variance of a duplex gamble is computed as $P_W(1-P_W)\$_W^2 + P_L(1-P_L)\$_L^2$ [Slovic, 1967, p. 223], where P_W and P_L are the probabilities of winning and losing, respectively, and $\$_W$ and $\$_L$ are the amounts to win and lose, respectively.

Slovic and Lichtenstein [1968b] reported three experiments based on choices between parallel standard and duplex gambles. These experiments varied the sizes of the variances, the differences between variances, and the response mode (whether subjects were required to choose between gambles or to state a price for which they would sell a ticket that would enable them to play each gamble). Slovic and Lichtenstein reasoned that subjects preferring low variance would find the duplex gamble (in Table 4.5) more attractive, while those preferring high variance would find the standard gamble more attractive. In contrast, subjects who do not make risky choices on the basis of variance should not exhibit strong preferences between parallel standard and duplex gambles.

Based on Experiment 1, Slovic and Lichtenstein [1968b, p. 649] concluded that "for the great majority of [subjects], the differences between parallel standard and duplex bets were no larger than the differences between the replications of the same standard bet, indicating the lack of any discernible variance preferences." This conclusion was substantially corroborated by Experiments 2 and 3.

These results were supported by Payne and Braunstein [1971]. While Slovic and Lichtenstein had held payoffs and probabilities constant across pairs of parallel standard and duplex gambles that had different variances, Payne and Braunstein displayed different values of payoffs and probabilities for pairs of duplex gambles whose variances were equal. An example of such gambles appears in Table 4.6. Payne and Braunstein reasoned that subjects who choose between such gambles on the basis of variance should not exhibit strong preferences for either member of a pair, while the choices of subjects who rely on explicitly stated payoff and probability dimensions should be systematically related to those dimensions. Such systematic preference patterns were found, again indicating that choices were not influenced by variance.

Further evidence was provided by Slovic [1967], who had subjects rate, on a ten-point scale, the risk inherent in several gambles. Correlations were computed between the risk ratings of each subject and the variance of the gambles. The highest correlation was .30 and the mean was .08, indicating that direct ratings of risk, as well as choices and bids, are virtually unrelated to variance. Payne [1973, p. 447] concluded a comprehensive review of moments studies by stating that "these abstractions of gambles, such as expected value and variance, may be good predictors of choices among pairs of gambles only because they correlate with the relevant variables."

4.2.2 Risk Dimensions Models

As the studies by Payne and Braunstein [1971], Slovic [1967] and Slovic and Lichtenstein [1968b] suggest, an alternative to moments models of risky decision

Tables 4.6

Pair of Duplex Gambles Equivalent in Variance

Duplex Gamble No. 1

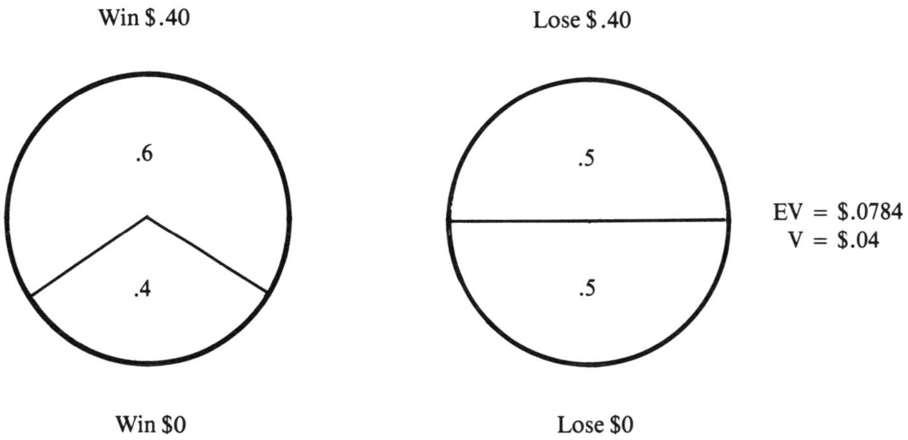

Duplex Gamble No. 2

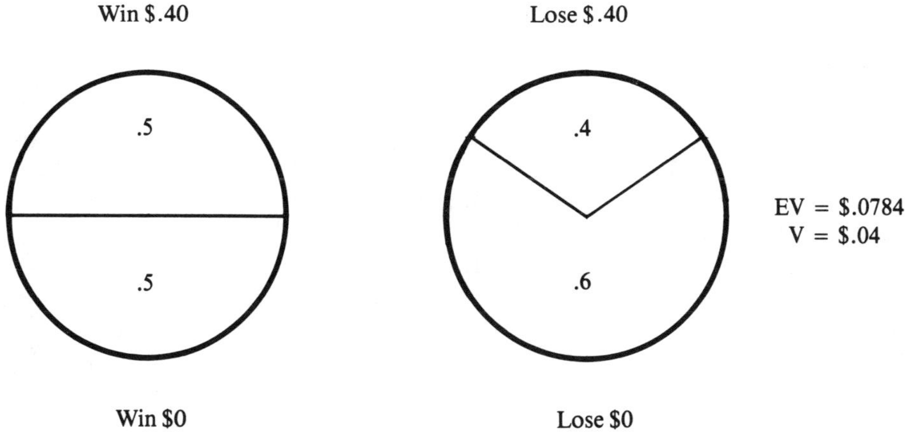

Source: Adapted from Payne and Braunstein [1971, p. 14]

making is a model that emphasizes explicitly stated probabilities and payoffs. Some researchers have argued that these "risk dimensions" offer the most promising basis for explaining (and perhaps predicting) risky choice behavior. An important feature of this view is the contention that one risk dimension may be most influential for some individuals (or in some circumstances), while a different risk dimension may be most important for other individuals (or circumstances). Risk dimensions may be evaluated separately instead of being combined into a summary measure such as expected value or variance.

Studies by Edwards [1953, 1954a, 1954b] and Coombs and Pruitt [1960] reported finding probability preferences. For example, Edwards [1953] found that for two-outcome gambles of equal positive expected value subjects preferred gambles in which the probability of winning was .50 and disliked gambles in which the probability of winning was .25 or .75. Coombs and Pruitt [1960] found probability preferences, but they were relatively weak compared to variance preferences. As noted earlier, however, the results of Edwards and of Coombs and Pruitt can be considered only suggestive because of the confounding inherent in two-outcome gambles.

Slovic and Lichtenstein [1968a] argued that risky decision making involves the independent evaluation of probabilities and payoffs. In the case of two-outcome gambles, they argued that four separate risk dimensions exist — probability of winning (P_W), probability of losing (P_L), amount to win ($\$_W$), and amount to lose ($\$_L$). They investigated these four dimensions, with particular emphasis on two basic ideas. First, the notion of "importance beliefs" implies that an individual relies to a greater extent on certain risk dimensions than on others because of the belief that certain dimensions are more important to a particular decision. "For example, a person with very little money and great fear of losing it may focus his attention on the amount to lose ($\$_L$) and base his decisions almost exclusively on this dimension, largely disregarding the other information provided in the bet" (p. 1). Second, Slovic and Lichtenstein emphasized information processing. An individual's ability to act on the basis of importance beliefs may be influenced by information processing limitations. Consequently, this view holds that decision making in risky choice situations is not fundamentally different from decision making in other types of situations.

To test these ideas, Slovic and Lichtenstein [1968a] conducted two experiments in which subjects indicated preferences for several duplex gambles. Correlation and regression analyses were used to quantify the influence of each risk dimension separately, and the four risk dimensions together, on expressions of preference. One group of subjects rated the attractiveness (or unattractiveness) of each gamble on a ten-point scale. Another group responded by bidding; some subjects in the bidding group stated the largest amount of money they would pay in order to play the gamble (in the case of attractive gambles) or the smallest amount they would have to be paid by the experimenter in order to play (in the case of unattractive gambles); other subjects stated the smallest amount for which they would sell a ticket that would enable them to play attractive gambles or the largest amount they would pay the experimenter in order not to play unattractive gambles; finally, some subjects were required to state a "fair price" for each gamble without knowing whether they or the experimenter owned the right to play the gamble. Since the subjects' responses were unrelated to the type of bidding procedure employed, the three bidding subgroups were combined in the analysis.

The results showed that the probability of winning (P_W) was the most important factor influencing the preferences of the *rating* group. The average correlation between P_W and attractiveness ratings was .48. For the *bidding* group, however, the amount to lose ($\$_L$) was most important. The average correlation between $\$_L$ and bids was -.50. Similar results were obtained in Slovic's [1967] earlier study in which subjects rated the risk inherent in several duplex gambles: The most influential factor was the probability of losing (P_L). The average correlation between P_L and risk ratings was .52. These two studies support the contention that individuals tend to be influenced more strongly by one risk dimension than others when formulating preferences in risky choice situations.[8]

Differential weighting of the four basic risk dimensions was an important finding in the Slovic and Lichtenstein [1968a] study. About two-thirds of the subjects were influenced more by P_W than by P_L. The authors noted (p. 9) that this result violates the independence axiom because it implies an interaction between subjective probabilities and utilities. Fitting such data would require a different subjective probability function when utility is positive than when utility is negative.

Slovic and Lichtenstein proposed a multiple regression model to represent the human information processing of individuals in risky choice contexts:

$$A(G) = u + W_1P_W + W_2\$_W + W_3P_L + W_4\$_L \qquad (4.4)$$

In this equation, A(G) is the subjective attractiveness of a gamble and the W_i ($i = 1 \ldots 4$) are regression weights that represent the importance of each risk dimension. Note that this model combines additively variables that the SEU model assumes are combined multiplicatively — P_W and $\$_W$, as well as P_L and $\$_L$. The model also assumes that the impact of the probabilities and payoffs is a linear function of their objective values. This assumption was tested via analysis of variance. It was found that, on average, approximately 75 percent of the variance in A(G) could be accounted for by a linear combination of the four risk dimensions. Less than one percent could be accounted for by interactions.

The predictive validity of the risk dimensions model (Equation 4.4) vis-à-vis the subjects' actual bids and ratings was assessed by Slovic and Lichtenstein. The model's outputs, A(G), correlated, on the average, .86 with both ratings and

---

[8] Note that a cue-response compatibility effect occurred in the Slovic and Lichtenstein [1968a] study. Subjects who evaluated gambles using monetary units (the bidding group) relied more heavily on payoff dimensons than did subjects whose evaluations were not made in terms of monetary units (the rating group). Later studies by Lichtenstein and Slovic [1971, 1973] and Lindman [1971] investigated such effects more rigorously by having each subject first choose the preferred gambles from pairs of gambles and later bid for each gamble separately. Within each pair of gambles, one bet had a higher probability of winning (the P bet), while the other offered a larger amount to win (the $ bet). When the P bet was chosen, the $ bet often received a higher bid — by the same subject. (Also see n. 2 of this chapter.)

bids, and very little shrinkage (.016, on the average) occurred on cross-validation. Average correlations between the gambles' expected values and the actual bids and ratings — .80 for bids and .79 for ratings — were lower than the correlations with the regression estimates. Thus, the risk dimensions model of risky decision making was a better predictor of actual responses than the expected value model.

The risk dimensions model has been investigated only in the case of relatively straightforward duplex gambles. However, such gambles are more complex than the simple two-outcome gambles for which the SEU model has been found globally predictive. Therefore, Slovic and Lichtenstein's risk dimensions model may be a significant building block in the development of descriptive theories of risky choice.

4.2.3 Lexicographic Models

Both the SEU and risk dimensions models are compensatory; that is, they entail the possibility that one attribute, or dimension, can be "traded off" for another.[9] Some models of risky choice are noncompensatory. An example is a lexicographic model, which maintains that alternatives are evaluated first on a specified attribute that is common to those alternatives. If one alternative is not superior on that attribute, then the alternatives are evaluated on another attribute. This process continues until one alternative is chosen.

Tversky's [1969] study of intransitive preferences (see Section 4.1.3.1) provides an example of a lexicographic choice strategy. In that study, it was argued that a decision maker might ignore small expected value (or probability) differences and choose between gambles on the basis of payoffs, but that large expected value (or probability) differences might result in greater reliance on that attribute. Tversky maintained that the use of a lexicographic choice strategy often will lead to instransitive choices in multidimensional settings where "the relevant dimension is noisy as a consequence of imperfect discrimination or unreliability of available information" [Tversky, 1969, p. 32]

Lexicographic choice strategies have been noted in several other studies of risky decision making. Lichtenstein [1965, p. 168], for example, concluded her study of higher moment preferences as follows: "These findings suggest that [subjects] approach bets with a lexicographic ordering of relevant variables: EV is of primary importance. When deciding between bets of equal EV, Ss prefer low V. When both EV and V are constant, Ss attend to the least likely amount, avoiding a small chance of large loss."

Payne and Braunstein [1971] also proposed a lexicographic model. Their model, developed in the context of risk dimensions, maintained that an individu-

---

[9] Several other types of risky choice models that involve tradeoffs have been proposed, e.g., mean-variance and mean-skewness tradeoff models. The risk component of such models may be defined in many ways. A review of the possibilities is provided by Libby and Fishburn [1977]. Examples include a mean-probability of below-target return model, a mean-probability of loss model, and a mean-semivariance model. A common feature of these and other models is that the risk component relates to a specific parameter (or to a portion) of the probability distribution of returns. These models are compensatory in that they encompass the notion of trading off one parameter for another, and they are similar to the risk dimensions model in emphasizing specific distributional parameters instead of summary measures such as variance and skewness.

al first compares P_W with P_L; if $P_W < P_L$, the gamble with the lower P_L is chosen; if $P_W > P_L$, the individual tries to maximize $\$_W$; if $\$_W = \$_L$, the gamble with the greater P_W is chosen. While Payne and Braunstein made no claim for the generality of this model, they did argue that this *type* of model is needed to adequately describe risky choice behavior.

Based on a study in which business executives evaluated hypothetical capital investment projects, Conrath [1973] proposed a model that involved both compensatory and noncompensatory components. Conrath found that investment projects which did not offer some minimum probability of earning at least a target rate of return were rejected, and that all projects surviving this criterion were evaluated according to a model that traded off expected value and the probability of earning the target rate of return. Similar models were suggested by several business executives interviewed by Mao [1970]. Their descriptions of their own investment strategies suggested that moments of probability distributions were relatively unimportant, that risk was generally conceived as the probability of failing to achieve some minimum return (or the probability of catastrophic loss), and that the relevant variables were most often processed via a lexicographic choice strategy. Several other studies have produced results consistent with this description. Libby and Fishburn [1977, p. 286] concluded an exhaustive review of risk studies in psychology and business with this remark:

> While final conclusions must await further research, the studies tentatively suggest that risk is combined with return in a hybrid model that combines noncompensatory and compensatory decision rules. A model in which risk first plays a role as a ruin constraint and then interacts with the mean as a trade-off parameter defined as target semivariance, probability of below-target return, or as some other below-target parameter would seem the most promising. All of the business parametric model studies support the need to incorporate a ruinous loss constraint. Further study will be necessary to determine more specifically which definition of the negative-return risk trade-off parameter will provide the most accurate predictions. However, it is clear that the concept of risk as variance is the least promising of those discussed.

4.2.4 The Additive Difference Model

Tversky [1969] noted that the conventional additive model specifies that alternative x will be preferred to alternative y or the individual will be indifferent between them (i.e., $x \gtrsim y$) if and only if

$$U(x) = \sum_{i=1}^{n} u_i(x_i) \geq \sum_{i=1}^{n} u_i(y_i) = U(y),$$

where the u_i are weights or utilities representing the contributions of each of the n dimensions, or attributes, to the overall evaluation. Multiple regression models and SEU models are examples of additive models. In contrast, Tversky proposed an additive difference model, in which $x \gtrsim y$ if and only if

$$\sum_{i=1}^{n} \phi_i \left[u_i(x_i) - u_i(y_i)\right] \geq 0,$$

and $\phi_i(-\delta) = -\phi_i(\delta)$ for all i. This model implies that an individual considers differences, $\delta_i = u_i(x_i) - u_i(y_i)$, between alternatives x and y on the ith dimension, applies a difference function, ϕ_i, to determine the contribution of that difference to the overall evaluation, and sums the $\phi_i(\delta_i)$ differences to determine whether $x \gtrsim y$.

The additive and additive difference models imply different ways of processing and evaluating alternatives, although the two models are mathematically equivalent when all the difference functions, ϕ_i, are linear. Referring to the diagram below [from Tversky, 1969, p. 42], the additive model suggests that each alternative is processed "horizontally" and a choice made by comparing the sums resulting from addition of the component values.

$$x = (x_1, \ldots x_i, \ldots, x_n) \rightarrow \sum_{i=1}^{n} u_i(x_i)$$

$$y = (y_1, \ldots y_i, \ldots, y_n) \rightarrow \sum_{i=1}^{n} u_i(y_i)$$

$$\downarrow$$

$$\sum_{i=1}^{n} \phi_i \left[u_i(x_i) - u_i(y_i)\right]$$

The additive difference model, on the other hand, suggests that the alternatives are processed "vertically" via intradimensional comparisons and a choice made by adding the results of these vertical comparisons. Tversky shows that one consequence of vertical evaluation is that transitivity is not guaranteed.

Tversky argues that the use of either model may be determined by the manner in which the data are displayed: Sequential display of the alternatives is more likely to result in the use of an additive choice strategy, while sequential display of the dimensions of those alternatives is more likely to lead to an additive difference strategy. Tversky maintains that an additive difference choice strategy should appeal to decision makers because intradimensional comparisons can simplify the evaluation process. For example, differences between alternatives on some dimensions might be "cancelled out," thus reducing the number of alternatives that must be considered. Further, it may be simpler to make comparisons between quantities that are expressed in terms of the same units than to evaluate the combined effects of attributes expressed in different units. In short, the use of an additive difference model for risky decision making is consistent with the contention that individuals employ simplified techniques, approximations and heuristics to reduce complex decision situations to more manageable tasks.

4.2.5 The Elimination-by-Aspects Model

Tversky [1972] also proposed the elimination-by-aspects model, which views choice as a covert sequential elimination process. Tversky described the model as follows: "Suppose that each alternative consists of a set of aspects [or dimensions], and that at every stage of the process, an aspect is selected (from those included in the available alternatives) with probability that is proportional to its weight. The selection of an aspect eliminates all the alternatives that do not include the selected aspect, and the process continues until a single alternative remains. If a selected aspect is included in all the available alternatives, no alternative is eliminated and a new aspect is selected. Consequently, aspects that are common to all the alternatives under consideration do not affect choice probabilities" (pp. 284-85).

This model involves a type of lexicographic choice strategy. However, it relaxes the requirement of lexicographic models that a fixed prior ordering of relevant aspects, or attributes, is specified. In the elimination-by-aspects model, the ordering of attributes is probabilistic. Tversky argues that the elimination-by-aspects model combines compensatory and noncompensatory features: It is compensatory "globally" with respect to choice probabilities but is noncompensatory "locally" after the ordering of aspects has been established. According to Tversky, a major appeal of the model is its simplicity: It is easy to apply, it involves no numerical computations, and it is easy to explain and justify — to oneself and to others — in terms of a priority ordering defined on the attributes. Like the additive difference model, it represents an attempt to reduce the complexity of risky choice situations via the use of heuristics and approximations.

To sum up, it appears that efforts to describe human information processing in risky choice contexts will ignore important features of the choice process if these efforts are guided only by normative models of choice. Beginning with a normative model and adjusting its form or parameters in response to experimental results may provide useful insights into human decision making. It has not, however, completely described actual decision making in complex choice situations. Descriptive studies of risky choice have discovered numerous features of actual decision making that may serve as components of a descriptive theory (or theories) of risky choice.

CHAPTER FIVE

Probability Assessment and Revision

Probabilities are a central component of the risky choice models discussed in Chapter 4. There it was seen that different choice models entail different implications for the manner in which probabilities are used in decision making. The initial assessment of probabilities for use in these (and other) choice models, and the revision of probabilities upon the receipt of new data, are other important dimensions of human information processing. This chapter considers the assessment and revision of probabilities.

The first major section examines three aspects of subjective probability assessment: (1) elicitation methods; (2) the "goodness" of the assessed probabilities; (3) ways of improving assessments. While several studies have focused on these three areas, few consistent findings have emerged. Reviews of various portions of the subjective probability assessment literature are available (e.g., Beach [1975], Chesley [1975], Hogarth [1975], Huber [1974b], Slovic, Fischhoff, and Lichtenstein [1977]), and all point to the mixed nature of the existing empirical results. Consequently, the present coverage tends to be issue-oriented instead of results-oriented. However, consistent research findings are presented when they exist.

The second major section of the chapter relates to intuitive probability revisions by individuals. Intuitive revisions are evaluated relative to the optimal revisions prescribed by Bayes' theorem. An important result of probability-revision studies — the "conservatism phenomenon" — is discussed, and several task characteristics that mediate the extent of conservatism are emphasized. Finally, a technique designed to reduce or eliminate conservatism (when it exists), called a "probabilistic information processing" system, is discussed. The third and final section of the chapter discusses cognitive processes involved in probability assessment and revision.

5.1 ASSESSING SUBJECTIVE PROBABILITIES

Subjective probabilities reflect an individual's degree of belief, or confidence, that a particular outcome or event will occur [Savage, 1954]. Such probabilities often are contrasted with objective probabilities, which usually are viewed from a relative frequency standpoint and are based on historical information related to repetitive events. While this distinction may be instructive, it can easily be overdrawn. One could argue that all probabilities are subjective when interpreted and used by an individual [Beach, 1975], or that the many subjective judgments involved in obtaining frequentistic information (e.g., selection of data base, choice of sample size, inclusion or elimination of outliers) cause the distinction between subjective and objective probabilities to be unclear [Huber, 1974b].

When should one assess and use subjective probabilities? A typical answer to this question is that subjective probabilities should be used "when the historical data that would otherwise be used are either (1) of unacceptable quality, (2) known to be unrepresentative of future events, or (3) unavailable" [Huber, 1974b, p. 432]. One might also add "too costly" to this list. Hogarth [1975, pp. 277-79] considers this question in a broader sense and suggests three criteria for subjective probability assessment and usage:

> First, the task should be meaningful to the assessor in that it concerns a domain with which he is reasonably familiar.
>
> Second, since a probability assessment is one form of "clinical judgment" . . ., its justification necessarily depends on the extent to which it can add something to predictive accuracy over and above that which could be achieved by the best available statistical model.
>
> A third criterion of meaningfulness . . . is that judgments expressed in probabilistic form are both more *accurate* (as evaluated by subsequent events) and useful than those expressed normally.

Concerning Hogarth's first criterion, a distinction may be made between normative experts and substantive experts [Winkler and Murphy, 1968a]. The former are experts in statistics and probability, while the latter are experts in a particular field of specialization. Hogarth maintains that for a probability assessment task to be meaningful the assessor should be either a normative expert, a substantive expert, or both. Hogarth notes, however, that most probability assessment studies have employed subjects (e.g., college students) who are neither normative nor substantive experts.

Of course, it cannot necessarily be concluded that expert subjects (of either type) making real-world assessments will produce results that are more generalizable or enlightening than will student subjects making "laboratory" assessments, because of "the difficulties inherent in establishing controls in realistic settings and/or the often small number of experts used as subjects in [real-world] studies" [Beach, 1975, p. 17]. In fact, studies employing both normative and substantive experts, and studies employing subjects with various degrees of expertise, do not allow straightforward conclusions concerning the role of expertise. For example, studies by Staël von Holstein [1970, 1971, 1972] have shown that stock market experts outperformed statisticians [1972], that statisticians performed as well as meteorologists [1971], and that teaching assistants in meteorology outperformed meteorologists [1970]. Studies by Winkler [1967a, 1971] have shown that normative experts (Ph.D.-level statisticians) assess similar probability distributions using different elicitation methods, that students with a knowledge of introductory statistics do not, and that sportswriters and bookmakers predict football scores better than do students and faculty members. On the other hand, Tversky and Kahneman [1971] found that normative experts made the same types of probabilistic judgment errors that were made by students [Tversky and Kahneman, 1973], and Snapper, Edwards, and Peterson [1972] found that substantive experts (experienced gamblers) made errors similar to those made by students in an information-purchase experiment.

Hogarth's second criterion, that the use of subjective probabilities should increase predictive accuracy relative to the use of a statistical model that incorporates objective probabilities, has been researched in medicine, meteorology and finance [Beach, 1975], and in the prediction of football scores. In medicine, Gustafson [1969] found that subjective likelihoods outperformed actuarially-determined likelihoods when both were processed by Bayes' theorem, and Lodwick [1966] found that a type of clinical synthesis (modifying actuarial probabilities based on personal experience) outperformed the use of actuarial probabilities alone. In meteorology, Murphy and Winkler [1974], Root [1962], Sanders [1963, 1973], and Winkler and Murphy [1968b] found that meteorologists' subjective probabilities in various types of weather forecasts were superior to actuarial probabilities based on climatological expectancies; Staël von Holstein [1971] found the opposite. Further, Staël von Holstein [1972] found that only three of 72 subjects (including both normative and substantive experts) in a stock-price prediction task outperformed a uniform distribution over the percentage-price-change classes considered. Finally, Winkler [1971] found that past relative frequencies were better than most subjects in terms of predicting the point spreads of National Football League games, but that subjects outperformed the past relative frequencies for college games.

The third criterion proposed by Hogarth concerns the accuracy and usefulness of probabilistic assessments versus point estimates. Studies that have compared the accuracy of probabilistic and deterministic assessments have focused on the mode of the probability distribution. DuCharme and Donnell [1973] and Martin and Gettys [1969] found deterministic responses more accurate, but Dalkey [1969] found the opposite. In addition to these three critria for the meaningfulness of probability assessments, a potential problem noted by Hogarth is that the recipients of probabilistic information may find it difficult to interpret and use.

5.1.1 Elicitation Methods

The number of probability elicitation methods available is quite large, especially when one considers that different features of two or more methods can be combined to form a "hybrid" method and that multiple methods can be used in the same elicitation effort. Consideration of the various methods is important because different methods may result in different assessments, and because some methods may be easier to teach than others. Chesley [1975], Hampton, Moore, and Thomas [1973], and Huber [1974b] discuss the principal elicitation methods, and the latter two sources provide "how to do it" commentary on the application of several methods.

Chesley [1975] provides a useful classification scheme, based on Savage [1971], for the principal methods. The most basic dimension of Chesley's scheme concerns the "directness" of the assessments. Direct assessment procedures require the assessor to answer relatively direct elicitation questions, while indirect methods allow the assessor's probabilities to be inferred from actions or choices (generally among bets). A second dimension relates to self-elicitation versus the use of a trained interviewer to question the assessor. A third dimension distinguishes between responses made in terms of probabilities and those made in terms of the scale of the independent variable of interest. While these three dimensions are not mutually exclusive, such a classification scheme may be a useful way of organizing elicitation methods.

Criteria for judging the effectiveness of elicitation methods include the accuracy of the resulting distributions, the consistency of assessed distributions across elicitation methods, and the understandability of the methods. Empirical evidence pertaining to the effectiveness of the methods is quite mixed and allows few conclusions. While greater consistency exists between the results produced by direct and indirect methods in the case of discrete events than in the case of continuous quantities [Hogarth, 1975, p. 279], one review concluded that no clearly preferable response mode exists even for discrete events [Slovic, Fischhoff, and Lichtenstein, 1977].

Since lengthy reviews of various elicitation methods are available, the methods are not described in detail here. However, a brief description of some of the more popular methods may be useful at this point to portray the "flavor" of the principal methods.[1]

Two direct elicitation methods are the variable interval and fixed interval methods. The former requires the assessor to subdivide the independent variable continuum into intervals containing certain portions of the probability density function, e.g., quartiles or deciles. This method does not require assessments in terms of probabilities, which could be advantageous for assessors who have difficulty stating probabilities. With appropriate modification, this method could be used to elicit cumulative probability functions instead of probability density functions. However, some subjects have found that working with probability density functions is easier [Schaefer and Borcherding, 1973; Winkler, 1967a].

The fixed interval method requires probability responses from the assessor for specific intervals of the independent variable scale. The odds associated with one interval versus another may also be used as a response measure, but odds generally are not understood well by subjects and may be especially difficult to use when more than two intervals are employed [Edwards, Phillips, Hays, and Goodman, 1968; Winkler, 1967a]. Another modification of this approach is to have the assessor express responses via graphical techniques, but Winkler [1967a] has noted a tendency for subjects to draw normal probability functions.

Two other elicitation methods, which are somewhat less direct than requiring probability or independent variable responses, are the equivalent prior sample and hypothetical future sample methods. The former, useful in a binomial setting, requires that the assessor specify two numbers — the number of "successes" (r) and the sample size (n) — such that the assessed probability is equivalent to having observed r successes in a sample of size n. The ratio of r to n is the assessor's subjective probability of a success. Schaefer and Borcherding [1973] found this method superior to the variable interval method, and Schaefer and Borcherding's and Winkler's [1967a] subjects found the method easier to use than either the variable interval or fixed interval method.

---

[1] Empirical studies employing one or more of these methods include DuCharme and Donnell [1973], Ford, Huber, and Gustafson [1972], Murphy and Winkler [1973], Peterson, Snapper, and Murphy [1972], Schaefer and Borcherding [1973], Staël von Holstein [1971, 1972], and Winkler [1967a, 1967b, 1971].

The hypothetical future sample method requires the assessor to state the change in his or her estimate of a proportion that would result from viewing a variety of hypothetical sample results. The assessor's subjective probabilities existing prior to viewing the samples are then inferred from his or her responses. While little research has been conducted on this method, Winkler [1967a] reported results very similar to those obtained via the equivalent prior sample method.

Indirect elicitation methods involve inferring the assessor's probabilities from his or her choices among gambles. Indirect methods seem to be favored by many normative decision theorists (e.g., Raiffa [1968], Savage [1954]). From an experimental standpoint, however, they involve a number of significant problems. For example, in order for indirect methods to be applied generally, the assessor's utility function must be known, it must not change during elicitation, and the assessor must choose among gambles so as to maximize expected utility. These requirements can be avoided to some extent by restricting the payoffs investigated. However, this simplification still requires that the assessor's choices correspond to an expected value maximization rule. Research reviewed in Chapter 4 suggests that the assumption of expected value maximization is sometimes unwarranted. Finally, the betting method can be quite time consuming [Beach and Wise, 1969].

Still another possible method of eliciting subjective probabilities is to have the assessor estimate the parameters of probability distributions (e.g., mean, median, variance, skewness). This is likely to be a most unsatisfactory method, however, given the extreme difficulties that individuals often have in understanding the concept of a distribution and in estimating certain distributional parameters. Section 5.3 reviews a great deal of evidence that supports this assertion.

The use of multiple elicitation methods is often suggested. The assessor could be presented with assessments elicited by several methods and required to reconcile any differences. The assessments are likely to need reconciling except, possibly, for those made by certain types of normative experts or those made in relatively simple tasks involving discrete events [Hogarth, 1975, p. 279]. However, the reconciliation process involves potential problems such as primacy or recency effects, and "splitting the difference" [Winkler, 1967a] in order to reduce the complexity of the reconciliation task.[2]

---

[2] Several elicitation methods for *utility* assessment have been developed and utilized in experimental studies (see Huber [1974a] and Hull, Moore and Thomas [1973] for reviews). Utility assessment is not discussed in this book because, in Lee's [1971c, p. 104] words, its " . . . net contribution . . . to behavioral decision theory . . . has been disappointingly slight." One of the principal problems of experimental assessments of utilities is that they typically involve only very small amounts of money. Lee [1971c] concluded an evaluation of utility assessment as follows: "Is it really important to measure 'utilities'? If utilities were really useful in understanding and predicting human behavior, the effort would be worthwhile. So far, such usefulness has not been very convincingly demonstrated. Various authors have compared predictions of choices between gambles based on expected utilities and on [objective] values. The predictions based on the utilities are typically superior, but only slightly so. It is doubtful that the gain is very often worth the effort, at least when relatively small amounts of money are involved . . . . Empirical studies of decision making typically forgo measurement of utilities; instead, behavior is analyzed in terms of objective quantities such as amount of money. Why is utility measurement neglected, when the theory of decision making emphasizes the importance of the subjective evaluation of consequences? Authors do not tell us, but we may speculate. I suppose utility measurement is neglected because it involves a lot of work, because people are not really sure which measurement technique or techniques are 'valid,' and because utilities would often make no important difference in the interpretation of the results" (p. 105). A more recent critique of utility assessment is offered by Slovic, Fischhoff, and Lichtenstein [1977].

5.1.2 "Goodness" of Subjective Probabilities

The accuracy of subjective probabilities can be assessed if "true" or agreed-upon probabilities exist for comparison purposes. Such comparisons can be made if extensive relative frequency data exist and subjective probabilities are essentially estimates of relative frequencies [Lichtenstein and Fischhoff, 1977]. Relative frequency data are unavailable, however, in many probability assessment tasks, e.g., in situations involving unique events. In these cases, other measures of the "goodness" of subjective probabilities are needed. Two primary criteria have been proposed for evaluating probability assessments in such cases — coherence and calibration.

5.1.2.1 Coherence

The coherence criterion asks whether subjective probabilities obey the probability axioms. One issue is simply whether an individual's probability estimates sum to 1. Very little evidence on this fundamental question is available because most studies use experimental devices that constrain such estimates to meet this criterion. However, a few studies have allowed "unrestricted" estimates. According to Peterson and Beach [1967], these studies have produced conflicting results, but there appears to be a tendency for probability estimates to sum to slightly more than 1. Most of the evidence for this tendency comes from studies of probability revision (e.g., Marks and Clarkson [1972], Phillips, Hays, and Edwards [1966]) instead of studies concerned solely with elicitation of priors. In contrast, the results of some studies depart from the tendency toward slight overestimation. For example, Teigen's [1974] subjects produced probabilities that summed, on average, to approximately 2.5, while Alberoni's [1962] subjects produced probabilities summing consistently to .85.

Another line of research has focused on the question of whether individuals' estimates of the probabilities of compound events are consistent with their estimates of the probabilities of the underlying elementary events. Again, the evidence is mixed. Some studies have concluded that probability estimates for conjunctive events are approximately equal to the products of the estimates for the component events, and that estimates for disjunctive events are approximately equal to the sums of the estimates for the component events, as they should be according to the combinatorial properties of probabilities.[3] Other studies have found, however, that the estimated probabilities for conjunctive events were too high, and those for disjunctive events were too low, relative to the estimated probabilities for the corresponding elementary events (e.g., Bar-Hillel [1973], Cohen and Chesnik [1970]). Bar-Hillel [1973, p. 396] noted that "the subjective probability of a compound event is systematically biased in the direction of the probability of its components . . . ."

The results of most studies of coherence do not clearly support either the hypothesis that the probability axioms are followed nor the hypothesis that they are not followed. Instead, most results permit alternative interpretations and em-

---

[3] See, for example, Barclay and Beach [1972], Beach and Peterson [1966], Cohen, Dearnaley, and Hansel [1958] and Peterson, Ulehla, Miller, Bourne, and Stilson [1965].

phases. The study reported by Barclay and Beach [1972] is an example. Their "goal was to see if verbally estimated personal probabilities for elementary events combine in the manner prescribed by probability theory to yield personal probabilities for complex events" (p. 177). Barclay and Beach investigated four situations (the proper combination rule is shown in brackets): (1) union of mutually exclusive events [$P(A \cup B) = P(A) + P(B)$]; (2) union of nonexclusive events [$P(A \cup B) = P(A) + P(B) - P(A \cap B)$]; (3) intersection of independent events [$P(A \cap B) = P(A)P(B)$]; (4) intersection of nonindependent events [$P(A \cap B) = P(A/B)P(B) = P(B/A)P(A)$]. They compared the degree to which the correct rule, when applied to the estimated elementary probabilities, accounted for the estimated compound probabilities — relative to the degree to which various incorrect rules (e.g., multiplying when one should add, treating nonexclusive events as though they were exclusive, etc.) could account for the estimated compound probabilities. Barclay and Beach found that (1) the estimated compound probabilities could be accounted for best by the correct rules, but that (2) the superiority of correct over incorrect rules was sometimes very small and (3) many subjects had a tendency to overestimate or underestimate the probabilities of various compound events relative to their own estimates of the probabilities of the elementary events. The authors (p. 183) interpreted these mixed results as follows:

> From a strict mathematical viewpoint these discrepancies require the conclusion that personal probabilities do not conform to the requirements of probability theory. However, a more lenient psychological viewpoint permits the conclusion that the approximation is probably good enough for most real-life intuitive decision making, and is sufficient to warrant their acceptance as legitimate probabilities.

5.1.2.2 Calibration

The second major criterion for evaluating the "goodness" of subjective probabilities is calibration. In the case of discrete events, an assessor is perfectly calibrated if, over the long run, for all events assigned a specific probability the proportion of events that is true is equal to the probability assigned. In the case of continuous probability density functions, an assessor is perfectly calibrated if, over the long run, the proportion of events falling below a given fractile of the distribution is equal to the fractile assessed. Note that an assessor's probabilities could be coherent, i.e., follow the probability axioms, yet the assessor could be poorly calibrated. Also note that calibration involves the comparison of subjective probabilities with relative frequency information; however, the relative frequencies are based on series of different events instead of repeated occurrences of the same event. Calibration studies have been reported by a number of researchers. Lichtenstein, Fischhoff, and Phillips [1977] provide an excellent review of published and unpublished work in this area.

Calibration results often are displayed via a "calibration curve," as in Figure 5.1. This example concerns the discrete-event case in which only two alternative answers — true and false — are allowed. Assessors in the Lichtenstein and Fischhoff [1977] study were required to choose one alternative and attach to it a probability between .5 and 1.0. Curve B represents perfect calibration: For all assess-

Figure 5.1
Calibration Curves

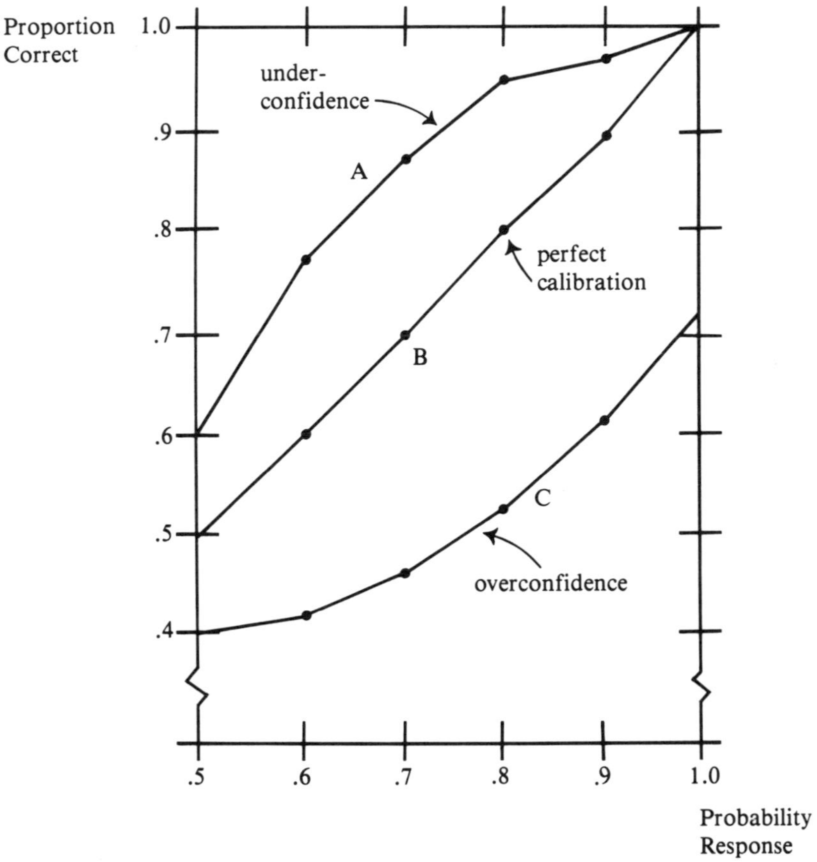

Source: Adapted from Lichtenstein and Fischhoff [1977], p. 162.

ments to which a probability of .6 is assigned, 60 percent are correct; for all assessments assigned .9, 90 percent are correct, and so on. Curve A represents underconfidence, and Curve C overconfidence, in the assessments; in these cases the assessed probabilities are too low and too high, respectively, relative to the proportion of events that is actually true.

Lichtenstein and Fischhoff [1977] used the following numerical measure of calibration [Murphy, 1973] for the discrete-event case:

$$\text{Calibration} = \frac{1}{N} \sum_{t=1}^{T} n_t(r_t - c_t)^2, \qquad (5.1)$$

"where N is the total number of responses, n_t is the number of times the response r_t was used, c_t is the proportion correct for all items assigned probability r_t, and T is the total number of different response categories used (e.g., T = 6 for subjects who limit their responses to the single digits .5, .6, .7, .8, .9, and 1.0)." The perfectly calibrated assessor will score zero on this measure. Lichtenstein, Fischhoff, and Phillips [1977] discuss this and several other measures of calibration, noting that none of the alternative measures has gained acceptance in the literature, none discriminates overconfidence from underconfidence, and nothing is known about the sampling properties of any of the measures. Lichtenstein and Fischhoff [1977] note, however, that over-and underconfidence can be measured simply by omitting the square from Equation 5.1; then overconfidence is indicated by a positive number and underconfidence by a negative number.

Some of the results from calibration studies are straightforward: (1) With the exception of experienced weather forecasters, individuals are very poorly calibrated; (2) Individuals are overconfident in their assessments; (3) Calibration does not seem to be related to expertise (except for weather forecasters) or to intelligence, but it is related to the degree of difficulty of the items being evaluated; (4) Less overconfidence (and sometimes underconfidence) often is found for very easy items [Lichtenstein and Fischhoff, 1977].

The results are similar for both the discrete and continuous cases. Assessments of continuous distributions that have been calibrated often have been elicited via the variable interval method or some variant of this method. The most common measures of calibration in such studies are the interquartile index and the "surprise" index. The interquartile index is the percentage of items for which the true value falls inside the assessed interquartile range. The perfectly calibrated assessor will have an interquartile index of 50. The surprise index is the percentage of items for which the true value falls outside the most extreme fractiles assessed. Thus, when the most extreme fractiles are .01 and .99 the perfectly calibrated assessor will have a surprise index of 2. A consistent finding is that assessed distributions are too tight. In the studies reviewed by Lichtenstein, Fischhoff, and Phillips [1977], between 20 percent and 50 percent, instead of two percent, of the true values typically fell outside the .01 to .99 fractiles of the distributions.[4]

5.1.3 Improving Subjective Probability Assessments

The limited evidence available suggests that improving unaided individual

---

[4] In February 1981, Joseph Kadane (Carnegie-Mellon University) and Sarah Lichtenstein (Decision Research) were conducting analytical research that raised serious questions about the entire area of calibration research. Interested readers may wish to obtain a copy of their manuscript when it becomes available.

probability assessments is possible, though extremely difficult. A general approach to improving assessments involves the use of a trained interviewer who motivates the assessor to respond conscientiously and structures the assessment task to reduce ambiguities. This approach includes various types of consistency checks designed to maximize the validity of the assessed distributions, e.g., determining if the assessed probabilities sum to 1, or using multiple elicitation methods for the same task. A detailed description of this approach is provided by Spetzler and Staël von Holstein [1975].

More specific means of improving individual probability assessment include training and the use of composite assessments. Training may include tutoring in statistics and probability, discussing with the assessor actual or potential cognitive biases, and various forms of feedback. Tutoring in statistics is supported by studies showing that normative expertise is related to the validity of probability assessments. Most studies that have found training to be useful have involved the discussion of potential assessment biases with the assessors (e.g., exhorting assessors to avoid making distributions too tight) and the provision of periodic feedback reports concerning calibration, over-and underconfidence, and other features of the assessments.

5.1.3.1 Scoring Rules

One type of feedback involves scoring rules, or "penalty functions." A scoring rule assigns a numerical score to an assessed probability (or to a vector of probabilities) as a function of both the actual outcome of an event and the assessed probability of that outcome [Slovic, Fischhoff, and Lichtenstein, 1977, p. 19]. A "strictly proper" scoring rule is one for which the assessor can maximize an expected score only by stating his or her true beliefs without hedging. Hedging may be a popular bias in subjective probability assessment; for example, "People are much less likely to criticize a weather forecast that leads them to carry an umbrella when it doesn't rain than one that leads them to be umbrellaless when it does" [Lichtenstein, Fischhoff, and Phillips, 1977, p. 282]. Since scoring rules are designed to encourage the assessor to report his or her true beliefs, they could be used as a third means (in addition to coherence and calibration) of evaluating the "goodness" of subjective probabilities, as well as a means of training assessors to improve their assessments. Scoring rules are discussed by Murphy and Winkler [1970, 1971], Savage [1971], and Shuford and Brown [1975].

An example of a scoring rule is the Brier score [Brier, 1950], a strictly proper scoring rule used in meteorology. Murphy [1972, 1973, 1974] showed that the Brier score can be partitioned into three additive components, one of which is calibration as defined in Equation 5.1. The second component is called "resolution," or the assessor's ability to successfully assign probabilities that differ from the overall proportion of correct responses:

$$\text{Resolution} = \frac{1}{N} \sum_{t=1}^{T} n_t(c_t - c)^2, \qquad (5.2)$$

where c is the overall proportion of correct responses, c_t is the proportion correct for all items assigned a specific probability r_t, and other terms are as defined earlier (see Equation 5.1). The higher the resolution score, the better. The third component is called "knowledge," and is measured such that the lower the score, the better:

$$\text{Knowledge} = c(1\text{-}c). \tag{5.3}$$

The Brier score is an additive combination of knowledge, calibration, and resolution such that the lower the score, the better:

$$\text{Brier Score} = c(1\text{-}c) + \frac{1}{N} \sum_{t=1}^{T} n_t(r_t\text{-}c_t)^2 - \frac{1}{N} \sum_{t=1}^{T} n_t(c_t\text{-}c)^2. \tag{5.4}$$

This scoring rule provides an overall measure of the "goodness" of assessed probabilities, and it adds dimensions not captured by calibration measures alone.

Strictly proper scoring rules other than the Brier score exist (e.g., see Stael von Holstein [1972]), but they typically do not produce differential improvement in performance. In fact, the evidence relating any scoring rule to improved probability assessments is mixed [Hogarth, 1975]. However, the review by Lichtenstein, Fischhoff and Phillips [1977] indicates that scoring rule feedback, calibration feedback, discussion of actual and potential biases, and exhortations to improve assessment performance sometimes results in more valid assessments.

There appear to be several potential reasons why the use of scoring rule feedback has not produced overwhelming evidence in favor of improvement. Some reasons concern the assumptions underlying the use of scoring rules. Winkler [1967b, p. 1107] lists three assumptions:

> The Assessor possesses the following ideal properties:
> 1. He never violates the postulates of coherence. Following Savage [1954, p. 11]: "This person is idealized; unlike you and me, he never makes mistakes, never gives thirteen pence for a shilling, or makes such a combination of bets that he is sure to lose no matter what happens."
> 2. He fully understands both the methods used to obtain his probability assessments and the methods used to encourage careful assessments. That is, he understands the alternatives open to him and the implications of each alternative.
> 3. He has a utility function which is linear with respect to money in the relevant range (that is, the range of monetary amounts used in conjunction with the assessment procedure). Furthermore, he chooses his responses in such a way as to maximize his expected utility.

Evidence reviewed earlier in this chapter indicates that the first assumption is not always correct. Evidence discussed in Chapter 4 suggests that the third assumption is also problematic. Relative to the second assumption, Murphy and Winkler's [1974] survey of 689 weather forecasters revealed that most rejected the notion that their forecasts could be evaluated by a single quantitative measure, and that 14 percent had hedged in an effort to improve their Brier scores. Several experimental studies have indicated that subjects find scoring rules, as well as various elicitation methods, difficult to understand.

Hogarth [1975] mentions other problems with the use of scoring rules: (1) They presume that the assessor has a "true" subjective probability distribution, and that the assessor knows his or her "true" distribution; (2) They ignore the cost of the assessment procedure; (3) They are relatively insensitive to different stated probabilities. Gonedes and Ijiri [1974] argue that scoring rules will not necessarily prevent hedging if a conflict exists between the assessor's payoff from the scoring rule and the payoff from implementation of an action based on a hedged assessment. In sum, it appears that scoring rules are "a conceptually ingenious device . . ., [but] from a practical viewpoint, they are subject to a number of flaws" [Hogarth, 1975, p. 280].

Notice that the types of feedback employed in probability assessment studies — e.g., "scores," calibration measures, and resolution measures — resemble outcome feedback (see Chapter 3). It was observed earlier that outcome feedback generally is the least effective form in multiple-cue probability learning studies. Hogarth [1975] points out that no probability assessment studies have employed task properties feedback, despite the fact that task properties feedback has been found most effective in other types of tasks.

5.1.3.2 Composite Assessments

Another method for improving the accuracy of subjective probability assessments involves the use of composite assessments. Two broad approaches for developing such composites are the behavioral and mathematical approaches [Winkler, 1968]. The behavioral approaches are distinguished according to whether the individual assessors are allowed to interact with each other in arriving at consensus distributions. One behavioral approach allows assessors to discuss their individual assessments and the reasons for these assessments, and to reach a consensus through group processes. This approach involves the possibility that individual assessors will falsify their assessments in an effort to influence other assessors. It also is subject to the "risky shift" phenomenon (see Kogan and Wallach [1967]). Another behavioral approach involves providing feedback to each assessor about the distributions assessed by the other individuals, and allowing the individuals to alter their assessments after receiving such feedback. The assessors do not interact with each other. This approach is sometimes based on the "Delphi" technique (see, e.g., Dalkey and Helmer [1963]). Unfortunately, very little is known about the relative merits of these two behavioral approaches [Beach, 1975; Hogarth 1975], or about the merits of behavioral approaches relative to mathematical approaches.

Several studies have investigated mathematical approaches (e.g., Sanders [1963, 1973], Staël von Holstein [1971, 1972], Winkler [1971]. A popular mathematical approach is the "opinion-pool" method, in which several individuals' assessments are combined via some arithmetical weighting scheme. The principal effect of forming such composites is to reduce the random error inherent in individual assessments. This effect was noted earlier when composite judgments within the lens model approach were discussed (see Chapter 3). Several weighting schemes have been proposed [Winkler, 1968] and used in various studies. Weighting schemes have been based on (1) the assessors' past performance in the task,

(2) self-ratings of expertise, (3) more objective measures of expertise and (4) equal weighting. Two major results have emerged: First, consensus distributions are more accurate than the majority of the individuals' distributions. Second, differential weighting provides very little [Staël von Holstein, 1971, 1972], if any [Winkler, 1971], increase in accuracy relative to equal weighting. Further, the various types of differential weighting have produced results that differ very little, although assessors sometimes express preferences for certain types of weighting schemes [Winkler and Cummings, 1972].

Winkler [1968] suggested another mathematical approach to obtaining a consensus distribution, the natural-conjugate method, which involves treating each individual's distribution as sample evidence that can be represented by a conjugate prior distribution, and then combining these distributions via successive applications of Bayes' theorem. (For a discussion of conjugate priors, see Winkler [1972]). This approach has not received much attention, apparently because of its complexity (Hampton, Moore and Thomas [1973], Hogarth [1975]). Hogarth [1975] discusses other complex mathematical approaches that seldom have been applied in experimental studies.

One final point should be mentioned in concluding this section on subjective probability assessment. In some situations, it may be unnecessary for assessors to have highly accurate probability distributions. Prior probabilities often are overwhelmed by sample evidence, especially when the amount of sample evidence is large and strongly favors one hypothesis over the others [Epstein, 1962; Lodwick, Turner, Lusted, and Templeton, 1966; Edwards, Lindman, and Savage, 1963]. Prior distributions that differ considerably may lead to very similar posterior distributions after they have been combined properly (via Bayes' theorem) with new evidence. In many real-life situations, however, new evidence may be impossible, or too expensive, to collect. Moreover, the negative payoff resulting from small differences in posterior distributions may be so large that accurate subjective priors will be important.

5.2 REVISING PROBABILITIES

To this point, Chapter 5 has focused on the initial assessment of subjective probabilities, the extent to which unaided assessments satisfy certain criteria of "goodness," and ways of improving unaided individual assessments. A related issue is the revision of probabilities upon the receipt of new data. Probability revision is relevant for both subjective and objective probabilities.

5.2.1 Bayes' Theorem

If a particular hypothesis, say H_i, about the state of the world is held, one should be able to increase or decrease his or her degree of belief in the truth of that hypothesis by making appropriate observations. If, for example, H_i implies D, and D is observed, then the credibility of H_i is likely to be increased. Further, if both H_i and H_j imply D, but the likelihood of observing D given that H_i is true exceeds the likelihood of observing D given that H_j is true, then the observation of D should increase one's confidence in H_i to a greater extent than it increases confidence if H_j.

These intuitive notions are expressed formally in Bayes' theorem, a logical consequence of conditional probabilities that prescribes the optimal revision of probabilities upon receipt of new data. Studies of human probability revision typically compare individuals' revisions with the optimal revisions produced by Bayes' theorem. In a typical Bayesian study, a subject will specify a probability distribution over two or more hypothesized states of the world. This may be contrasted to a typical lens model study, in which the subject estimates a single fractile of the probability distribution (e.g., the most likely value). Bayes' theorem often is linked to normative decision theory (e.g., Savage [1954], von Neumann and Morgenstern [1974]), in which revised probability distributions may be combined with payoff information to implement the decision rule of expected utility maximization. However, optimal probability revision is important regardless of the choice criterion employed.

The Bayesian approach is described in some detail by Edwards [1968], Edwards, Lindman, and Phillips [1965], Nickerson and Feehrer [1975], and Slovic and Lichtenstein [1971]. A more rigorous exposition of the Bayesian approach, and an excellent discussion of its relevance for psychology, is given by Edwards, Lindman, and Savage [1963].

For discrete hypotheses, Bayes' theorem may be written as

$$P(H_i \mid D) = \frac{P(D \mid H_i)P(H_i)}{P(D)}. \tag{5.5}$$

In Equation 5.5, $P(H_i)$ is the prior probability that hypothesis H_i is true. This probability is conditional on all information about H_i available to the individual before the observation of a new datum, D. Similarly, $P(H_i \mid D)$, called the posterior probability of H_i, is the probability of H_i conditional on that same background information together with D. In addition, $P(D \mid H_i)$ is the conditional probability of observing D given that H_i is true. $P(D \mid H_i)$ represents the impact of D on the hypothesis H_i. It reflects the extent to which one's posterior probability, $P(H_i \mid D)$, should differ from the prior probability, $P(H_i)$, as a result of having observed D. As such, $P(D \mid H_i)$ is a measure of the diagnosticity of the datum D.

Bayes' theorem reveals that if both the prior probability that a hypothesis is true, $P(H_i)$, and the probability of observing a particular datum given that the hypothesis is true, $P(D \mid H_i)$, are known for all hypotheses, then the probability that the hypothesis is true given that the datum has been observed, $P(H_i \mid D)$, may be calculated easily. In many decision situations, $P(H_i)$ and $P(D \mid H_i)$ are not known, but must be estimated "subjectively" using, perhaps, the methods discussed in Section 5.1.1. The calculational importance of Bayes' theorem is based on the assumption that individuals are better able to estimate $P(D \mid H_i)$ values than $P(H_i \mid D)$ values. If individuals could provide accurate estimates of $P(H_i \mid D)$ directly, then the use of Equation 5.5 to make the calculations would be unnecessary [Nickerson and Feehrer, 1975].

The denominator in Equation 5.5, P(D), is a normalizing constant that makes the $P(H_i \mid D)$ values sum to 1.0 over the set of mutually exclusive hypotheses being considered. It can be computed as $P(D) = \sum_i P(D \mid H_i)P(H_i)$. However, P(D) is more often eliminated than calculated in Bayesian revision studies. One way to eliminate P(D) is to restate Bayes' theorem in its odds-likelihood ratio form. If one considers an alternative hypothesis, say H_j, that is mutually exclusive of H_i, and modifies his or her beliefs about H_j after observing datum D, then

$$P(H_j|D) = \frac{P(D|H_j)P(H_j)}{P(D)}. \tag{5.6}$$

Dividing Equation 5.5 by Equation 5.6 gives the odds-likelihood ratio form of Bayes' theorem,

$$\frac{P(H_i|D)}{P(H_j|D)} = \frac{P(D|H_i)}{P(D|H_j)} \cdot \frac{P(H_i)}{P(H_j)}$$

or

$$\Omega_1 = LR \cdot \Omega_0, \tag{5.7}$$

where Ω_1 is the posterior odds in favor of H_i over H_j, Ω_0 is the prior odds, and LR is the likelihood ratio.

The form of Bayes' theorem expressed in Equation 5.7 often is more convenient from an experimental standpoint, especially if the number of alternative hypotheses being considered is small. Some individuals may find it easier to estimate likelihood ratios than to estimate $P(D|H_i)$ or $P(D|H_j)$ values directly. Estimates of likelihood ratios often are used as dependent variables in Bayesian revision studies. In terms of Equation 5.7, $LR > 1.0$ implies that the posterior odds in favor of H_i over H_j have increased relative to the prior odds, $LR < 1.0$ implies that the posterior odds in favor of H_j over H_i have increased, and $LR = 1.0$ implies that the observation of D did not change the prior odds.

Bayesian revision studies often compare an individual's subjective likelihood ratios (SLR) with optimal Bayesian likelihood ratios (BLR). A variant of this comparison involves $\log_{10}$ likelihood ratios (SLLR and BLLR), or the log of the posterior odds minus the log of the corresponding prior odds. Logs are used to make the optimal responses linear with the amount of evidence favoring one hypothesis over the other. Peterson, Schneider, and Miller [1965] introduced SLLR ÷ BLLR (called the "accuracy ratio") as an additional measure of the extent to which an individual's performance is optimal. The accuracy ratio can serve as a revision measure for each datum, or as a summary measure across many responses to several data. In the latter case, SLLR ÷ BLLR is the slope of the regression line relating SLLR's to BLLR's and is similar to a regression weight in the lens model approach [Slovic and Lichtenstein, 1971]. An accuracy ratio of 1.0 indicates optimal revision, while an accuracy ratio less (greater) than 1.0 implies conservative (extreme) revision relative to that prescribed by Bayes' theorem.

5.2.2 Conservatism

Slovic and Lichtenstein's [1971] exhaustive review of the Bayesian revision literature concluded that conservatism was the principal experimental finding:

> Upon receipt of new information, subjects revise their posterior probability estimates in the same direction as the optimal model, but the revision is typically *too small;* subjects act as if the data are less diagnostic than they truly are. Subjects in some studies . . . have been found to require from two to nine data observations to revise their opinions as much as Bayes' theorem would prescribe for one observation (p. 693).

Most studies demonstrating conservatism have used simplified laboratory tasks involving some variant of the bookbag-and-pokerchip task (e.g., Peterson, Schneider, and Miller [1965], Phillips and Edwards [1966], Pitz and Downing [1967], Pitz, Downing, and Reinhold [1967], although a few studies have found conservatism in more complex tasks (e.g., Edwards, Phillips, Hays and Goodman [1968], Gustafson [1969]). Bookbag-and-pokerchip tasks typically involve binomial situations in which only two alternative hypotheses are considered. Moreover, symmetric binomial tasks involving further simplification often are employed.

Edwards, Lindman, and Phillips [1965] provide an example of a symmetric binomial bookbag-and-pokerchip task: Two bookbags are filled with pokerchips, one containing 70 red chips and 30 blue chips, and the other containing 30 red chips and 70 blue chips. A sample of chips is drawn from one bag, and the subject is required to estimate the likelihood ratio (or posterior probability or posterior odds) that the bag sampled is the predominantly red bag instead of the predominantly blue bag. The experimenter flips a fair coin to determine which bag will be sampled, indicating that the prior probability of selecting either bag is .5 and that the prior odds is 1.0. The experimenter then draws, with replacement, eight red chips and four blue chips from the bag. Since the prior odds that the predominantly red bag was sampled is 1.0, the posterior odds is equal to the likelihood ratio. In the symmetric binomial case, the likelihood ratio is given by $(p/1\text{-}p)^{2r-n}$, where (in this example) p is the proportion of red chips in the bag, 1-p is the proportion of blue chips, r is the number of red chips in the sample, and n is the sample size. Therefore, the likelihood ratio is $(7/3)^4 = 29.6$. In other words, it is 29.6 times as likely that the predominantly red bag was sampled instead of the predominantly blue bag. This corresponds to a posterior probability for the predominantly red bag of .97. Research by Edwards, Lindman, and Phillips [1965] found that intuitive estimates in this situation typically are between .75 and .80.

The extent of conservatism found in laboratory tasks is influenced substantially by various characteristics of the tasks. Slovic and Lichtenstein's [1971] review indicates that the extent of conservatism is greater when (1) the subject is not offered a payoff for good performance, (2) prior probabilities are less extreme, (3) the subject must estimate probabilities instead of odds, (4) the subject observes new data that tend to disconfirm, instead of confirm, a currently-favored hypothesis, and (5) the diagnosticity of the new data is relatively high.[5] To elaborate on the latter determinant of conservatism, diagnosticity may be increased by

---

[5] Note that this discussion refers to characteristics of the task, and not to characteristics of individuals. Alker and Hermann [1971] found that the extent of conservatism was unrelated to six measures of individual differences, including dogmatism [Rokeach, 1960], integrative complexity [Schroder, Driver, and Streufert, 1967] and risk-taking propensity [Kogan and Wallach, 1964].

increasing the sample size of the new observations, by increasing the disparity between the number of "reds" and "blues" in the bookbag (e.g., an 80:20 split is more diagnostic than a 70:30 split), and by other means. Regardless of the manner in which diagnosticity is manipulated, greater diagnosticity results in greater conservatism. In tasks of very low diagnosticity, the opposite of conservative revision has been found.

Three explanations of conservatism have been offered [Edwards, 1968], and some evidence supports all three: (1) misperception; (2) misaggregation; (3) response bias. The *misperception* explanation maintains that individuals misperceive the conditional probability of the data given the truth of the hypothesis, $P(D|H_i)$, or that they misperceive the likelihood ratio, $P(D|H_i) \div P(D|H_j)$, but that they aggregate the likelihood ratio with the prior odds appropriately. The misperception explanation implies, for example, that individuals' estimates for posterior probabilities, $P(H_i|D)$, are biased in the same way as their estimates of $P(D|H_i)$, and some studies (e.g., Peterson, DuCharme and Edwards [1968]) have found this to be the case.

Rappaport and Wallsten [1972] discuss various forms of misperception. One is a tendency to underestimate the informativeness of rare events. Suppose, for example, that in the bookbag-and-pokerchip example presented earlier, the number of red chips and blue chips drawn had been 1004 and 1000, respectively, instead of eight and four. The Bayesian posterior probability that the predominantly red bag had been sampled is still .97, just as it is with eight reds and four blues. However, individuals typically view this "unusual" combination of reds and blues as quite uninformative, i.e., they misperceive $P(D|H_i)$, and revise the prior probability conservatively.

The *misaggregation* explanation focuses on individuals' difficulties in aggregating several data in order to produce a single response. Support for the misaggregation explanation comes from studies finding that conservatism occurs to a smaller extent on the first trial of a data sequence than on subsequent trials (e.g., DuCharme and Peterson [1968]). Supporting evidence also includes research on "probabilistic information processing" systems (e.g., Edwards, Phillips, Hays, and Goodman [1968]). Edwards and his colleagues have reported several experiments in which some subjects gave $P(D|H)$ estimates that were aggregated via Bayes' theorem into $P(H|D)$ estimates, while other subjects gave $P(H|D)$ estimates directly. The latter subjects (who had to aggregate the data themselves) were far more conservative than the former. Edwards [1968] has argued that misaggregation is the major source of conservatism.

The third explanation maintains that conservatism is artifactual. Instead of reflecting information processing errors, as implied by the misperception and misaggregation explanations, conservatism may reflect a *response bias*. For example, DuCharme [1970] presents some evidence that individuals' revisions are near optimal when dealing with odds between 1:10 and 10:1, but are conservative outside that range. The response bias explanation of conservatism is difficult to refute, as noted by DuCharme [1970, p. 67]: "A response bias will, of course, explain the occurrence of conservatism in general. Any time a sequence of data favors a particular hypothesis strongly enough, [subjects'] responses will appear conservative. They will be loath to estimate numbers as extreme as those called for by the optimal model." Such a response bias would explain the finding that conservatism increases as the diagnosticity of a datum increases, as well as the finding that conservatism increases as more data in a sequence are observed. Both situations increase the extremeness of the response required for optimality.

5.2.3 Moderating Effects on Conservatism

The response bias explanation and the impact on conservatism of various task characteristics suggest that conservatism may be a less general finding than some early research had implied. Moreover, Winkler and Murphy [1973] argue that the simplified bookbag-and-pokerchip tasks in which conservatism often is demonstrated may be less familiar to individuals than many real-world tasks that are more complex, and that unfamiliarity may be linked to suboptimal performance. Probabilistic situations in the real world may differ from those in bookbag-and-pokerchip experiments in several ways, including (1) data diagnosticity, (2) data reliability, (3) the stationarity and types of data-generating processes, (4) the frequency of multistage inferences, and (5) the existence of conditionally nonindependent data.

Some evidence suggests that the extent of conservatism decreases when experiments are modified to capture more fully the complexity of the real world. For example, subjects who make conservative revisions in bookbag-and-pokerchip tasks may be generalizing from real-world situations in which data tend to be relatively undiagnostic. Closely related to the effects of diagnosticity, Winkler and Murphy suggest, is the additional uncertainty in real-world situations that results from unreliable data and from nonstationarity of the underlying process that generates the data. These authors argue that treating perfectly reliable bookbag-and-pokerchip data as if they were unreliable, and treating stationary bookbag-and-pokerchip data generators as if they were nonstationary, could lead to conservative revisions.

Another way in which the typical bookbag-and-pokerchip task differs from many real-world settings is its reliance on a binomial data generator. Data in real life often vary along a continuum rather than being restricted to only two values. DuCharme and Peterson [1968] found that conservatism was about half as great in a normally-distributed population as observed in experiments involving binomial populations.

A related issue is that of cascaded, or multistage, inferences (e.g., Steiger and Gettys [1972], Youssef and Peterson (1973]). The conventional bookbag-and-pokerchip task represents single-stage inference involving unambiguously-observed raw data. Multistage inference, on the other hand, consists of a series of single-stage inferences in which the output (i.e., an inference) from one stage becomes input for the next stage. "While you always know with certainty what your data are in a single-stage inference, in multistage inference your data are often the result of previous probabilistic inferences. Thus, succeeding stages of inference are based on probabilities of events, rather than the certain knowledge that an event occurred" [Steiger and Gettys, 1972, p. 1].

Gettys and Willke [1969] developed an optimal model for probability revision in multistage settings. A great deal of research (see, for example, the entire December 1973 issue of *Organizational Behavior and Human Performance*) has shown that the performance of individuals in multistage settings is described well by a "best guess" model; that is, at stage n + 1 individuals proceed primarily on the basis of the most likely event at stage n (their best guess) and tend to ignore the impact of the less likely events at stage n. While the resulting inferences often are conservative relative to those prescribed by the optimal model, they typically are much less conservative than inferences made in corresponding noncascaded settings [Youssef and Peterson, 1973].

The typical bookbag-and-pokerchip task involves conditionally independent data. For example, the color of the nth chip drawn from a bag is independent, conditional on a given bag, of the colors of the first n-1 chips drawn. Conditional independence implies that $P(D_2 | H_i, D_1) = P(D_2 | H_i)$, where D_1 and D_2 are two data. It further implies that $P(D_1, D_2 | H_i) = P(D_1 | H_i)P(D_2 | H_i)$. The data are conditionally nonindependent if the equalities in these two expressions are violated [Schum, 1966]. Winkler and Murphy [1973] maintain that most real-world decision tasks involve conditionally nonindependent data, and that individuals who treat conditionally independent data as redundant will appear conservative in bookbag-and-pokerchip tasks. Bayes' theorem may be modified such that it is appropriate for conditionally nonindependent data. Studies that have compared individuals' probability revisions based on conditionally nonindependent data with those prescribed by the appropriate Bayesian model often have found that conservatism is reduced or eliminated (e.g., Domas and Peterson [1972], Schum [1966]).

5.2.4 PIP Systems

Relying on early research that suggested the prevalence of conservatism, and on the belief that conservatism is caused primarily by misaggregation, several studies have investigated a technique designed to eliminate or reduce conservatism. This technique, which corresponds somewhat to replacing the individual by a model in the lens approach, is called a probabilistic information processing (PIP) system. It was developed by Edwards and his colleagues [Edwards, 1962b; Edwards and Phillips, 1964; Edwards, Phillips, Hays, and Goodman, 1968].

The seminal PIP study is Edwards, Phillips, Hays, and Goodman [1968]. These researchers conducted a complex experiment in a simulated military diagnosis context. The hypotheses being evaluated involved the likelihood of various wars vis-a-vis the continuance of peace. One group of subjects (the PIP group) estimated likelihood ratios for $P(D | H)$, the probability of observing a datum given that a particular hypothesis was true. These estimates were aggregated by Bayes' theorem, and the output of this aggregation was posterior probability, $P(H | D)$, estimates. Subjects in the other three groups had to perform the aggregation themselves. The POP group estimated posterior odds in favor of various war hypotheses relative to the peace hypothesis. The PEP group stated a fair price for an insurance policy that would pay them 100 points if a particular war occurred, and nothing if peace continued. This was a "disguised" posterior probability estimate. Finally, the PUP group estimated posterior probabilities directly.

The researchers could not evaluate the "goodness" of the subjects' estimates since the correct odds for war versus peace were not known. Instead, the subjects' estimates were evaluated according to the "extremeness" of the posterior odds. Based on this criterion, the PIP group, who did not have to perform the aggregation themselves, was far superior to the other three groups. For example, when the PIP group arrived at odds of 19:1, the other groups arrived at odds between 1.2:1 and 2.0:1; when the PIP group showed odds of 99:1, the other groups showed odds between 1.9:1 and 11.9:1.

The superiority of the PIP system was supported by two experiments reported by Kaplan and Newman [1966], while a third experiment showed that PIP and POP groups performed at approximately the same level. While the Edwards, Phillips, Hays, and Goodman [1968] and Kaplan and Newman [1966] experiments involved the use of conditionally independent data, a study by Schum [1966] employed conditionally nonindependent data. In this study, also a simulated military diagnosis task, individuals' posterior probability, $P(H|D)$, estimates were very near optimal. Domas and Peterson [1972], in a bookbag-and-pokerchip task, found POP to outperform PIP with conditionally nonindependent data, while the opposite occurred with conditionally independent data.

Slovic and Lichtenstein [1971] and Beach [1975] review studies that have compared the performance of PIP and POP systems, i.e., the assessment of $P(D|H)$'s or likelihood ratios that are aggregated by Bayes' theorem versus the assessment of $P(H|D)$'s or posterior odds. The evidence is somewhat mixed but generally supports a PIP system. Whatever PIP's merits in the laboratory, however, its utility outside the laboratory has been questioned. In a review of Bayesian research, Beach [1975, p. 24] observed:

> The evidence reviewed here appears to favor a PIP system, at least in a laboratory simulated military decision making context. However, there are some problems with diagnostic tasks in the real world that have not been studied extensively in a "laboratory PIP" system, so applying PIP systems elsewhere should be done with caution. There are problems in the real world of defining an exhaustive set of mutually exclusive hypotheses, of determining whether or not conditional dependencies exist among the data (either in pairs or higher orders), of determining the reliability of the sources of the data, and of the nonstationarity of the data sources . . . .

Beach mentions many of the same issues that limit the generalizability of the conservatism phenomenon. This is not surprising since the purpose of a PIP system is to eliminate or reduce conservatism. If less conservatism occurs in realistic situations, as Winkler and Murphy [1973] argue, then the utility of PIP systems will be decreased. Slovic, Fischhoff and Lichtenstein [1977, pp. 26-27] noted that very little research on PIP has appeared since about 1970, and that "apparently few, if any, PIP systems are operational today despite the mass of research refining its methodology."

5.3 COGNITIVE PROCESSES IN PROBABILITY ASSESSMENT AND REVISION

A number of studies have focused on the cognitive processes involved in probability assessment and revision. Some studies clearly relate to either assessment or revision; others relate to both. The experimental results are somewhat fragmented in that no comprehensive theory of cognitive processes exists to provide an integrative framework for the empirical findings. This section of the chapter is organized according to the apparent empirical generalizations that can be drawn from the results. Hogarth [1975] and Peterson and Beach [1967] summarize several studies upon which some of these generalizations are based.

In their review of the early probabilistic judgment literature, Peterson and Beach [1967] distinguished between studies of intuitive *descriptive* statistics and studies of intuitive *inferential* statistics. "Typically, experiments on descriptive statistics display a sample of data and ask the subjects for estimates of the proportion, mean, variance, correlation, or some other descriptive statistic" (p. 30). On the other hand, "[e]xperiments on intuitive inference explore how man uses samples of data to reach conclusions about characteristics of his environment" (p. 31). Studies of intuitive descriptive statistics relate primarily to probability assessment, while studies of intuitive inferential statistics relate primarily to probability revision. The criterion against which intuitive descriptive statistics are judged in accuracy, while the criterion for intuitive inferential statistics is optimality, i.e., the optimal responses produced by a normative model. Since intuitive descriptive statistics often underlie the intuitive inference process, many studies of descriptive statistics are relevant to inferential processes, and it is often difficult to classify a study as relating primarily to description or to inference.

5.3.1 Pervasive Shortcomings

It is useful to classify the experimental results according to the nature of the cognitive characteristics that limit an individuals' ability to deal effectively with probabilities. The results reveal three pervasive shortcomings of individuals as "intuitive statisticians": (1) Individuals do not have an adequate concept of a probability distribution; (2) Individuals have great difficulty in dealing with rare events; (3) In their attempts to handle uncertainty, individuals inappropriately search for patterns and avoid irregularity [A. Ashton, 1977].

5.3.1.1 The Concept of a Distribution

That individuals do not have an adequate concept of a probability distribution is supported by two types of evidence. An example of the first type is Cohen and Hansel's [1955a] finding that adolescents possess only primitive concepts of distributions, ranging from the idea that numbers can vary to the idea that some outcomes are more likely than others. These authors observed that "Instead of a tendency toward a distribution, we find a tendency away from it," and they noted a "marked preference for balance and the avoidance of asymmetrical arrangements" (p. 120).

Second, when individuals do acquire an intuitive understanding of distributions, they tend to think in terms of normal distributions. Winkler [1967a] attributes this tendency to the emphasis on normal distributions in statistical training, but Hogarth [1975] found a more basic psychological explanation in the work of

Allport [1955], who maintained that symmetry is a powerful organizer of perceptual phenomena.

5.3.1.2 Rare Events

Another generalization concerns rare events, or the extremes of probability distributions. It was noted earlier that individuals have difficulty estimating the extreme fractiles of a probability distribution. The importance of extreme odds assessments in determining the extent of conservatism in probability revisions also was discussed earlier. In addition, several studies involving intuitive judgments of central tendency, variance and proportion point to the difficulty of dealing with extreme occurrences.

For example, Peterson and Miller [1964] found that individuals could provide accurate estimates of the mode and median of a skewed frequency distribution. However, estimates of the mean were biased toward the median, revealing a reluctance to weight extreme occurrences heavily enough. In that study, "[t]he deviant events were also rare events, so subjects may have regarded them as unrepresentative and thus not more important than the most frequently occurring events" [Peterson and Beach, 1967, p. 34]. In a study of intuitive judgments of variance, Beach and Scopp [1968], using normally distributed samples, found that raising deviations from the mean by an exponent of .39 (instead of 2.0) best explained the judgments of their subjects. Again, such a result indicates a reluctance to weight extreme occurrences heavily enough. With respect to intuitive judgments of proportions, Peterson and Beach [1967, p. 34] review several studies showing both overestimation and underestimation of both low and high proportions, while mean judgments of nonextreme proportions generally were very near the sample proportion.

5.3.1.3 Patterns and Irregularity

The third generalization concerns searching for patterns and avoiding irregularity in samples of data. This cognitive bias is manifested in at least three ways. First, individuals have very poor conceptions of independence and randomness. Cohen and Hansel [1955b] found that young children who were asked to guess the binary outcomes of a series tended to make responses that "balanced" the outcomes of the series. Wagenaar [1970, 1972] found that individuals experienced a great deal of difficulty distinguishing random from nonrandom sequences. According to Wagenaar [1970, p. 348], subjects showed "a tendency towards too few repetitions and too many alterations." The subjects tended to impose regularity when none was present. This result is reminiscent of the "gambler's fallacy," i.e., the erroneous belief that probabilistic events which have not occurred for some time become more likely [Hogarth, 1975, p. 274].

A second set of studies relevant to intuitive judgments of independence and randomness concerns the "illusory correlation" phenomenon. Illusory correlation has been defined as "the report by observers of a correlation between two classes of events which, in reality, (a) are not correlated, (b) are correlated to a lesser extent than reported, or (c) are correlated in the opposite direction from that which is reported" [Chapman, 1967, p. 151].

The seminal illusory correlation study is Chapman and Chapman [1967]. Working with a psychodiagnostic device known as the Draw-a-Person Test, these researchers paired each of 35 drawings with a symptom statement supposedly representing various behavioral problems of the drawers. Actually, the drawings and symptom statements were combined in such a way that "each drawing characteristic occurred as often with one symptom statement as another" [Chapman and Chapman, 1967, p. 196]. Thus, there was *no relationship* between drawings and symptom statements. However, experimental subjects reported observing various relationships. For example, high percentages of subjects reported a high co-occurrence between figures with big eyes and the statement "He is suspicious of other people"; between muscular figures and the statement "He is worried about how manly he is"; between figures with enlarged heads and the statement "He is worried about how intelligent he is." Thus, the subjects "saw" popular relationships in the data although these relationships were nonexistent. Similar results have been reported by Chapman [1967], Chapman and Chapman [1969], Golding and Rorer [1972] and Starr and Katkin [1969].

While illusory correlation suggests a tendency to find nonexistent relationships, studies of "contingency judgments" reveal that individuals often are sensitive to certain types of relationships but not to others. Such studies follow a common pattern (e.g., Jenkins and Ward [1965], Smedslund [1963, 1966], Ward and Jenkins [1965]): If A_1 and A_2 represent two events (e.g., the appearance of symptom S and the nonappearance of symptom S, respectively), and B_1 and B_2 represent two other events (e.g., the diagnosis of illness I and the diagnosis that illness I is not present, respectively), then a contingency exists between A (the symptom) and B (the illness) to the extent that the probability of B_1 given A_1 differs from the probability of B_1 given A_2. In other words, a contingency exists between A and B to the extent that $a/(a+b)$ differs from $c/(c+d)$ in the joint-frequency table below. In judging contingency, however, individuals typically do not compare $a/(a+b)$ with $c/(c+d)$. Instead, they concentrate on cell a (and occasionally on cell d), ignoring both cell b (e.g., that symptom S is sometimes not associated with illness I) and cell c (e.g., that illness I sometimes occurs in the absence of symptom S). Such results imply, for example, that an individual who holds the hypothesis that A_1 co-occurs with B_1 may not even look for A_1 when B_2 occurs, nor for A_2 when B_1 occurs, thus avoiding a type of irregularity.

	B_1	B_2
A_1	a	b
A_2	c	d

A tendency to impose regularity has also been found in studies of intuitive judgments of variance. That judgments of variance are influenced too little by extreme outcomes was noted earlier. It has also been found that judgments of variance are influenced by the mean of the observations. The results of Beach and Scopp [1968] and Lathrop [1967] suggest that judged variability decreases as the mean increases, " . . . as though the subjects were estimating the coefficient of variation (standard deviation/mean) rather than the variance. Put another way, it is as though they were judging discrepancies from the mean in relation to the magnitude of the mean . . . ." [Peterson and Beach, 1967, p. 31]. The finding that variance is underestimated when the related mean is large reflects a tendency to impose regularity.

5.3.2 Heuristics and Biases

Results such as these suggest systematic cognitive biases in the assessment and revision of probabilities. Other research has focused on potential causes of such biases, and has discovered several heuristics that individuals seem to employ in order to reduce complex cognitive processes to simpler judgmental operations. The use of simplifying heuristics may be beneficial in that it reduces the time and amount of cognitive effort needed for probabilistic judgments. In addition, judgments based on heuristic processes may be "good" when evaluated against accuracy or optimality criteria. The danger in relying on heuristics, however, is that they often may lead to biased or incorrect judgments. Moreover, the potential detrimental effect of heuristics may not be recognized by the decision maker. Kahneman and Tversky ([1972, 1973], Tversky and Kahneman [1971, 1973, 1974]) have investigated three heuristics — representativeness, availability, and anchoring and adjustment — and several judgmental biases to which the use of these heuristics can lead. Fischhoff [1975, 1977] and Fischhoff and Byeth [1975] have studied the hindsight bias.

5.3.2.1 Representativeness

One of the most detrimental heuristics appears to be representativeness. "A person who follows this heuristic evaluates the probability of an uncertain event, or a sample, by the degree to which it is: (i) similar in essential properties to its parent population; and (ii) reflects the salient features of the process by which it is generated" [Kahneman and Tversky, 1972, p. 431]. Events that are more representative often are judged to have a higher probability of occurrence than less representative events. Tversky and Kahneman [1974] have documented several biases that may result from use of the representativeness heuristic. One is insensitivity to prior probability. Bayes' theorem makes it clear that probabilistic judgments should be affected by prior probabilities. However, prior probability has no effect on the representativeness of observed sample outcomes. Thus, if individuals make judgments of probability on the basis of representativeness they will tend to ignore prior probabilities. Kahneman and Tversky [1972, 1973] found this to be the case in several experiments. Subjects used prior probabilities only when they had no other information.

Insensitivity to sample size is another bias that results from use of the representativeness heuristic. The similarity of a sample statistic to the corresponding population parameter does not depend on the size of the sample. Thus, if probabilities are assessed by representativeness the judged probability of a sample statistic will be independent of sample size. Subjects have been found to assess identical distributions for sample sizes of 1000, 100 and 10. Of course, sampling theory entails that extreme outcomes are more likely to occur in small samples than in large ones.

Kahneman and Tversky [1972] note that to be representative an uncertain event should appear random, in addition to being similar to its parent population. Randomness, they argue, is captured by two general properties — irregularity and local representativeness. The latter entails that the characteristics of the parent population are represented not only globally in the entire sample, but also locally in each of its parts. However, a locally representative sample contains too many alterations and too few runs. (The belief in local representativeness may explain the "gambler's fallacy.") Other biases that can result from use of the representativeness heuristic are discussed in Kahneman and Tversky [1972, 1973]) and Tversky and Kahneman [1974].

5.3.2.2 Availability

Another heuristic identified by Tversky and Kahneman [1973, 1974] is availability. "A person is said to employ the availability heuristic whenever he estimates frequency or probability by the ease with which instances or associations can be brought to mind" [Tversky and Kahneman, 1973, p. 208]. The retrievability of instances or associations may depend on familiarity, salience, recency of occurrence, imaginability, or the effectiveness of a search set. For example, individuals have been found to believe (erroneously) that it is more likely that an English word starts with the letter r than that r is the third letter of the word. Retrieving from memory words that begin with r is easier than retrieving words with r in the third position.

The availability heuristic provides an explanation for the illusory correlation phenomenon discussed earlier. The association between two items is strengthened whenever the items co-occur. "Thus, when a person finds that the association between items is strong, he is likely to conclude that they have been frequently paired in his recent experience. However, repetition is not the only factor that affects associative strength. Factors other than repetition which strengthen the association between the members of a pair will, therefore, increase the apparent frequency of that pair. According to this account, illusory correlation is due to the differential strength of associative bonds" [Tversky and Kahneman, 1973, p. 224].[6]

5.3.2.3 Anchoring and Adjustment

The third heuristic identified by Tversky and Kahneman [1974] is anchoring and adjustment. They argue that individuals often make estimates by establishing

---

[6] Kahneman and Tversky [1972] point out that the heuristic, if any, used by an individual may depend in part on the manner in which a probabilistic judgment task is characterized. Either the representativeness heuristic, the availability heuristic, or both, may be evoked by the nature of the task. For example, the representativeness heuristic is more likely to be employed when events are characterized in terms of their general properties, whereas the availability heuristic is more likely to be employed when events are characterized in terms of specific occurrences.

some initial value (an anchor) that may be suggested by the task or may be the result of a partial computation, and then making some adjustment to this initial value. Such adjustments typically are insufficient. Anchoring and adjustment may explain many of the problems individuals have in probability assessment. For example, it was noted earlier that estimated probabilities of conjunctive events often are too high while those for disjunctive events are too low. That is, estimated probabilities of compound events are systematically biased in the direction of the probabilities of the simple events that comprise them (e.g., Bar-Hillel [1973]). Tversky and Kahneman [1974] suggest that the probability of an elementary event provides a natural starting point for the estimation of the probability of a compound event, and that adjustment from this initial value is insufficient.

Another way in which the anchoring and adjustment heuristic may lead to faulty probability assessments involves the use of the variable interval elicitation method. If the assessor first establishes an anchor (e.g., his or her best estimate of an uncertain quantity) and then makes insufficient adjustments from that anchor, the assessor will estimate probability distributions that are too tight. That is, the actual number of occurrences lying outside the most extreme fractiles will be greater than the assessed number of such occurrences. Evidence reviewed earlier indicates that this often happens in subjective probability assessment.

5.3.2.4 Hindsight

Fischhoff [1975, 1977] and Fischhoff and Byeth [1975] have studied the hindsight bias. It was found that the knowledge that an outcome had occurred increased its perceived *prior* probability of occurrence, while the knowledge that an outcome had not occurred decreased its perceived prior probability of occurrence — relative to a control group that possessed no knowledge of outcomes. Moreover, individuals seem to be unaware of the influence that outcome knowledge has on assessed probabilities. Fischhoff [1975, p. 298] notes that "Making sense out of what one is told about the past seems so natural and effortless a response that one may be unaware that outcome knowledge has had any effect at all on him." Thus, the hindsight bias may contribute to the overconfidence that has been observed in probability assessment. Together, the hindsight and overconfidence biases are likely to be very instrumental in inhibiting learning from past experience and, consequently, the improvement of probabilistic judgments.

Several researchers who have studied cognitive processes involved in probability assessment and revision have addressed the issue of whether normative principles, particularly Bayes' theorem, serve well as a first approximation to intuitive probabilistic judgments. Some researchers (e.g., Barclay, Beach, and Braithwaite [1971], Peterson and Beach [1967], Pitz, Downing, and Reinhold [1967]) have argued that one function of normative decision models is to serve as starting points in the search for adequate descriptive models of behavior. Students of conservatism in probability revision sometimes maintain that intuitive probability revision generally follows the Bayesian model, but that individuals simply fail to extract sufficient information from new samples of data. In their early literature review, Peterson and Beach [1967, pp. 42-43] concluded:

> Experiments that have compared human inferences with those of statistical man show that the normative model provides a good first approximation for a psychological theory of inference. Inferences made by subjects are influenced by appropriate variables and in appropriate directions.

However, other researchers have reached less optimistic conclusions.

> . . . performance in a probability revision task is nonoptimal in a more fundamental way than is implied by discussions of conservatism. Performance is determined in large part by task characteristics which are irrelevant to the normative model. [Pitz, Downing and Reinhold, 1967, p. 392]

> In his evaluation of evidence, man is apparently not a conservative Bayesian: he is not Bayesian at all. [Kahneman and Tversky, 1972, p. 450]

Like the descriptive research on risky choice models, much of the recent work on probabilistic judgment suggests that normative principles are violated qualitatively as well as quantitatively. Normative models often do not capture the essential determinants of human judgment.

Part III

Relation to Accounting

CHAPTER SIX

The Role of Human Information Processing Research in Accounting

A large number of studies have addressed a variety of human information processing issues in accounting and auditing. Studies relying on the lens paradigm are reviewed in Chapter 7, and SEU-related studies are the subject of Chapter 8. The authors of those studies offered specific motivations for conducting particular projects. Much of the rationale for the existing studies can be inferred from the reviews in Chapters 7 and 8, or from an understanding of the two paradigms employed.

Before reviewing the individual studies, however, it may be useful to consider, in a more general sense, the reasons for doing human information processing research in accounting. Further, it may be useful to consider the relationship of human information processing research to other perspectives within which accounting and auditing research is conducted. The present chapter discusses the role of human information processing research and its relationship to some other research perspectives.

6.1 THE USE OF ACCOUNTING INFORMATION BY DECISION MAKERS

The role of information in decision making typically is viewed from two perspectives: probability revision and predictive ability. The probability-revision perspective views information in terms of its impact on revisions of expectations of uncertain outcomes. For example, an auditor who holds certain prior beliefs about the error rate in some audit population (based on experience with similar clients, evaluation of internal controls, etc.) may use the results of substantive testing procedures to revise his or her probability distribution over possible error rates. The predictive-ability perspective views information in terms of its impact on the prediction of specific future events [Beaver, Kennelly and Voss, 1968]. For example, an auditor might use the results of substantive tests to predict the particular error-rate level in the population. Information is considered "useful" to the extent that it can impact probability revision or prediction.

The probability-revision and predictive-ability perspectives are compatible, interrelated viewpoints on the role of information in decision making. For example, predictions of specific events may be used in the assessment or revision of probability distributions over outcomes. In human information processing research, however, the probability-revision perspective typically entails a more complete formulation of the decision problem than does the predictive-ability perspective. In probability-revision studies, the decision maker is assumed to be concerned with the entire distribution of possible outcomes, while in predictive-ability studies, the decision maker is assumed to be concerned only with a particular fractile of that distribution, e.g., the most likely outcome.[1]

For decision problems that are formulated in terms of probability revision, Bayes' rule can be applied to yield the optimal revision. A type of optimality criterion also is available in the context of predicting specific events: The "best" series of predictions may be considered those that maximize some goodness-of-fit measure, such as the mean-squared-error criterion in regression analysis.

Therefore, it is possible to evaluate the role of information in decision making without considering the human decision maker. As a practical matter, however, people do make decisions that involve accounting information. External parties use accounting information, for example, to adjust investment portfolios and make credit-granting and regulatory decisions. Internal parties use accounting information, for example, in decisions concerning production, pricing, capital expenditures, sales promotion, and performance evaluation. Moreover, accountants themselves make decisions about which information to produce and supply. These decisions may impact the cost of information production, the cost incurred by individuals to process information, and the set of information that is available. Auditors make decisions about the sufficiency of evidential matter, the fairness of statement presentation, the type of audit opinion to issue, and so on. Such decisions impact the costs incurred by auditing firms and their clients, and they have other effects that reach beyond the parties who are immediately involved.

In all these decision-making activities, accountants, auditors and users of accounting information assess and revise expectations about possible future outcomes, and they attempt to predict specific events. Time and resource constraints do not always permit "good" subjective probability assessments, optimal probability revisions, nor maximization of predictive accuracy. Further, many decision problems faced by accountants, auditors and users of accounting information do not easily lend themselves to meaningful formalization. Therefore, exclusive reliance on formal characterizations of the role of information may systematically direct attention away from important decision-making issues in accounting. Empirical results based on applications of the perspectives and methodologies of human information processing research have enhanced our understanding of decision making. These results should complement the formal characterizations in a more comprehensive view of the role of information in decision making.

6.2 RELATION OF HUMAN INFORMATION PROCESSING RESEARCH TO OTHER ACCOUNTING RESEARCH PERSPECTIVES

The previous section mentions several "application" areas in which human information processing research is conducted, e.g., internal accounting, auditing, and credit-granting decisions. At a more fundamental level, it may be instructive to consider how human information processing research is related to other major perspectives within which accounting research is conducted. It is important to recognize that the perspective of human information processing research does not

---

[1] Wright [1978a] and the AAA Committee on Human Information Processing [1977] elaborate on this distinction.

conflict with these other research traditions. On the contrary, knowledge of the methods and results of human information processing research often can enhance the contributions made by research that derives from other perspectives. Of course, the nature and extent of that enhancement may differ among the alternative perspectives. The remainder of the chapter provides a framework for viewing the relationship of human information processing research to other major accounting research perspectives.

The framework is adapted from that of the Committee on Concepts and Standards for External Financial Reports [American Accounting Association, 1977]. This Committee reviewed three paradigms that have guided efforts to construct accounting theory. Two of the paradigms, the decision usefulness approach and the information economics approach, provide a basis for discussing the roles that the lens and SEU paradigms can play in accounting research. As presented by the Committee, the decision usefulness approach has two major branches. One branch focuses on decision *models*; the other on decision *makers*. The decision-maker branch is further subdivided into the individual user level and the aggregate, or market, level. The information economics approach is also subdivided — into the single-individual case and the multi-individual case. While the Committee was concerned with external accounting issues, the present use of the framework as a tool for viewing human information processing research is applicable to internal accounting[2] and auditing issues as well.

The Committee itself devoted very little attention to human information processing research. For the most part, the "behavioral accounting" studies mentioned by the Committee were studies of users' attitudes toward financial reporting alternatives and disclosure issues. The Committee also discussed briefly some literature on cognitive styles and cognitive complexity. As noted in Chapter 1, neither attitude surveys nor cognitive-styles studies is discussed in this book. The Committee's neglect of human information processing research may have been due to its principal concern with external accounting issues and/or the relatively small amount of published research on human information processing in accounting at the time the Committee deliberated. Hopefully, the use of this framework as a vehicle for viewing the role of human information processing research in accounting will help to alleviate this omission by the Committee.[3]

---

[2] Demski and Feltham [1976] distinguish between the user decision model approach and the information economics approach in the context of internal accounting.

[3] At least three other frameworks for viewing human information processing research in accounting could have been selected. For example, the two paradigms for human information processing research — lens and SEU — could have been emphasized in this chapter. This approach, used by Libby and Lewis [1977, 1981], would have led to an exposition similar to that resulting from use of the Committee's framework, since research issues within the decision usefulness approach typically are addressed via the lens paradigm, and those within the information economics approach via the SEU paradigm. However, certain issues within the decision usefulness approach can be studied via the SEU paradigm and, similarly, the lens paradigm is relevant for some information-economics issues. Second, the role of human information processing research could be viewed in terms of the three research perspectives discussed in Chapter 4 — prescriptive, descriptive and predictive. Most accounting research emanates from (at least) one of these perspectives, and human information processing research is relevant to all three. Finally, the usefulness of human information processing research in each of three traditional areas of application — external accounting, internal accounting, and auditing — could have been emphasized. These alternative frameworks for viewing human information processing research are mentioned at later points in this chapter.

6.2.1 The Decision Usefulness Approach

As noted earlier, the Committee discussed two major branches of the decision usefulness approach — decision models and decision makers — and it subdivided the decision maker branch into the individual and aggregate levels of analysis. The individual/aggregate distinction is more important for human information processing research in accounting than is the model/maker distinction. Consequently, the individual and aggregate levels of analysis are considered separately in this section, and the distinction between decision models and decision makers is addressed at the individual level.

6.2.1.1 The Individual Level

The decision usefulness approach at the individual level has occupied a central place in accounting research for several years. An emphasis on individual decision makers and the information "needs" implied by their decision models pervades reports issued by the AICPA [1974] and the FASB [1976, 1978].

According to the Committee, those who stress decision *models* argue that accountants should "become involved in the evaluation, refinement, and construction of decision models and then . . . educate the receivers [users] in the use of these models . . . ." (p. 14). While both normative and descriptive models are included, normative models seem to predominate. It often is suggested that such models be used in a prescriptive sense, i.e., to specify the information that users "should" want. Investment decision models and cost variance investigation models are examples. Of course, SEU models also could be included in this category.

The decision *maker* branch of the decision usefulness approach relies on users' reactions to accounting information "as a means for inductively deriving preferred reporting alternatives" (the Committee, 1977, p. 10). According to the Committee, those who emphasize this approach argue "that we ought to focus on users and ignore the difficult, perhaps impossible, problem of determining when a decision model is right or wrong" (p. 14). This approach is descriptive in nature. The Committee maintains that this approach entails (1) asking users what information they want, perhaps via attitude or opinion surveys, and then supplying users with the requested information, and (2) descriptive modeling of users' decision processes to determine whether (and how) they use various types of information.

The decision usefulness perspective is also prevalent in recent internal accounting and auditing research. Libby and Fishburn [1977, p. 273] emphasize the importance of descriptive research on decision making in internal accounting contexts involving the evaluation of risky alternatives:

> A better understanding of how managers actually evaluate risky alternatives may lead to the development of techniques that help decision makers better achieve their goals. For example, investment techniques based upon accurate risk preference assumptions might be constructed. Accurate descriptive models could also be useful in training and in monitoring company policy . . . . A complete specification of the decision model should also lead to better specification of information which would be useful to decision makers. Finally, the models themselves can provide useful in-

> formation to be employed in the decisions . . . . All of these techniques for helping individuals to make better decisions depend to a large extent on a detailed understanding of how managers actually evaluate risky alternatives.

A similar rationale for descriptive research on decision making in auditing contexts has been offered by Ashton [1974a, 1979c].

Human information processing research is closely related to the decision usefulness approach at the individual level. Descriptive models of decision makers can be established and used for a variety of purposes, including those mentioned by Libby and Fishburn. They also can be used to promote agreement among the judgments of different decision makers. Moreover, the results of modeling can be used to improve the quality of decisions. Three options for improving decisions have been suggested in the human information processing literature [Libby, 1976c; Ashton, 1979a]. First, the decision maker may be educated to make improved decisions. Second, the decision maker may be replaced by a decision model. Finally, the information set upon which decisions are based may be altered. Of course, combinations of these three strategies could be employed. For example, the information set could be changed and the decision maker educated to use it, or the decision maker could be educated to make improved decisions and then be replaced by a model of his or her own decision process. Note that the goal of applying these options is improved decisions. It matters little whether the impetus for improvement derives from the decision *model* viewpoint, the decision *maker* viewpoint, or some combination of both.

Human information processing research conducted within the decision usefulness framework typically has relied on the lens paradigm, and the criterion for evaluating improvement has been a correlational criterion (see Chapter 3). The type of model that typically has been considered a candidate for replacing the human decision maker is a model of the decision maker's own decision process. However, other types of models could be used, e.g., statistical models of the environment or SEU models. Moreover, other decision improvement options could be used in conjunction with the various types of models. Decision makers could be educated to use their own descriptive models, SEU models, Bayesian revision models, and others. In addition, the estimates used in such models could be the focus of training. For example, decision makers could be educated to make better subjective probability assessments for use in SEU models. The basic point is that human information processing research can add an important dimension to accounting research conducted from a decision usefulness viewpoint by focusing on the understanding, evaluation and improvement of decision making.

6.2.1.2 The Aggregate Level

Accounting research conducted at the aggregate level often incorporates the efficient market hypothesis. A securities market is said to be efficient, conditional upon a specified information set, if security prices act as if there is universal knowledge of that information. If security prices possess this property, they are said to "fully reflect" the information set [Beaver, 1981a, p. 142).[4] The indi-

[4] Beaver [1981b] discusses definitions of market efficiency at some length.

vidual investor is assumed to use the information to revise assessments of the expected return and riskiness associated with securities. The individuals' assessments are assumed to be aggregated, by some unknown process, to form the market's assessment of the expected return, risk and price of each security.

In a "semi-strong" efficient market, the individual investor faces a "fair game" with respect to publicly-available information, including accounting information. Portfolio theory and the efficient market hypothesis imply that individual investors, facing a market-determined set of risk-return relationships, should avoid holding undiversified investment portfolios, selecting undesired risk levels, and incurring excessive transactions costs in the belief that they can "beat the market" with publicly-available information. While the question of abnormal returns to innovative information processing has not been settled, this research area maintains that consistently superior investment performance for a given risk level is rare.[5]

Casual observation, the existence of security analysis services, and the results of a recent survey [Mayer-Sommer, 1979] suggest that a large number of individual investors act as if they are ignorant of, or do not accept, these implications of portfolio theory and the efficient market hypothesis. One important feature of an efficient market, however, is that naive decision making at the individual level does not deny the operation of a sophisticated market at the aggregate level. The "sophistication differential" between the individual and the aggregate may cause the relevance of human information processing research at the level of the individual investor to be questioned. It appears, however, that accounting policy makers are interested in predicting the consequences of policy alternatives for both the aggregate securities market *and* for individual investors. It is well accepted that reliance on the efficient market approach cannot completely determine the policy alternatives that should be chosen. Alternatives that produce accounting numbers having the highest associations with market prices are not necessarily the preferred alternatives (for elaboration, see Gonedes and Dopuch [1974a], May and Sundem [1973]). Human information processing research at the individual-investor level may be able to provide desired input for accounting policy decisions.

There are three areas in which human information processing research might complement accounting research conducted from an aggregate market perspective. These areas relate to (1) the revision of expectations concerning the expected returns and riskiness of securities, (2) the aggregation of individuals' expectations into the opportunities established by the market, and (3) the assumptions on which the market model and the capital asset pricing model are based. It should

---

[5] The phrase "superior performance," or "abnormal returns," has a very specific meaning in this context. That meaning derives from the market model of Markowitz [1952] and Sharpe [1963], which asserts that the stochastic process that generates security returns is $R_{it} = \alpha_i + \beta_i R'_{mt} + u_{it}$, where R_{it} is the return of security i in period t, R'_{mt} is the general market factor in period t, α_i and β_i are the intercept and slope, respectively, of the (assumed) linear relationship between R_{it} and R'_{mt}, and u_{it} is a stochastic component reflecting the portion of security i's return that varies independently of R'_{mt}. The expected value of u_{it} is assumed to be zero, and a securities-trading strategy that implies nonzero u_{it} also implies that abnormal returns are associated with that strategy. The market model and the capital asset pricing model [Sharpe, 1964], the latter a model of equilibrium security prices in the market, have been the cornerstones of empirical research in this area.

be emphasized, however, that virtually nothing is known about the potential value of human information processing research in these three areas. Consequently, the following brief discussion is intended only to suggest some of the ways in which human information processing research might be relevant within an aggregate perspective.

It was stated earlier that individual investors should hold diversified portfolios, select desired risk levels, and avoid incurring excessive transactions costs. Research conducted within the lens and SEU paradigms may help explain and predict investors' choices among alternative levels of diversification, risk and transactions costs by focusing on investors' reactions to accounting information (cf. Beaver [1973, p. 54]).

An example is the investor's use of accounting data for predicting the systematic riskiness (β_i) of a security. Beaver, Kettler, and Scholes [1970] found significant associations between accounting-based risk measures and β_i. They also found that accounting-based risk measures predicted future levels of β_i better than extrapolations of past trends by β_i. They concluded that accounting data have predictive ability with respect to a security's β_i which affects the expected return from holding that security.[6] Beaver [1972, p. 417] points out that the notion of predicting future levels of β_i based on accounting information is "applicable from the point of view of the individual investor in assessing the risk of securities, such that he can select an optimal portfolio." Human information processing research methods can be used to study the prediction of β_i by individual investors, and several methods for improving such predictions could be pursued.

The aggregation of individuals' assessments of expected return and risk into the market's determination of security prices is the second area in which human information processing research could be useful. Virtually nothing is known about this aggregation process when heterogeneous expectations are admitted, except for results derived under very restricted forms of probability assessments and individual preference functions (e.g., Lintner [1969]). However, the similarities in information processing that have been found across a variety of tasks and subjects may provide groundwork for research on the aggregation process. At the least, there is no compelling reason to believe that decision making at the individual level is irrelevant to the aggregation process or to market-level phenomena. This point was made by May and Sundem [1976, pp. 756-57]:

> . . . we see no inherent conflict as long as theories of individual behavior are not themselves taken to be ideal predictors of market behavior. A predictive theory of capital market equilibria could, of course, be constructed without regard to individual decision making, but there is no intrinsic superiority to such an approach. Moreover, although individual actions are not necessarily one-for-one with competitive market phenomena, there is no inherent reason suggesting that theories predicting market phenomena *cannot* be constructed based on theories of individual "rivalrous

---

[6] A study by Eskew [1979] produced results largely consistent with those of Beaver, Kettler, and Scholes, but a study by Elgers [1980], which incorporated several methodological refinements, produced contrary results. Elgers cited other research, however, which found that accounting-based and market-based risk measures used *in combination* may enable predictions of systematic riskiness that are superior to those obtained by using accounting-based measures alone.

price-taking" behavior. Indeed, precisely because market equilibria are established (at least as manifested by observable exchange prices) by the interactions of individuals, this approach would seem to be very promising a priori.

It may be possible to draw an analogy between the relationship of individual decision making to market-level phenomena and the relationship of individuals' predictions and probability assessments to composite predictions and assessments. The consistent finding in the human information processing literature that composite predictions and assessments are superior to those of almost all individuals included in the composite was discussed in Chapters 3 and 5. If security price is viewed as a composite across individual investors, then, by analogy, security price can be viewed as diversifying away the idiosyncratic components of the individuals' knowledge. Then the quality of knowledge reflected in security prices will be considerably greater than the average quality of knowledge at the individual level (cf. Beaver [1981a, pp. 160-62]).

The third area in which human information processing research may be relevant within an aggregate perspective concerns the assumptions on which the market model and the capital asset pricing model are based. Human information processing research may be relevant to the extent that these assumptions are necessary for the predictive validity of the models with respect to security returns (or to the extent that other assumptions which are descriptively more valid can be used to improve predictive validity).

Two such assumptions have significant "behavioral" interest: (1) All investors are risk-averse, single-period, expected-utility-of-terminal-wealth maximizers who choose portfolios of securities on the basis of the means and variances of the probability distributions of returns; (2) All investors have homogeneous expectations, i.e., they have identical subjective estimates of the means, variances and covariances of returns among all securities. These and other assumptions are discussed by Jensen [1972] and Dyckman, Downes, and Magee [1975].

With respect to the mean-variance assumption, research reviewed in Chapter 4 suggests that individuals have preferences for the skewness of returns, as well as for mean and variance. At the aggregate level, Arditti's [1967, 1971] results suggest that skewness is important in explaining security returns. Kraus and Litzenberger [1976] added a measure of systematic skewness to the traditional two-parameter model, and found the resulting three-parameter model superior in explaining security returns. It may be that expected return is a function of systematic skewness as well as β_i. This provides an example of how a parameter that is descriptively valid at the individual level can be incorporated in an existing model to produce greater predictive validity.

The second assumption mentioned above is that of homogeneous expectations. Heterogeneous expectations result in the incurrence of transactions costs to buy and sell securities. Recall that one implication of the efficient market hypothesis is that individuals should avoid excessive transactions costs in an attempt to earn abnormal returns. It is clear from the results of human information processing research that heterogeneous probability assessments and heterogeneous predictions are the rule, not the exception. At the aggregate level, the finding that trading volume increases substantially during the weeks of the annual [Beaver, 1968b] and interim [Kiger, 1972] earnings announcements also supports the existence of heterogeneous expectations. Human information processing research methods might be used to estimate the association between various types of accounting information and the extent of heterogeneous expectations. The clustering models discussed in Chapter 3 may be useful for isolating groups of individuals whose expectations are more or less homogeneous. Finally, research at the individual level may be useful for evaluating ways of decreasing the heterogeneity of expectations. Dyckman, Downes, and Magee [1975, p. 92] comment on this possibility:

> . . . even if the equilibrium price structure in the market does reflect all publicly available information — in this sense the price structure is unbiased — there will remain a dispersion of individual expectations around what can be thought of as the market's average response. This distribution of expectations leads to transactions, and hence to transactions costs. If an alternative (accounting) information system could decrease the dispersion of individual expectations, it would represent an improvement in the operation of the market by decreasing transactions (subject, of course, to cost considerations). In other words, research on the process by which individuals process information is still very relevant.

6.2.2 The Information Economics Approach

The Committee on Concepts and Standards for External Financial Reports [1977] noted that the decision model branch of the decision usefulness approach often utilizes economic theory to specify the kinds of information needed for normative decision models. Information typically is treated as a free good and is not incorporated directly into the economic theory being applied. In contrast, the information economics approach "treats information as a conventional economic commodity, the acquisition of which constitutes a problem of economic choice" [p. 21]. In other words, the information economics approach focuses on the demand for information. This approach can be applied at both the single- and multi-individual levels.

6.2.2.1 The Single-Individual Case

Implications of the information economics approach at the single-individual level have been explored often in auditing (e.g., Kinney [1975a, 1975b]) and internal accounting contexts (e.g., Demski [1972, 1980], Feltham [1972], Demski and Feltham [1976]). Such implications rely on the assumption that individuals make choices that maximize (subjectively) expected utility.[7] Thus, the outlook of

---

[7] Watts and Zimmerman [1978] (also see Watts [1977]) assume SEU maximization by corporate managers, elected and appointed government officials, and standard setters. In this context, the purpose of the assumption is to facilitate the development of a *positive* theory of the determination of accounting and financial reporting standards. Such a theory, if and when developed, "will be able to *explain* the existing set of generally accepted accounting standards and *predict* how that set will be altered with changes in the underlying variables" [Zimmerman, 1980, p. 107]. Much of the income-smoothing literature also relies on a utiity-maximization argument to explain certain behavior of managers (see, e.g., Ronen and Sadan [1978]).

the information economics approach in the single-individual case is both prescriptive — i.e., it prescribes a choice criterion for the decision maker — and predictive, i.e., the decision maker's choices can be predicted if his or her preferences do not violate the axioms of rational choice.

Suppose the decision maker must choose some action, a, from a set of alternative actions, A. The preferred action, a*, is the action that maximizes SEU, which can be represented as

$$E(U|a^*) = \max_{a \epsilon A} \sum_{s \epsilon S} U(s,a)\phi(s), \tag{6.1}$$

where $E(U|a^*)$ is the (subjectively) expected utility of the optimal action, $U(s,a)$ is the utility associated with a unique state-action combination, and $\phi(s)$ is the (subjective) probability that state $s \epsilon S$ will obtain. Now assume that some signal (or piece of information, or cue), $y \epsilon Y$, is transmitted to the decision maker by some information system $\eta \epsilon H$. The effect of receiving signal y from system η is to change $\phi(s)$ to $\phi(s|y,\eta)$. This revision of ϕ is assumed to follow Bayes' rule, and the decision maker's optimal action after receiving signal y from system η is

$$E(U|y,\eta,a^*) = \max_{a \epsilon A} \sum_{s \epsilon S} U(s,a)\phi(s|y,\eta). \tag{6.2}$$

If the four elements of Equation 6.2 (A, S, U and ϕ) are completely specified, then the role of information is that of probability revision [Demski, 1972, Ch. 2].

The information economics approach offers a normative specification of information use (Bayesian revision) and a normative criterion for designing an accounting information system (SEU maximization). While the approach has substantial theoretical appeal, a number of operational difficulties exist. According to the Committee, the "[m]ost obvious [difficulty] is the practical issue of how one operationalizes the expected utility measures. With the proper axiomatic foundation, the mathematical existence of such measures surely is guaranteed. But this theoretical existence provides little guidance for constructing such a measure and incorporating actual numbers — as must be done to implement the approach in a real-world setting" (p. 36).

The SEU paradigm of human information processing is relevant for researching certain implementation issues within the information economics approach. The extent to which individuals' preferences can be represented by the global SEU maximization hypothesis and the extent to which individuals' choices conform to the utility theory axioms will condition the ability to implement the information economics approach. The performance of individuals in subjective probability assessment and probability revision is also relevant.

Information processing and economic cost considerations preclude complete specification of the A, S, U and ϕ elements of Equation 6.2 in realistic settings. While analytical work in information economics often relies on the "costless analysis" assumption, proponents of this approach recognize that simplification of the complete information economics model is necessary. An extremely large number of alternative simplifications could be made, resulting in a plethora of simplified models.[8]

Simplification may involve any of the four basic elements of the complete model. Some action choices may be excluded from consideration, and some state differentiations may be ignored. An example of the latter is the omission of a decision's future-period effects. Similarly, rough utility approximations may be employed, or utility values may be ignored altogether. Further, certain types of information, or cues, may be excluded from consideration. One area in which simplification is likely to occur is probability assessment and revision. For example, the revision of probabilities after new information is received may not follow Bayes' rule. Instead, the decision maker may employ the heuristics discussed in Chapter 5. Moreover, the decision maker may choose to assess (or revise with respect to) a fractile instead of the entire probability distribution. These and other types of simplifications can be studied via human information processing research.

6.2.2.2 The Multi-Individual Case

The information economics approach is also relevant at the multi-individual level. A common type of analysis at this level involves two individuals — a decision maker and an information evaluator (e.g., an accountant). In this case, the information economics approach emphasizes the choices made by the *evaluator*. Essentially, the job of the information evaluator is to choose the information system, η, that will generate signals, y, on which the decision maker will base action choices, a. This formulation introduces additional considerations, relative to the single-individual case, for which human information processing research is relevant.

The two-person information evaluation paradigm assumes that the decision maker and the information evaluator share the same state specification and perceive the same set of action choices available to the decision maker. The role of the evaluator is to select η. For any particular action choice, however, the evaluator has no control over the y that will be generated by η and transmitted to the decision maker. In the case of a complete model, the evaluator is assumed to associate some utility with each possible combination of $s \epsilon S$, $y \epsilon Y$ and $\eta \epsilon H$, and to select the information system, η^*, that will maximize the evaluator's expected utility, as follows:

$$E(U \mid \eta^*) = \max_{\eta \epsilon H} \sum_{y \epsilon Y} \sum_{a \epsilon A} \sum_{s \epsilon S} U(s,a,y,\eta)\phi(s \mid y,\eta)\phi(a \mid y,\eta)\phi(y \mid \eta). \tag{6.3}$$

Note that this formulation requires the evaluator to assess three probability distributions, whereas the decision maker must assess only one. The evaluator (and

[8] Hilton [1980] partially relaxes the costless analysis assumption of information economics and demonstrates that human information processing paradigms are not necessarily incompatible with the normative information economics model. A "synthesis" of the lens and information economics models is presented by Mock and Vasarhelyi [1978].

the decision maker) must assess the probability that state s will occur, given that signal y is produced by system η, i.e., $\phi(s|y,\eta)$. In addition, the evaluator must assess the probability that signal y will be produced by system η, i.e., $\phi(y|\eta)$, and the probability that the decision maker will choose action a, given the receipt of signal y from system η, i.e., $\phi(a|y,\eta)$. Obviously, the SEU paradigm of human information processing research is relevant in a two-person information economics context.

Modeling the decision maker via either the SEU or lens paradigm is also relevant in the two-person case. The probability distribution $\phi(a|y,\eta)$ in Equation 6.3 indicates that the evaluator must be concerned with actions that the decision maker might choose. The decision model used by the decision maker can be an important input to the evaluator's own decision process. Newman [1978] showed that an information evaluator who held erroneous beliefs about the model employed by a decision maker could make sub-optimal choices in the selection of η; that is, the evaluator could fail to maximize expected utility.

Demski [1972] points out that the evaluator might consider "refining his perception of the decision maker's action choice process" (p. 124). For example, the evaluator might construct a "parallel" model to predict the decision maker's choices (see Feltham and Demski [1970]). If the evaluator could acquire perfect knowledge of the decision maker's model, then the probability distribution $\phi(a|y,\eta)$ could be replaced by a functional equation, say $a = m(y,\eta)$, relating any (y,η) pair to a specific $a \epsilon A$. Equation 6.3 would then become

$$E(U|m,\eta^*) = \max_{\eta \epsilon H} \sum_{y \epsilon Y} \sum_{s \epsilon S} U(s,m(y,\eta),y,\eta)\phi(s|y,\eta)\phi(y|\eta). \qquad (6.4)$$

In other words, with perfect knowledge of the decision maker's model, $\phi(a|y,\eta)$ would be either zero or 1.00 for every $a \epsilon A$, given $y \epsilon Y$ and $\eta \epsilon H$. Moreover, the acquisition of additional imperfect knowledge of the decision maker's model would reduce one source of uncertainty in the evaluator's analysis [Demski, 1972, Ch. 7]. Therefore, modeling the decision maker could improve the *evaluator's* decision making, as well as that of the decision maker. The various decision improvement options reviewed in Chapter 3, which typically are discussed within a lens-paradigm context, are also relevant within the information economics approach.[9]

The use of simplified models by decision makers was mentioned earlier. Information evaluators are also likely to employ simplified models relative to the complete model in Equation 6.3. The evaluator's use of a simplified model may affect the evaluator's ability to use information about the decision maker's

---

[9] Note that, like the single-individual model, the two-person information economics model has both predictive and prescriptive orientations. The evaluator is interested in predicting the action choices that the decision maker will make, and the expected-utility formulation of the evaluator's choice process prescribes how this prediction should be used, along with the evaluator's other specifications, in the selection of an information system. Moreover, the relevance of predicting the decision maker's choices does not require that the decision maker employ a complete model. Knowledge of the decision maker's simplified model also could be beneficial to the evaluator.

model [Uecker, 1980]. Simplifications employed by evaluators, and their impacts on SEU maximization by evaluators, are additional issues for which human information processing research can be useful within the two-person information economics framework.

Extending the information evaluation approach to the social level introduces complexities not encountered in moving from the single-individual case to the two-person case. At the social level, the users of accounting (and nonaccounting) information are the decision makers, and some type of policy body that formulates accounting standards is the information evaluator.[10] Extension of the approach to the social level is complex, in part, because nonusers as well as users of accounting information are affected by the accounting standards (information systems) that are chosen. Further, this extension is predicated on the assumption of utility-maximizing behavior at the individual level (see, e.g., Demski [1974], Ng [1978]). While characterization of individuals as expected utility maximizers enables their preferences to be predicted, it does not permit the prescription, at the social level, of the information system that should be chosen. This result is based on Arrow [1963], who proved that no method of moving from individual to social preference will, in general, satisfy four seemingly desirable conditions (Pareto optimality, nondictatorship, complete and transitive preferences, and independence of irrelevant alternatives). Human information processing research may be useful for determining which of Arrow's conditions, if any, the affected individuals would choose to violate. Since these conditions involve some axioms of rational choice, the types of research discussed in Chapter 4 may be relevant.

---

[10] While the information evaluation approach focuses on the relationship between the policy body and information *users,* the "information control" approach suggested by Ijiri [1975] focuses on the relationship between the policy body and information *evaluators* (accountants). The information control approach involves predicting accountants' choices of the information to be supplied, and it recognizes that one purpose of issuing accounting standards is to control such choices by "eliminating much of the discretionary activity of accountants" [Ijiri, 1975, p. 45].

CHAPTER SEVEN

Lens Studies in Accounting

Experimental studies in accounting and auditing contexts that are based on the lens paradigm are reviewed in this chapter.[1] The review is comprehensive in that it includes relevant studies published in *Accounting, Organizations and Society,* the *Journal of Accounting Research* and *The Accounting Review* through 1980, several studies published elsewhere, and a number of unpublished working papers.

The main purpose of this chapter is to organize and describe these studies. A detailed critical evaluation of each study is beyond the scope of this book and, consequently, few critical remarks are offered. However, the studies vary markedly in terms of the issues addressed, their comprehensiveness, and their quality. The interested reader should examine the original studies if a more detailed understanding is desired. Moreover, methodological and technical issues are not explained in this chapter. Interested readers may wish to refer to Chapters 2 and 3 to refresh their memories about technical aspects of lens studies.

The studies reviewed here are organized under seven principal headings that denote the general types of issues addressed: internal control evaluation, materiality judgments, audit report messages, bankruptcy prediction, stock recommendations and price predictions, functional fixation, and managerial accounting. A miscellaneous category is also included. The final section of the chapter is devoted to some summary comments on lens studies in accounting.

7.1 INTERNAL CONTROL EVALUATION

Independent auditors' evaluations of internal control have been studied by several researchers [Ashton, 1974a, 1974b; Ashton and Brown, 1980; Ashton and Kramer, 1980; Gaumnitz, Nunamaker, Surdick and Thomas, 1980; Hamilton and Wright, 1977, 1980; Joyce, 1976; Mock and Turner, 1979; Reckers and Taylor, 1979; Weber, 1978]. Most of these studies have required subjects to rate the strength of various hypothetical internal control systems, although some have involved audit planning decisions and the selection of sample sizes for substantive testing.

Ashton [1974a, 1974b] presented 63 auditors, who typically had two or three years of experience, with 32 hypothetical payroll internal control cases, each of which contained six internal control questions that had been pre-answered yes or no by the researcher. A yes (no) answer always represented a strength (weakness) in the system. The 32 cases were chosen according to a ½ fractional replication of the 2^6 factorial experimental design. The auditors were required to evaluate the

---

[1] Non-empirical discussions of the lens paradigm and its application to accounting and auditing issues are provided by Ashton [1974c, 1976b], Casey [1976], Committee on Human Information Processing [AAA, 1977], Jiambalvo [1976], Kennedy [1977], Libby [1975b, 1976c], Libby and Lewis [1977], Mock and Vasarhelyi [1978], Salamon, Uecker, and Simmons [1976], and Wright [1978a].

strength of internal control in each case on a six-point scale. After responding to all cases the subjects allocated 100 points to the six questions to indicate the (subjective) importance of each cue to their judgments. The entire experiment was repeated with 58 of the 63 subjects between six and 13 weeks later in order to assess the stability of internal control judgments over time.

The data from each subject were analyzed via analysis of variance, and ω^2 statistics showed that the six main effects (representing linear cue utilization) explained, on average, 80.2 percent of the variance in judgments, while the 15 two-cue interactions (representing configural cue utilization) explained only 6.4 percent. Two cues that pertained to separation of duties explained an average of 51.4 percent of judgment variance. Intersubject consensus, intrasubject stability and judgment insight were evaluated via correlation analysis. The mean correlation between the ratings of all pairs of subjects (consensus) was .70. The mean correlation between the ratings of each subject on the two administrations of the experiment (stability) was .81. Finally, mean self-insight, or the correlation between the subjective weights assigned by a subject and the ω^2 values from the same subject's analysis-of-variance model, was .89. Length of experience was unrelated to insight, stability, and the proportion of variance explained by the separation-of-duties cues or by total main effects. Individual differences in cue utilization across subjects were substantial.

This study was replicated and extended by Ashton and Brown [1980], Ashton and Kramer [1980] and Hamilton and Wright [1977, 1980]. Ashton and Brown used two additional internal control questions (one of which pertained to separation of duties) and five times as many hypothetical cases. Thirty-one auditors, whose mean experience level was slightly less than that of subjects in the original study, participated. A total of 128 cases was generated according to a ½ replication of the 2^8 factorial design, and 32 of these cases were repeated (unknown to the subjects) in order to assess judgment stability. This design allowed Ashton and Brown to assess the impact of far more interactions than did the design used by Ashton. An average of 71.9 percent of judgment variance was explained by the eight cues, 6.1 percent by the 28 two-cue and 56 three-cue interactions, and 50.9 percent by the three separation-of-duties cues. Average values of consensus (.67) and insight (.86) were very near those found in the earlier study. The average stability value (.91) was higher than that found in the original study in which the two evaluations of the same cases were separated by several weeks. Again, the subjects' length of experience was unrelated to any of the judgment measures evaluated.

The Ashton [1974a, 1974b] study was also repeated with a group of 30 auditing students [Ashton and Kramer, 1980]. The original six internal control questions explained a smaller amount of variance (65.6 percent) in the students' judgments than in those of the auditors, and this finding was traced to the fact that the two separation-of-duties questions were less important for the students. On average, these two cues explained only 36.9 percent of the variance in the students' judgments. The mean values of both consensus (.66) and insight (.77) were slightly lower for the students than for the auditors. When the results from the 63 auditors in the original study were combined with those from the 30 students, the

Pearson correlations between length of experience (zero, one, two, or three or more years) and several judgment measures were statistically significant ($\alpha < .05$), though small, ranging from .215 to .276. Point-biserial correlations, computed by dichotomizing the 93 subjects into those having *no* experience versus those having *some* experience, ranged from .256 to .357. This result suggests that having some experience, as opposed to no experience, was more important than the specific amounts of experience the auditors had.

The original study was also replicated, with some modifications, by Hamilton and Wright [1977]. These researchers omitted two of the original six questions and divided the two original separation-of-duties questions into three questions. All 32 combinations of the resulting five questions were presented to 17 practicing auditors. Hamilton and Wright used multiple regression analysis to model the judgments of each subject. The results were consistent with those found in the earlier study. The mean values of consensus and insight were .66 and .87, respectively. The average proportion of judgment variance explained by the five cues was 82 percent, and the importance of the separation-of-duties cues was virtually identical for the two studies. To evaluate the effects of experience, Hamilton and Wright divided the 17 subjects into two groups — those with three or fewer years of experience ($n = 10$) and those with more than three years of experience ($n = 7$). The auditors with more experience had more judgment variance explained by the five cues (85 percent vs. 80 percent), greater consensus (.78 vs. .62) and greater insight (.93 vs. .84), on the average, than did the auditors with less experience. Further analysis of self-insight values found the Spearman correlation between length of experience and judgment insight to be .50 ($\alpha < .05$).

A later study by Hamilton and Wright [1980] presented their same 32 cases to 78 auditors from five firms who had a greater range of experience levels than subjects in earlier studies. Again, the results were similar to those of prior studies. For example, mean consensus and insight were .72 and .77, respectively; the main effects from an analysis of variance of each auditor's judgments accounted for a large proportion of judgment variance, while interactions accounted for very little variance; separation-of-duties cues were again very important. Consensus and insight differed among auditing firms, and insight was positively related to experience. When the study was replicated with a group of 31 auditing students, the results were virtually identical to those obtained with auditors, except that separation-of-duties cues explained less judgment variance.

Reckers and Taylor [1979] investigated the consensus of payroll internal control evaluations in a study involving five hypothetical cases, each of which involved 36 cues. Thirty auditors assigned to each of the five hypothetical internal control systems a reliability rating that could range from zero percent to 100 percent, as suggested by Statement on Auditing Standards No. 1 [AICPA, 1979]. A group of 40 auditing professors also evaluated the five cases. The mean correlation, across the five cases, between the ratings of all pairs of auditors was .16. Auditors with greater than the median level of auditing experience (7.5 years) had a mean consensus index of .36, while those with less than median experience had mean consensus of .14. Mean consensus for the auditing professors was .13. In other words, the ratings of the more experienced auditors agreed better than did those of the less experienced auditors or the auditing professors. Moreover, the ratings of the less experienced auditors and the auditing professors generally were lower than those of the more experienced auditors.

These results led Reckers and Taylor to assert that less experienced auditors and auditing professors would "overaudit," which, they stated, was a "common complaint registered by managers and partners" (p. 51). Reckers and Taylor also interpreted their results to indicate that professional judgment cannot be taught — since the auditing professors disagreed about reliability ratings in these five cases. Ashton [1979c] took exception to such assertions. The Reckers and Taylor study does serve to emphasize, however, the low levels of judgment consensus that may obtain in relatively complex tasks.

Weber [1978] also studied internal control evaluaton, based on a case study of one hypothetical inventory system. The subjects, 40 auditors, studied simulated transactions data and working papers that indicated internal control strengths and weaknesses. The subjects were required to perform several tasks, including (1) estimating the dollar error in three types of inventory, (2) estimating the sensitivity of the dollar error to the occurrence of several types of internal control weaknesses, and (3) estimating the number of hours required to complete the inventory audit. After these and other responses had been made, the actual dollar error in the inventory was communicated to the subjects, and they were allowed to revise their initial audit plans (the hours estimates) in light of this new information. One group of subjects had access to an interactive computer-based simulation decision aid, while the other group did not. The decision aid allowed the subjects to simulate the impacts of various frequencies and types of errors on the financial statements. The subjects also completed psychological tests related to dogmatism and risk-taking propensity.

The results showed that subjects who had access to the decision aid made more "accurate" decisions and took less time than those who did not have access to the decision aid.[2] However, access to the decision aid did not affect the number of hours estimated to complete the inventory audit, and those subjects who had access to the decision aid specified a wider range of possible error amounts than did the other group. Weber [1978, p. 378] interpreted these results to mean that the decision aid improved an auditor's ability to determine the range of possible error, although he concluded that use of the decision aid is not practically viable until much more is known about its effects.

Only three of 12 statistical tests related to the effects of dogmatism, risk-taking propensity and length of experience reached significance, and two of these three were in the opposite direction from that hypothesized by Weber. For example, the estimated number of hours required to complete the inventory audit was *positively* related to length of experience. As Weber [1978, p. 382] noted, this result " . . . runs counter to the often-voiced contention that inexperienced auditors tend to 'over-audit'" (cf. Reckers and Taylor [1979]). Finally, no relation-

[2] Accuracy had a somewhat unusual definition in this study: " . . . decision accuracy was measured on two bases: the absolute difference between the mean of the distribution [of dollar error] produced by the system simulator and the mean of the distribution specified by the subject, and the absolute difference between the range of the distribution produced by the system simulator and the range of the distribution specified by the subject" (pp. 373-74).

ship existed between the estimated dollar amount of error in inventory and the extent of the audit plan (i.e., hours) proposed for substantiating the inventory. Moreover, informing subjects of the actual amount of dollar error in inventory did not result in systematic revisions of the hours estimates. Fourteen subjects made *no* revisions to their initial audit plans. Weber concluded (p. 386) that ". . . the current research shows that auditors may not adjust the scope of their substantive testing plans to reflect their assessment of the internal control system."

Joyce [1976] also focused on time estimates in a study of internal control evaluation. Referring to the relatively high mean level of consensus found by Ashton [1974a, 1974b], Joyce argued that auditors might tend to agree in their evaluations of internal controls yet disagree about the relative amounts of audit effort to be devoted to various types of substantive testing procedures. Disagreement at this stage could have important implications for the cost of the audit and/or the quality of audit evidence collected. Joyce had 35 practicing auditors with a mean experience level of 6.7 years evaluate several hypothetical internal control cases pertaining to the accounts receivable area. Each case contained five cues, and each cue could assume one of two levels. Nineteen subjects (Group 1) responded to 16 cases (a ½ replication of the 2^5 factorial design), and the other 16 subjects (Group 2) responded to 32 cases (a full 2^5 design). All subjects specified the number of hours they would plan for each of five categories of audit procedures (e.g., confirmation procedures, review of subsequent cash collections, and review of year-end sales cutoff).

A univariate analysis of variance on the *total* time specifications of each subject revealed large individual differences in cue utilization. The mean proportion of judgment variance explained by the five cues (the interactions — for Group 2) was 74.7 percent (3.7 percent). An average of 28.1 percent of judgment variance was explained by one cue that pertained to separation of duties. Both the total planned time and the allocation of total time across the five categories of procedures varied considerably across subjects. Consensus, based on the first 16 total time judgments for each subject, ranged from -.687 to .937, with a mean of .373. The mean *canonical* correlation for the first 16 time allocations of each subject was much higher (.930, with a range of .359 to 1.000), but Joyce pointed out significant problems with the interpretation of canonical correlations as measures of consensus. Consensus (based on the univariate analysis) was *inversely* related to length of experience: Mean consensus was .566, .236 and .140 for subjects having three to five years, six to ten years, and 11 to 25 years of experience, respectively ($\alpha < .001$). Judgment stability, based on total time specifications for four repeat cases, was high (mean = .863), but judgment insight, based on the 100-point allocation technique, was moderate (mean = .53; median = .64). Insight was not related to length of experience.

Gaumnitz, Nunamaker, Surdick, and Thomas [1980] tried to reconcile Ashton's finding of high mean consensus for internal control evaluations with Joyce's finding of low mean consensus for audit hours estimates. They pointed out that it is not known whether Ashton's subjects would have agreed on the extent of substantive testing, nor whether Joyce's subjects agreed or disagreed on internal control evaluation. These researchers had 35 auditors make an explicit internal control evaluation, followed by an audit hours estimate, for 20 hypothetical cases adapted from Joyce [1976].

Mean inter-subject consensus was relatively high for both internal control evaluations (.70) and audit hours estimates (.62). In addition, mean intra-subject consistency between internal control evaluations and audit hours estimates over the 20 cases was high ($r = .83$). This finding implies that the extent of audit tesing would vary inversely with the auditor's reliance on internal control, as required by professional auditing standards. Although mean consensus among audit hours estimates was relatively high in correlational terms, the absolute numbers of hours specified differed greatly among some auditors, and the authors discussed some potential explanations for these differences.

Mock and Turner [1979] (also see Mock and Turner, forthcoming) reported some preliminary results from a large-scale research project in which auditors were required to specify sample sizes based on their evaluations of the internal controls in a revenue cycle. Seventy-three auditors studied a revenue cycle adapted from an actual company. These subjects were given almost all the information normally available in an actual audit, e.g., the completed audit program of the previous year, the partially completed program of the current year, results of interim compliance tests, and accounting system flowcharts. The subjects were required to specify sample sizes for each of four types of substantive tests. Overall internal control strength in the revenue cycle was described as having changed during the current year. Half the subjects were given information intended to represent substantial improvement in internal controls (a change from "weak" to "strong"), while the remainder were given information intended to represent a lower level of improvement (a change from "weak" to "fair"). In addition, half the subjects were provided with "explicit guidance" pertaining to the restriction of testing because of reliance on internal controls, while the remainder were not provided with explicit guidance.

A group-level analysis indicated that subjects in the weak-to-strong condition restricted their sample sizes to a greater extent (i.e., chose smaller samples) than those in the weak-to-fair condition. This effect was statistically significant ($\alpha < .05$) for all four types of tests. The effect of explicit guidance was not significant for any of the tests. Further analyses showed that while intersubject variability in suggested sample sizes was considerable, it was smaller for the weak-to-strong group for all four tests, and that neither the length nor type of the subjects' experience was related to their sample size choices. This study also found a "halo effect." Although no improvement occurred in the specific controls relating to one of the four types of audit tests, the mean sample size chosen for this test was significantly smaller for the weak-to-strong group than for the weak-to-fair group. Mock and Turner [1979, p. 291] suggested that "the reduction may be attributable to the impact of a perceived improvement in the general control environment created by improvements in specific controls." Finally, limited evidence of an "anchoring" effect was found. The 73 subjects in the main experiment had an "anchor" available for each of the four tests, i.e., the current year's planned sample size, while a separate group of 43 subjects in a follow-up experiment were not informed of planned sample sizes. For three of the four tests, the mean sample sizes of the subjects who were given an anchor were closer to that anchor than were those of the no-anchor group. This evidence was described as weak (p. 288) because several features and requirements of the experimental task differed between the main study and the follow-up study.

7.2 MATERIALITY JUDGMENTS

Boatsman and Robertson [1974], Hofstedt and Hughes [1977], Messier [1979], Moriarity and Barron [1976, 1979], and Firth [1979] have studied materiality judgments. Boatsman and Robertson [1974] generated 30 sets of values for eight cues that had, within sampling error, the same means, standard deviations and cue intercorrelations as those contained in a sample of 103 actual financial statements. They presented these 30 cases, each in narrative form and containing numerical values of the eight cues, to 18 audit partners and 15 securities analysts. Each subject was required to sort the 30 cases into three piles according to how the subject thought a particular item should be disclosed. The piles correspond to (1) no separate disclosure (because of lack of materiality), (2) footnote disclosure and (3) line-item disclosure in the financial statements. The item in question varied across the 30 cases; each case involved either a gain or loss on the sale of noncurrent assets, a change in an accounting principle, or an uncertainty.

A discriminant analysis based on all 33 subjects classified 63 percent of the cases like the subjects classified them. About three-fourths of the predictive power of the model was contributed by one cue — the relationship of the item to current-year net income. When the model tried to classify the cases into only two groups — no disclosure vs. either footnote or line-item disclosure — the results agreed with the subjects' classifications in 84 percent of the cases. A simple "4 percent of net income" rule-of-thumb would have predicted correctly 65 percent of the subjects' classifications, but this rule was judged inferior to the multivariate model because it tended to err on the side of underdisclosure. Several additional analyses found no important differences between the classification decisions of the audit partners and the securities analysts.

In a similar study, Firth [1979] examined the disclosure recommendations of 90 auditors, 30 chief accountants in industrial and commercial firms, and 30 investment analysts and bank lending officers in the United Kingdom. The task involved whether to recommend separate disclosure (as an extraordinary item) of a gain or loss from the sale of a portion of a firm's activities. Thirty cases, involving 15 gains and 15 losses ranging in size from less than .5 percent to more than 7 percent of profit before extraordinary items, were employed.

While there were large within-group differences in disclosure recommendations for many of the 30 items, the chief accountants generally recommended fewer separate disclosures, and the analysts and bankers more separate disclosures, than the auditors. The size of the item as a percentage of net assets and total assets and, especially, as a percentage of profit before extraordinary items, was positively associated with disclosure recommendation. The extent of recommended disclosure did not differ between the gain and loss items.

Hofstedt and Hughes [1977] had 19 second-year MBA students specify the probability of their recommending that a loss from the write-down of a subsidiary be disclosed separately as an extraordinary item (versus being aggregated with "Other Expenses"). Probability of separate disclosure was considered a surrogate for "perceived materiality." Three numerical levels were used for each of three cues, making a full 3^3 factorial design. A group-level analysis found that all three cues were statistically significant, explaining approximately 40 percent of judgment variance. An individual-level analysis of each subject found sizable inconsistencies in judgments both within and across individuals. The individual analyses also found that linear regression models based only on the three cues typically represented the subjects' judgment policies virtually as well as regression models that included interactive effects, although some differences among individuals were noted. Judgment consistency (R_s^2), based on the three-cue regression models, ranged from .40 to .94 and averaged at .70. A percent-of-net-income cue had a significant regression weight (b_{si}) for all subjects, while the other two cues were significant for one-half to two-thirds of the subjects.

Messier [1979] had 29 audit partners make both a materiality judgment and a disclosure judgment for 32 hypothetical cases based on five cues. The cases were constructed according to a ½ replication of the 4×2^4 factorial design.[3] The item in question concerned an inventory write-down. Materiality judgments were made on a seven-point scale, and disclosure judgments on a zero-to-100 percent probability scale (the probability that the subject would require separate disclosure in the income statement). The 100-point allocation technique was used to elicit subjective weights for the five cues. The subjects responded to 16 of the 32 cases on a second occasion, typically between five and 60 days after making their first judgments, so that judgment stability could be assessed. The subjects were from eight national (including seven "Big Eight") and three regional public accounting firms.

Analysis of the materiality judgments revealed that the effect on net income accounted for an average of 72.9 percent of judgment variance (for the 26 auditors for whom this cue reached statistical significance). The other four cues typically accounted for much less variance. Significant interactions accounted for only 4.8 percent of judgment variance. Judgment consensus and insight were relatively high, with means of .67 and .86, and ranges of -.10 to .95 and .53 to 1.00, respectively. Analysis of the disclosure judgments revealed similar results: Effect on net income accounted for 69.1 percent, and total interactions for 4.4 percent, of judgment variance; mean consensus and insight were .67 and .85, respectively. Judgment stability, based on a canonical correlation analysis, ranged from .53 to 1.00 and averaged at .90. Multivariate analysis-of-variance results were consistent with the two separate univariate analysis-of-variance results. Further, the correlations between the materiality and disclosure judgments of the subjects ranged from .75 to .99, with a mean of .93.

Messier found significant differences across firms and experience levels for the disclosure judgments (and across firms for the materiality judgments). For these analyses, the firms were divided into "Big Eight" (n = 7) and other (n = 4), while experience level was partitioned as 11 to 15 years (n = 14) and 16 or more

[3] In personal communication [May 1980], Messier pointed out that this study inadvertently contained a small number of nonsensical cases. The results should be interpreted in light of this limitation.

years (n = 15). The higher mean responses for subjects from non-Big Eight firms implied that these subjects had lower materiality and disclosure thresholds than did the subjects from Big Eight firms. Similarly, the less experienced subjects had lower disclosure thresholds than did the more experienced subjects. These materiality and disclosure differences occurred at lower levels (3 percent and 5 percent) of the percent-of-net-income variable, while mean materiality and disclosure judgments between groups differed very little at higher levels (10 percent and 20 percent) of this variable.

Moriarity and Barron [1976, 1979] reported two materiality studies based on conjoint measurement analysis. In the first study, they argued that materiality should be viewed as an ordinal variable, thus removing materiality thresholds (see, e.g., Rose, Beaver, Becker, and Sorter [1970]) as a source of differences in the materiality judgments of different individuals. The item in quesion was a decrease in the estimated useful life of equipment — caused by an "inadvertent error in a judgment estimate" (p. 338) — which would reduce before-tax net income. Three variables — before-tax income (3 levels), firm size (3 levels) and earnings trend (2 levels) — were combined in a full $3^2 \times 2$ factorial design to produce 18 cases, each represented by a different set of financial statements. The subjects, 15 audit partners, were required to rank the 18 cases in terms of the materiality of the item.

Axiomatic conjoint measurement analysis found that eight of the 15 auditors' judgment models were additive. Within these eight, there were three distinct rank orderings of cue importance. The models of three additional subjects were judged to be "nearly additive," i.e., only a "small" number of the necessary axiomatic conditions for the existence of an additive model were violated. The other four subjects were judged to have a "large" number of such violations, and their judgments were not considered to be represented adequately by additive models. Moreover, their judgments could not be represented by any of the other three combination rules — multiplicative, distributive or dual-distributive — that axiomatic conjoint measurement methods are capable of diagnosing. Numerical conjoint measurement analysis, using Kruskal's [1965] MONANOVA, was performed on the 11 additive (or nearly additive) models in order to find part-worth functions depicting the contribution to materiality judgments of each level of each cue. Net income was the most important cue for all 11 subjects, and two of these subjects seemed to place almost no weight on either of the other two cues.

Moriarity and Barron's [1979] second study utilized numerical conjoint measurement. They reported results from five audit partners who estimated overall pre-audit materiality levels for 30 hypothetical firms, based on five variables that could assume four levels each. The methodology combined additive conjoint measurement with overlapping fractional factorial designs to produce two models of the judgments of each auditor. The qualitative features of the part-worth functions (e.g., shape) showed a great deal of diversity across subjects. A quantitative analysis based on the two models that represented each person also suggested low consensus, but high stability and response consistency. When correlational analyses were used to evaluate how well Model 1(2) could predict the actual judgments used to derive Model 2(1), the median r was .85. This is comparable to the R_s levels often found in other linear model studies. The median within-subject correlation between the predictions derived from the two models was .928 ($r^2 = .861$), and the median such correlation across all subjects and all models was .527 ($r^2 = .278$).[4]

7.3 AUDIT REPORT MESSAGES

Libby [1979a, 1979b] reported two studies of the message communicated by various types of audit reports. The first study [Libby, 1979a] examined the question of whether the message intended by auditors when they choose a type of opinion is consistent with users' perceptions of that message. The user group studied was commercial loan officers. Libby had 30 audit partners and 28 experienced commercial loan officers consider ten types of audit reports that involved unqualified opinions, qualified opinions, disclaimers of opinion and unaudited statements. The qualified opinions and disclaimers represented both uncertainties and scope limitations. The uncertainties were further subdivided into litigation and asset-realization uncertainties, and the scope limitations into those imposed by clients and those imposed by circumstances. Each subject rated, on a ten-point scale, the similarity of the message intended by each pair of the ten report types.

The data were analyzed via Carroll and Chang's [1970] multidimensional scaling model in order to establish the dimensions that affected the subjects' judgments and the relative importance weights for those dimensions. An analysis of the data from all subjects found that a two-dimensional model accounted for 61 percent of the variance. Dimension 1 split the reports into three distinct groups — unqualified opinions, qualified opinions and disclaimers. The perceived "distance" between qualified opinions and disclaimers was much greater than that between unqualified opinions and qualified opinions. Further, little difference existed between the litigation and asset-realization types of uncertainties, within either the qualified opinions or the disclaimers. Dimension 2 split the reports by type of scope limitation — none, circumstance-imposed, and client-imposed. Dimension 1 was slightly more important to the subjects' judgments than was Dimension 2.

When the judgments of the auditors and bankers were analyzed separately, and several additional analyses performed, virtually no differences were found between the auditors' and the bankers' perceptions of the messages intended by the various reports. The only possible exception was that the auditors perceived the client-imposed and circumstance-imposed scope restrictions as more similar than the bankers did. Libby [1979a, p. 118] concluded that " . . . fears of miscommunication of the messages intended by audit reports to more sophisticated users may not be justified."

Libby's [1979b] second study concerned the effects on bankers' loan decisions of disclosing an uncertainty in the footnotes of financial statements, and of adding a "subject to" uncertainty qualification in the audit report. Libby reasoned that the perceived risk of a loan should be greater when a material uncer-

[4] Note that these numbers are correlations between $\hat{Y}_s$ values, not Y_s values as is typically reported in lens model studies. Using $\hat{Y}_s$ removes the random error component of judgments.

tainty is disclosed than when it is not disclosed, since a contingent liability would decrease the mean and increase the variance of the expected future cash flows available to repay the loan. Moreover, if additional information related to the uncertainty suggested an unfavorable resolution of the uncertainty, then the perceived risk should be greater than if a favorable resolution was indicated. With respect to the incremental effect of adding a "subject to" qualification to the footnote disclosure of the uncertainty, Libby suggested: "If bankers believe . . . that (1) an adverse outcome is no more likely for uncertainties accompanied by a qualified report and footnote disclosure than for those disclosed in footnotes alone, and (2) there is no change in the default risk absorbed by the auditor when he adds his qualification to footnote disclosure alone, or if such information is redundant with information from other sources, adding the 'subject to' qualification to the footnote disclosure should have no additional effect. However, a belief that the addition of the uncertainty qualification affects either or both of these factors (and this information is *not* redundant) should manifest itself in a further increase in perceived loan risk" (p. 38).

Libby had two groups, each consisting of 17 experienced commercial loan officers, specify the interest rate premium (above the prime rate) that they would require (or that they believed another lender would require if they were unwilling to grant the loan) for each of 12 hypothetical loan applicants who had applied for a loan for a specified amount, term and purpose. Each subject group responded to four cases in which no uncertainty disclosure was made. One group also responded to eight cases that included footnote disclosure of an uncertainty pertaining to a lawsuit against the applicant. The second group responded to eight cases in which a "subject to" qualification was added to the footnote disclosure. For some cases in which an uncertainty was disclosed, additional information that indicated a favorable probable resolution was provided; for the other cases, the additional information suggested an unfavorable resolution.

As expected, disclosure of a material uncertainty resulted in significantly higher interest rate premiums specified by the subjects. Moreover, the additional information had a major impact on this lending decision; the effect was so strong that cases in which an uncertainty disclosure was accompanied by favorable additional information were considered no riskier than cases in which no uncertainty was disclosed. Finally, addition of the auditor's uncertainty qualification to the footnote disclosure and the supplemental information had no effect on the perceived risk of the loan. Libby suggested that the most plausible explanation for this lack of effect is that the information conveyed by the "subject to" uncertainty qualification was redundant with the information conveyed by the footnote disclosure and/or the supplemental information about the probable resolution of the uncertainty.

7.4 BANKRUPTCY PREDICTION

The predictive ability of accounting and other financial information in a business failure context has been studied extensively in the accounting and finance literature (e.g., Altman [1968], Altman and McGough [1974], Beaver [1966, 1968a], Deakin [1972], Edmister [1972]). Another set of studies has examined the ability of individual decision makers to use such information for predicting failure. Since a criterion is available and measurable in this prediction task, such studies can assess the *accuracy* of intuitive bankruptcy predictions, along with the other characteristics of judgment that typically are assessed when criterion values are *not* available — for example, in the case of internal control evaluations or materiality judgments. Human information processing studies relative to bankruptcy prediction have been reported by Libby [1975a, 1975b, 1976a] (also see Libby [1976b] and Libby and Blashfield [1978]), Zimmer [1980, 1981], Casey [1980b], Abdel-khalik and El-Sheshai [1980], Kida [1979], and Moriarity [1979].

Libby [1975a] had 43 experienced commercial loan officers predict whether 60 actual firms had failed or not failed based on five financial ratios. The ratios were chosen by performing a principal components analysis of the 14 ratios studied by Beaver [1968] and Deakin [1972], and selecting one ratio to represent each of the five components that emerged. Very little predictive ability was sacrificed when the set of ratios was reduced from 14 to five. The subjects were told that (1) half the 60 firms had failed — to set equal the priors of all subjects, and (2) their performance would be scored +1 (-1) for each correct (incorrect) prediction — to establish a symmetric loss function. Each subject was required to classify each firm as having failed or not failed within three years and to rate his or her confidence in each prediction on a three-point scale. Ten repeat firms (five failed, five not failed) were included in order to assess judgment stability.

Environmental predictability for this task was 51; that is, 51 of the 60 firms could be predicted successfully via a discriminant model based on the five cues. Thirty-seven correct predictions were necessary to achieve better than random accuracy (at $\alpha < .05$). Forty of the 43 subjects performed at a nonrandom level, with a range of 27 to 50 correct predictions and a mean of 44.4 of 60. Length of experience was unrelated to accuracy. Predictions of the "composite judge," formed by computing the average response across all subjects for each firm (i.e., an equal-weighted majority "voting" rule), were correct for 49 of 60 firms. This level of performance was only one prediction less accurate than the best individual, and two predictions less accurate than the optimal discriminant model.

Libby [1975a] also assessed the consensus and stability of the subjects' predictions. Consensus, or agreement between the failed/non-failed predictions of all pairs of subjects, ranged from 31 to 57 of 60 and averaged at 48. Intrajudge stability ranged from six to ten of the ten repeat cases and averaged at 8.9. Forty-one of the 43 subjects made the same prediction on at least eight of the ten repeat firms (necessary for nonchance stability), and 13 subjects exhibited perfect stability.

Some results that pertain to the subjects' *models,* as opposed to their actual predictions, also were reported by Libby [1975b]. Discriminant models constructed to represent the judgment policy of each subject correctly predicted between 47 and 58 of the subjects' actual predictions, with a mean of 52.9, indicating substantial linear predictability. The ability of the subjects' models to capture the subjects' judgment strategies was stable over a one-week time period. (Some of the subjects made 30 predictions one week after having made the first 30, while the other subjects made all 60 predictions at one experimental sitting.) The subjects' models also were found to be stable over "response thresholds" (determined by combining the two-point prediction scale with the three-point confidence scale). This result was interpreted to indicate that the results were not specific to only one set of priors and one implicit loss function.

Libby [1976a] further analyzed this data relative to the "man versus model" issue that had been explored by Goldberg [1970] and others. That is, he compared the accuracy of the predictions made by each subject's discriminant model with the accuracy of the subject's actual predictions. On average, the subjects' models predicted 43.3 cases correctly, while the subjects themselves predicted 44.4 cases correctly. This difference was statistically significant. Twenty-six subjects outperformed their models, ten subjects were outperformed by their models, and there were seven ties between subject and model. Moreover, the model of the composite judge predicted only 46 cases correctly, compared to 49 for the composite judge. Finally, Libby found that the more valid a subject's predictions, the better the subject performed relative to his or her model; the correlation between the subject's validity and the incremental validity of the subject's model over the subject was -.44.

Three possible reasons for the fact that the subjects generally outperformed their models were discussed by Libby [1976a]: (1) The criterion, business failure, is well defined and reliably measured; (2) commercial bankers are experts at this prediction task; (3) the actual distributions of the ratios used are skewed. Libby concluded that the subjects employed valid nonlinear judgment strategies. Goldberg [1976], noting the extreme skewness in four of the five cues used by Libby, transformed these cues to make them more normally distributed and performed several analyses on both the dichotomous (failed/nonfailed) and continuous (i.e., combining the dichotomous scale with the confidence ratings) forms of the response scale. Using regression analysis, Goldberg concluded that 31 (instead of ten) of the subjects were outperformed by their models. Libby [1976b] rejoined that the use of correlational statistics and data transformations was not appropriate for this prediction task. For example, Libby maintained that the squared-error loss function in the correlational validity measure (r_a) is inappropriate because the crucial distinction in failure prediction is simply whether the judge is correct or incorrect — not how incorrect the judge is. Libby also noted that two subjects who had identical hit rates could produce different r_a values because of different relationships between accuracy and confidence. He further contended that Goldberg's transformations were nonlinear and argued that Goldberg had shown only that nonlinear models outperformed most subjects. The "man versus model" argument typically had been restricted to linear models, and Libby argued that his results were in conflict with all prior studies that had investigated this issue.[5]

Libby's study was replicated by Zimmer [1980, 1981]. Thirty Australian bank loan officers used five financial ratios to predict whether 42 firms (21 failed; 21 nonfailed) listed on the Sydney stock exchange had failed. The subjects were told

---

[5] Libby and Blashfield [1978] used Libby's data to study the incremental performance of a composite judge (relative to individual judges) as a function of the number of judges included in the composite. This study was discussed in Chapter 3.

that "approximately half" the firms had actually failed. A discriminant analysis established environmental predictability at 37 of the 42 firms. Consistent with Libby's results, 28 of 30 subjects achieved a nonchance level of accuracy (more than 27 correct predictions), with a range of accuracy of 19 to 39 and a mean of 32.4. The composite judge correctly predicted 36 firms and was at least as accurate as 28 of the 30 subjects. Virtually identical results were obtained in a replication with 30 students. A majority of Zimmer's subjects, unlike those of Libby's, were outperformed by their own models. On average, the subjects' models correctly predicted 33.7 of the 42 firms, compared to 32.4 for the subjects themselves.

Casey [1980b] reported a bankruptcy prediction study that produced some results inconsistent with both Libby and Zimmer (also see Casey [1980a]). Forty-six bank loan officers made predictions for 30 firms, half of which had actually failed. The subjects were *not* told the number of firms that had failed. Casey employed six ratios as cues, including the five used by Libby. On average, the subjects correctly predicted only 17 of the 30 firms (13 of the 15 nonfailed firms, and 4 of the 15 failed firms). The accuracy of the composite judge was almost identical to the mean accuracy of the individual subjects (14 of 15 for the nonfailed firms, and 4 of 15 for the failed firms). Seventeen subjects were at least as accurate as the composite for the nonfailed firms, and 28 were at least as accurate for the failed firms. Casey suggested that since the subjects were not told the proportion of failed firms in the sample, they might have used their own (low) subjective prior probabilities of failure in making their predictions. Indeed, almost 80 percent of all predictions were for nonfailure.

Abdel-khalik and El-Sheshai [1980] reported a similar study in which 28 commercial lending officers predicted loan default for 32 firms. These researchers, however, allowed the *subjects* to select the cues they wished to use from a list of 18 financial ratios and trends. The cues were "purchased" with hypothetical "points" with which the subjects had been endowed, and when a subject purchased a cue, he or she received its value for all 32 firms. This feature of the experimental design represented a substantial departure from the typical lens study, in which a small number of cues is established by the researcher. Half the sample firms had actually defaulted on loans, but the subjects were told only that "some" firms had defaulted and that the proportion of defaulted firms in the sample was not representative of the actual proportion of defaulted firms in the real world.

Predictive accuracy was computed for four combinations of cue selection and cue processing: (1) both selection and processing by the subject; (2) selection by the subject, but processing by the subject's paramorphic model; (3) selection by the subject, but processing by the optimal environmental model; (4) both selection and processing by the optimal environmental model. The environment and the subjects were modeled by discriminant analysis. The percentages of correct predictions achieved by the four combinations of cue selection and cue processing were: (1) 62.5 percent; (2) 62.5 percent; (3) 67.5 percent; (4) 90.6 percent. These results indicate that, on average, the subjects' models performed no better than the subjects themselves when both modes of processing were based on cues selected by the subjects; that the optimal environmental model slightly outperformed both the subjects and the subjects' models when cues had been selected by subjects; and that processing via the optimal environmental model substantially outperformed all other selection/processing combinations when the model-selected cues were employed. It appears, therefore, that the primary reason for the subjects' sub-optimal performance was related to cue selection instead of processing.

Abdel-khalik and El-Sheshai also reported the predictive ability of two common rule-of-thumb predictors — a current ratio of 2.0 or greater, and a total debt to equity ratio of 1.0 or greater. These rules of thumb correctly predicted 84 percent and 72 percent of the sample firms, respectively. These levels of predictive accuracy exceeded, on average, those of the subjects, the subjects' models, and the optimal environmental model based on the subjects' selected cues. Other "benchmark" models involving various cues also outperformed the subjects. A replication of part of the study, conducted between five and six months later with ten of the 28 subjects, involved disclosing to the subjects that half the sample firms had actually defaulted. Surprisingly, only four subjects improved their prediction accuracy in the replication, six made less accurate predictions, and the mean accuracy level of these ten subjects decreased from 61.3 percent to 59.0 percent of the firms.

Kida [1979] conducted a study similar to Libby's, using 27 audit partners as subjects. This study was motivated by Altman and McGough's [1974] finding that Altman's [1968] bankruptcy prediction model correctly predicted failure for 82 percent of a sample of problem firms, while going-concern problems were mentioned in the audit reports of only 44 percent of the firms one year prior to their entering bankruptcy proceedings. Kida argued that factors other than the perceived likelihood of going-concern problems, such as the perceived consequences to the auditing firm or the client of qualifying versus not qualifying the audit opinion, may be considered by auditors when choosing the type of opinion to issue. Therefore, Kida sought more direct evidence on the ability of auditors to predict bankruptcy.

The subjects predicted whether 40 firms (20 failed; 20 nonfailed) would experience going-concern problems within one year of a particular financial-statement date. The occurrence of any one of six events (e.g., entering receivership or liquidating assets) was specified as indicative of going-concern problems. The cues were five financial ratios that had been selected via factor analyses and stepwise discriminant analyses from a set of 20 ratios. The auditors were told that there was "not necessarily an equal number" (p. 511) of firms in the sample that had and had not experienced going-concern problems. The auditors' judgments were made on a six-point scale labeled "I believe this firm does/does not have going-concern problems."

The optimal discriminant model correctly predicted 36 of the 40 firms. The accuracy of the auditors' predictions ranged from 24 to 37 of 40, and averaged at 33.22. Only two of the 27 auditors failed to exceed chance accuracy (27 of 40). Discriminant models of the individual auditors correctly predicted their classifications, on average, for 36.3 of the firms, with a range of 25 to 40. When the auditors' models were used to predict going-concern problems, the models were found to be (nonsignificantly) more accurate than the auditors. The average accuracy of the auditors (33.22) and the auditors' models (33.66) was virtualy identical. Ten auditors outperformed their models, 11 auditors were outperformed by their models, and there were six ties. A transformation of Kendall's W to the Spearman r showed a relatively high level of consensus (.755) among the predictions of the 27 auditors.

These results suggest that Kida's subjects were capable of predicting going-concern problems quite accurately. Kida also asked these subjects to specify the type of audit opinion they would prefer to issue for each of the 40 firms. While the subjects predicted going-concern problems for 17.5 of the 40 firms (on average), they preferred to issue a qualified opinion or a disclaimer of opinion for only 13.2 firms. In other words, the subjects would issue an unqualified opinion in 24 percent of the cases for which they predicted going-concern problems. Further results reported by Kida linked the auditors' propensity to qualify or not qualify the opinion to several perceived consequences that might accrue to the auditor or the client, in addition to their predictions of going-concern problems.

Moriarity [1979] also reported a study concerning bankruptcy predictions. In the main experiment, he divided 227 undergraduate accounting majors into four groups and had them predict whether 22 discount department stores (7 failed; 15 nonfailed) had gone bankrupt. The actual number of bankrupt firms in the sample was not revealed to the subjects. All groups received information covering a six-year time period. Two groups received numerical information (either 13 financial ratios or the financial statement balances that could be used to compute these ratios). The other two groups received nonnumerical information in the form of Chernoff faces (see Chernoff and Rizvi [1975]). Certain features of the faces (e.g., nose width, ear diameter, pupil position) represented the financial ratios, and changes in facial features (e.g., bigger eyes that look increasingly to the left) represented trends in the ratios over the six-year time period. One group of subjects who received faces was told the ratio that each feature represented, and the other group was not.

Analysis of the number of correct predictions revealed that subjects who received Chernoff faces with the accompanying explanations outperformed all other groups. Those who received financial ratios were the poorest performers. In fact, even the subjects who received the faces with no explanations significantly ($\alpha < .05$) outperformed those receiving the ratios. The mean numbers of incorrect predictions were 7.1, 7.3, 7.5 and 8.6 for the faces/explanation, faces/no explanation, financial statement balances, and financial ratios groups, respectively.[6]

Sensitive to the fact that his subjects were unsophisticated in the use of financial ratios, Moriarity repeated part of the study with a group of 20 members of the Oklahoma City Chapter of the American Society of Women Accountants. Half these subjects received financial ratios, and the remainder received faces with explanations. On average, the ratios group made 6.5 incorrect predictions

[6] The results in favor of the faces were much more dramatic when the accuracy data were adjusted for the amount of time that the four groups used. The faces groups rendered their (more accurate) predictions faster than the financial-data groups rendered their (less accurate) predictions.

compared to 8.6 for the students. However, the faces group made an average of only 4.7 incorrect predictions compared to 7.1 for the students, suggesting that sophistication differences between these two groups did not impact the effectiveness of the ratios vis-à-vis the faces. Finally, all subject groups in these two experiments outperformed Altman's [1968] bankruptcy prediction model. The Altman model made either nine or 11 errors, depending on the cut-off criterion used. Moriarity posited several reasons for the poor showing of the Altman model, and he discussed several caveats that should be considered when interpreting the usefulness of the faces. He also suggested several possibilities for further research based on faces (e.g., their potential usefulness in analytic review in auditing — see also Moriarity and Roach [1977]).

7.5 STOCK RECOMMENDATIONS AND PRICE PREDICTIONS

Lens model methodology has been used in several studies concerning stock recommendations (McGhee, Shields, and Birnberg [1978], Savich [1977], Slovic [1969], Slovic, Fleissner, and Bauman [1972]) and the prediction of stock price changes [Wright, 1977a, 1977b, 1979a]. The earliest application of the lens paradigm in an accounting-related context, by a psychologist and published in the *Journal of Applied Psychology* [Slovic, 1969], involved two stockbrokers who rated the attractiveness of 128 hypothetical stocks on a scale from one ("strong recommendation not to buy") to nine ("strong recommendation to buy"), based on judgments of the likelihood that the prices of the stocks would increase substantially in the following six to twelve months. The 128 cases were chosen according to a 1/16 replication of the 2^{11} factorial design. The levels of the 11 cues were presented as up versus down, good versus poor, etc. Analysis-of-variance results showed that main effects accounted for 72 percent (80 percent), and interactions accounted for seven (five) percent, of the variance in the judgments of Broker 1 (Broker 2). Six (seven) main effects and six (five) two-cue or three-cue interactions were significant ($\alpha < .05$) for Broker 1 (Broker 2). The correlation between the two brokers' ratings of the 128 stocks was .32.

Slovic, Fleissner, and Bauman [1972] extended this study with a group of 13 stockbrokers and five MBA students. The brokers had between one-half year and 15 years of experience with a median (mean) of two (4.5) years. A ¼ replication of the 2^8 factorial design was used to generate 64 hypothetical stocks. The subjects rated the stocks on a scale from one (substantial expected decrease in value) to nine (substantial expected increase in value) for a six- to 18-month time horizon. On average, main effects explained 75 percent, while two-cue and three-cue interactions explained 4 percent, of judgment variance. While substantial individual differences were found, the cue "earnings yearly trend" (denoted as up or down) was most important for the majority of subjects. Inter-subject consensus was better among the students than among the brokers. The mean insight index was higher for the students (.79) than for the brokers (.34). Moreover, the Spearman r between insight and length of experience for the 13 brokers was -.43, indicating an inverse relationship between insight and experience.

Similar experiments were reported by Savich [1977] and McGhee, Shields, and Birnberg [1978]. Savich [1977] had 26 undergraduate accounting majors rate

64 hypothetical stocks on a scale from one (indicating a "sell attitude") to nine (indicating a "buy attitude"). The eight cues employed were taken from APB Opinion No. 28 [Accounting Principles Board, 1973]. A group-level step-wise regression suggested that five of the eight cues were approximately equally important, and that the other three were virtually unrelated to the ratings. The R_s^2 from the group regression was .44, while the median individual R_s^2 was .71 and the range was .37 to .87. Mean insight was .92. Individual differences in response consistency and cue weighting were substantial.

McGhee, Shields, and Birnberg [1978] employed the same cues used by Savich. A nine-point response scale was used again, but the end-points were labeled against (1) or for (9) further consideration of the stock for possible inclusion in an investment portfolio. The subjects were 24 MBA students. McGhee, Shields, and Birnberg found that the same five cues that were important in Savich's study were also important in their study. The R_s^2 values of the 24 individual judgment models ranged from .07 to .88, and the mean R_s^2 (of the 22 significant ones) was .79. When the models included the 28 two-cue interactions in addition to the eight cues, the mean R_s^2 (of the 23 significant ones) was .91. Again, large individual differences in cue weighting were reported.

While the four studies reviewed above focused on stock recommendations, Wright [1977a, 1977b, 1979a] had subjects estimate price changes for common stocks. Thus, Wright was able to assess judgment accuracy in addition to policy-capturing measures. Wright [1977a, 1977b] had 39 second-year MBA students estimate price changes for 60 common stocks for a one-year period, based on seven cues that involved both accounting and capital-market information. Certain cues were later combined such that only five independent variables were used in the data analysis. Cue values were taken from actual companies, reflecting the cue validities and intercorrelations that actually existed.

When price change was used as the dependent variable in a multiple regression analysis of each subject, environmental predictability (R_e) was .58 (R_e^2 =.34). The median accuracy level (r_a) was .16, and only 40 percent of the subjects achieved better than chance ($\alpha<.05$) accuracy. Few subjects had a significant nonlinear component (C) of accuracy. Judgment consistency (R_s^2) ranged from .13 to .79 with a median of .49. When *percentage* price change was the dependent variable, R_e was .49 (R_e^2 =.24), median r_a was .20, and median R_s^2 was .48. The ranges of r_a and R_s^2 were very near those found when price change was the dependent variable. The consensus of the subjects' percentage price change estimates was low: The median correlation between the predictions of all pairs of subjects was .27. Moreover, substantial disagreement among subjects was apparent in the estimated percentage price changes for the 60 stocks. The mean percentage ranged from -21 percent to +42 percent. A tendency to overestimate the percentage price changes for low-priced (less than median price) stocks was found. Finally, a cluster analysis based on the percentage price changes (using the JAN algorithm) resulted in four separate clusters, or "four basic types" [Wright, 1977a, p. 686], of judgment models, although Wright did not attempt to delineate the specific differences among these four types.

Wright [1977b] examined judgment insight in two ways.[7] First, he correlated each subject's objective cue-utilization coefficients (b_{si}) with his or her subjective weights (elicited by the 100-point allocation technique). The mean (median) Pearson correlation was .415 (.345). Second, Wright used the subjective weights of each subject in a linear model to predict the subject's actual judgments, and then correlated the predicted judgments with the actual judgments. The median squared correlation was .28. When equal (unit) weights were used instead of the weights supplied by the subjects, the median squared correlation with actual judgments was .15. Thus, subjective weights were more successful at reproducing judgments than were equal weights, but neither was as successful as the subject's multiple regression model (median $R_s^2 = .43$).

Wright [1979a] replicated this study with a group of first- and second-year MBA students, using 50 stocks and four cues, and modeling subjects' judgments in terms of percentage price changes. Task predictability (R_e) was .59, and the 35 first-year (12 second-year) subjects produced a median r_a of .20 (.31). Chance achievement ($\alpha < .05$) was .24. Only 37 percent of the first-year students had r_a values of at least .24, while 75 percent of the second-year students reached this level of accuracy. Application of the lens model equation showed that for the first-year (second-year) students the median matching (G) index was .48 (.46), median R_s was .53 (.62), and median non-linear cue utilization (C) was .03 (.20). Further, median consensus was .38 (.54), and median insight was .34 (.65), for the first-year (second-year) students. Generally, the performance of the first-year students was similar to that found in Wrights' first study, while the second-year students, who were more knowledgeable about contemporary stock market theory and accounting information, performed better. Finally, Wright constructed aggregate, or composite, judgment models for each subject group by using the group's mean judgment for each stock as the dependent variable. Aggregate performance substantially exceeded median individual performance.

7.6 FUNCTIONAL FIXATION

Four studies of functional fixation at the individual level have appeared [Abdel-khalik and Keller, 1979; Ashton, 1976a; Chang and Birnberg, 1977; Swieringa, Dyckman and Hoskin, 1979]. An individual who is fixated with respect to accounting numbers will be unable to change his or her utilizaion of those numbers when the underlying accounting methods that generate the numbers change. Ashton [1976a] tested the functional fixation hypothesis at the individual level in a task involving the establishment of selling prices for hypothetical products based on accounting and nonaccounting cues. Subjects were required to establish a selling price for each of 30 products, using three pieces of information, one of which was unit product cost. Some subjects received full cost data, while others received variable cost data. After the 30 selling prices had been set, subjects in four experimental groups were told that an accounting change had oc-

---

[7] For these analyses, Wright modeled the subjects' judgments using *either* price change *or* percentage price change as the dependent variable, depending on how the subjects described their models. Therefore, the median R_s^2 values reported in Wright [1977b] are somewhat different from those in Wright [1977a].

curred. Those who previously had received full (variable) cost data would now receive variable (full) cost data. Subjects in the full-to-variable (variable-to-full) condition were also told that the accounting change increased (decreased) the usefulness of unit product cost for establishing selling prices. In addition, the amount of information about the change that was provided to subjects differed. Some subjects within each cost condition were given more information about the change than were other subjects. Subjects then established selling prices for each of 30 additional products, using the new type of cost data. Two control groups made 60 pricing decisions based on the type of cost data they were given initially; in other words, an accounting change did not occur for the two control groups. The subjects were 106 MBA students.

Each subject's decision model was represented by a multiple regression equation based on the first 30 selling-price decisions. Then each subject's model was applied to the data for the second set of 30 decisions. The output of the model represented the 30 selling prices the subject would have established if he or she had been completely fixated, i.e., if the subject's "old" decision model had been used in the "new" situation in which the meaning of unit product cost had changed. The average absolute difference between the price set by the model and the price set by the subject on the 30 products in the second set was divided by the average selling price set by the model to obtain a "percentage average difference score" for each subject. Lower scores corresponded to greater fixation.

A group-level analysis indicated that subjects in the four experimental conditions (those informed of the change in accounting method) changed their decision models significantly more than did subjects in the two control groups (those for whom an accounting change did not occur). Analysis of the percentage average difference scores for individual subjects, however, showed that approximately half the experimental-group subjects changed their decision models no more than did control-group subjects. This result suggests that functional fixation occurred for a sizable proportion of the subjects. An analysis of variance of the experimental-group results suggested that subjects in the increase (full-to-variable) condition exhibited significantly less fixation than those in the decrease (variable-to-full) condition. However, this effect was caused largely by a few extreme percentage average difference scores in the increase condition. A nonparametric test found no difference between the medians of the percentage average difference scores for the increase and decrease groups. Both parametric and nonparametric analyses found that the amount of information about the accounting change provided to the subjects had no effect on fixation.

Swieringa, Dyckman, and Hoskin [1979] used Ashton's experimental task to assess the replicability of his results. This study was motivated, in part, by Libby's [1976d] observations about some potential weaknesses in Ashton's experimental design. Libby noted that Ashton's results could have been confounded because (1) the control groups received different cue values than the experimental groups, (2) the full-cost and variable-cost data sets differed, thus creating a possible sequence effect, and (3) the experimental groups were given a suggested weighting for unit product cost, making it possible that the effect of the accounting change was confounded with the effect of the suggested weighting. Six groups of subjects were used: variable-cost and full-cost control groups for whom no accounting change occurred; variable-to-full and full-to-variable experimental groups who were told only that a change had occurred; two variable-to-full experimental groups who were given different amounts of information about the accounting change and its effects. All subjects received the same set of observations on the three cues and made decisions in the same sequence. The observations were those used by Ashton [1976a] in his variable-to-full (decreasing importance) condition. The subjects were 201 students enrolled in an introductory accounting course.

Based on the percentage average difference score used by Ashton [1976a], Swieringa, Dyckman, and Hoskin [1979] found that the experimental groups altered their decision making more than the control groups, i.e., the accounting change had an effect. It was also found that the amount of information about the change that was communicated to subjects had no consistent effect on the percentage average difference scores. Both of these results agreed with Ashton's earlier findings. On average, however, the amount of information and the extent of cognitive change were *inversely* related.

Libby [1976d] had also suggested that Chow [1960] tests should have been applied to the Ashton data. Roughly, the Chow test would compare the residuals from a multiple regression equation based on all 60 products with the residuals of two other multiple regression equations based on products 1-30 and 31-60, to determine if a change in information processing occurred. Swieringa, Dyckman, and Hoskin tabulated the proportion of subjects whose models changed according to this test. The results were consistent with those based on average difference scores in that a larger proportion of experimental-group subjects changed their models vis-à-vis control-group subjects. Moreover, the proportion was larger for groups receiving more information about the change. However, the proportions were not significantly different across groups. Further analysis of the F-ratios used in the Chow test revealed higher mean and median F's for the experimental groups than the control groups, but not for subjects receiving more information about the change versus those receiving less. Thus, the various analyses yielded similar results, and these results were consistent with those of Ashton [1976a].

Swieringa, Dyckman, and Hoskin speculated about the unexpected results with respect to the amount of information. They suggested that the fact that the cost figures were higher for products 31-60 than for products 1-30 could have increased the perceived importance of unit cost for products 31-60. Yet the subjects who received additional information were told that unit cost was less useful for products 31-60 than it had been before the change occurred, possibly causing the subjects to de-emphasize unit cost. The authors suggested that the effects of the additional information may have resulted from a complex interaction among the higher unit cost numbers, the accounting change and the additional information. They suggested that the accounting numbers reported after the change may have been important — as well as information about the change itself.

In another study of functional fixation, Abdel-khalik and Keller [1979] had 61 bank investment officers and security analysts evaluate the attractiveness of six real (disguished) firms as investment opportunities. Given the objective of maximizing investment return over a specified holding period, the subjects predicted three levels (optimistic, most likely, pessimistic) of the expected price of each stock at the end of the holding period. The researchers used these predictions to compute each subject's expected return for each stock. The subjects also ranked the stocks in terms of their expected ability to meet the investment objective.

Each subject made price predictions and ranked the six stocks three times. For the first set of evaluations, all firms were using the FIFO method of inventory valuation. For the second set, Firm E had changed to LIFO, and this fact was clearly communicated to the subjects. The subjects did not know, however, that Firm E had been created by the researchers as a "twin" of Firm A by multiplying all the numbers on A's financial statements by 1.02. For the third set of evaluations, Firms A, B, and C had also changed to LIFO, leaving only Firms D and F on FIFO.

Since an inflationary period was assumed, a change from FIFO to LIFO would result in lower earnings but greater net cash inflow than would have been the case without the change. Therefore, given a firm valuation model based on net cash inflow and dividend-paying ability, Firm E should be valued higher than Firm A in the second set of evaluations. If the decision maker were fixated on earnings, however, Firm E would be valued lower than Firm A.

Several statistical tests on the within-subject differences in the expected returns of Firms A and E showed no significant differences when both firms were on FIFO or when both were on LIFO. When Firm A was on FIFO and Firm E on LIFO, however, the expected return on E was lower than that on A. This result, which was corroborated by an analysis of the rankings of Firms A and E before and after Firm E changed to LIFO, supports the functional fixation hypothesis. When expected returns were reassessed for Firms A, B, and C after these firms had changed to LIFO, the results largely supported the fixation hypothesis for A and B, but not for C.[8]

Chang and Birnberg [1977] distinguished between two types of fixation. One refers to the inability to adjust to changes in the methods used to compute data inputs. "The other is when the same method is used to calculate a data input, but new numbers are produced" (p. 302). Ashton [1976a], Swieringa, Dyckman, and Hoskin [1979], and Abdel-khalik and Keller [1979] studied the former type of fixation. Chang and Birnberg [1977] studied the latter.

Chang and Birnberg had 44 MBA students make decisions with respect to a manufacturing process that could be either "under control" or "out of control." The subjects were given base rates for these two states based on a sample of observations from prior periods. The subjects were required to examine, sequentially, 25 cost variance reports and to state for each (1) whether they would investigate the process and (2) how large a variance would have to be to justify an investigation (called the subject's "decision criterion"). Half the subjects were told that the standard cost against which the actual costs should be evaluated was $6000; the other half were told that the standard was $5000. The true state of the process was disclosed to subjects on every fifth trial. After the 25 decisions had been made, the subjects were told that $6000 was the accurate standard. This rep-

---

[8] Additional observations on this study are provided in R. Ashton [1980a].

resented a change for the group that previously had been told the standard was $5000, but did not represent a change for the other group. All subjects made 25 more decisions after receiving this information.

The experimental ($5000-to-$6000) group had significantly lower average decision criteria for the second set of decisions than for the first set. They responded to the information by altering their decision making. However, a comparison of the experimental and control ($6000-to-$6000) groups on the second set of decisions showed that the control group had significantly lower average decision criteria. Since both groups were given the same standard for the second set of decisions, Chang and Birnberg argued, their average decision criteria should have been equal. The authors suggested that some type of "inhibiting behavior" occurred for the experimental group, although it was more complex than that typically implied by the fixation hypothesis.[9]

7.7 MANAGERIAL ACCOUNTING

Only two lens studies have directly addressed managerial accounting issues. Harrell [1977] investigated two assumptions of Anthony's [1965] framework for management planning and control: " . . . (1) that middle-level managers' management control decisions are influenced strongly by the organizational goals emphasized by their senior managers and (2) that middle-level managers accurately can incorporate a specified importance of organizational goals into their management control decisions . . . ." [Harrell, 1977, p. 833]. To test these assumptions, Harrell had 75 Air Force officers, ranging in rank from first lieutenant to lieutenant colonel, rate the overall performance of 32 hypothetical pilot training wings on a scale from one (highly unsatisfactory) to eight (highly satisfactory), based on five cues that were denoted either as satisfactory or unsatisfactory. The cues were goals that the pilot training wing wished to achieve.

A pretest/post-test design was used [Campbell and Stanley, 1963], and all subjects, divided into five groups of 15 each, evaluated the same cases for both the pretest and the post-test. Before administering the post-test, groups 2, 3, 4 and 5 were given a "policy statement" indicating the relative importance (weights) that they should attach to each of the five cues. In addition, groups 3, 4 and 5 received feedback after each of the 32 cases. This feedback indicated the rating their immediate superior had given to each hypothetical wing. For group 3 (4) the feedback suggested that their superior had made decisions that agreed (disagreed) with the relative weighting specified in the policy statement. (The subjects had to infer their superior's weighting scheme from the feedback information.) Group 5 received feedback generated by the use of a random number table; it was unrelated to the policy statement. Harrell used Hoffman's [1960] relative weight measure to infer each subject's cue weights, and he compared the subjects' overall ratings to those made by a linear scoring model that incorporated the weights specified in the policy statement.

---

[9] This study used two different payoff (cost) tables for the variance investigation decision. Although no hypotheses were offered about their expected effects, they did result in significantly different average decision criteria.

A group-level analysis of the pretest decisions found no significant differences among the five groups, indicating that the random assignment to groups was successful. Analysis of the post-test data showed that group 2 made significantly different decisions than group 1, suggesting that the policy statement had some effect. For 21 of the 32 cases, on average, the subjects in group 2 made the same decisions as the "optimal" scoring model that incorporated the specified weights. However, these subjects had significantly different cue weights vis-a-vis the policy statement for three of the five cues. On average, the cue weights of group 3, who received "consonant" feedback, were nearer the policy weights than were those of group 2. The decisions of group 3 agreed with those of the scoring model for 29 of the 32 cases. However, these subjects also had significantly different cue weights vis-à-vis the policy statement for three of the five cues. Group 4, who received the same policy statement but "dissonant" feedback, made different decisions than the subjects in groups 2 and 3. The group 4 subjects made the same decisions as the scoring model for only ten of the 32 cases. Their cue weights were heavily influenced by the feedback information which suggested that their superiors had used a different weighting scheme than that contained in the policy statement. Finally, subjects who received random feedback (group 5) did not make different decisions than subjects who received no feedback (group 2).

Harrell concluded that his results support Anthony's first assumption but not the second. That is, decisions are influenced by the goals emphasized by superiors, but decision makers are not able to incorporate accurately into their decision making a specified level of importance of organizational goals. Harrell suggested that the problem is primarily cognitive, not motivational.

A. Ashton [1980a] evaluated the accuracy of individual decision makers, models of the individuals, and composite predictions in a budgeting task. Thirteen executives made 42 predictions of the annual number of advertising pages appearing in *Time* magazine over a 14-year period. The executives worked for Time, Inc. magazines other than *Time*. They were experienced in making this type of prediction, which is an important initial step in the budgeting process for a magazine, as part of their normal job responsibilities. The predictions were based on five cues.

Environmental predictability was .944 for this task. The accuracy of the subjects ranged from .61 to .92, with a median of .69. Unlike most lens studies, median consistency (.96) was greater than median matching (.89), suggesting that subjects were less able to acquire appropriate task knowledge than to apply task knowledge consistently. No subject outperformed his or her paramorphic model, but there were three ties when the achievement indexes were rounded to two decimal places. The median difference between the accuracy of the models and that of the corresponding individuals was .044, in favor of the models. The accuracy of the composite predictions, based on equal weighting of the 13 individuals' predictions for each of the 42 cases, was .936, which was greater than that of every individual and very near environmental predictability. Accuracy was not improved by modeling the composite. These results were used as a basis for discussing the costs and benefits of several decision-improvement options associated with the lens paradigm.

7.8 OTHER STUDIES

Five additional lens studies have been reported. Kessler and Ashton [1980] reported a study of the effects of feedback on prediction achievement in a bond-rating task. Barefield [1972] studied the effects of data aggregation and redundancy on decision making. Danos and Imhoff [1980] reported a study of auditors' judgments of the reasonableness of financial forecasts. Schultz and Gustavson [1978] studied factors that affect actuaries' perceptions of public accounting firms as professional liability insurance risks. Eggleton [1976] studied intuitive predictions based on sequences of numbers.

Kessler and Ashton [1980] had 69 MBA students predict the bond ratings assigned by Moody's to a sample of 34 industrial bond issues based on the values of three financial ratios for each firm. Four types of feedback were employed, and improvement in prediction achievement over a series of four trials was assessed. The feedback, presented at the beginning of each of the last three trials, involved (1) the number and percentage of predictions that were correct and the number and percentage that were off by one rating category (Type A), (2) Type A feedback plus cue utilization (r_{si}) coefficients (Type B), (3) Type A feedback plus cue validity (r_{ei}) coefficients (Type C), and (4) Types A, B and C combined (Type D). Note that Types A and B involve only information about the subject's performance (cognitive feedback) while Type C relates to properties of the task and Type D (called "lens model" feedback) combines cognitive feedback and task feedback.

The environmental predictability (R_e) of the data set used by Kessler and Ashton was .74. Prediction achievement (r_a) for the individual subjects typically was between .55 and .65. A group-level analysis showed that subjects receiving Feedback Types C and D improved their mean r_a in Session 2 and maintained that level of performance, without further improvement, for the following two sessions. The finding that these two groups improved their r_a over sessions, while subjects receiving Feedback Types A and B did not improve, is consistent with several prior studies conducted with abstract tasks. Further analysis based on the lens model equation showed that the improvement in achievement was influenced by improvements in both matching (G) and consistency (R_s), but that matching was slightly more important. The subjects were slightly better at acquiring knowledge of optimal cue weighting than at applying that knowledge consistently. The authors concluded that task properties and lens model feedback were the most effective types, although neither resulted in significantly higher r_a values than Feedback Type A during the terminal session. Furthermore, neither type enabled the subjects to perform as well as a multiple regression model of the cue-criterion relationships.

Using statistical decision theory to develop an optimal "environmental" model and discriminant analysis to model the decision maker, Barefield [1972] examined both acquisition of knowledge and consistent application of knowledge as determinants of performance in a process control setting. Barefield had 28 graduate students judge whether or not labor had been used efficiently in each of 40 simulated periods. The subjects' priors on efficient/inefficient labor usage were set at .50. Two independent variables were manipulated across two levels —

the extent to which labor and materials variances were aggregated, and the degree of redundancy (correlation) between labor and materials variances. When the difference between the optimal number of correct decisions (based on the theoretically optimum decision rule) and the actual number of correct decisions was used as the performance measure, neither independent variable reached statistical significance; that is, neither the level of aggregation nor the level of redundancy was related to performance.

Barefield also separated performance into two components by modeling, via discriminant analysis, the judgments of each subject. The difference between the optimal number of correct decisions and the number of correct decisions the subject would have made had his or her own decision rule (as represented by discriminant analysis) been applied consistently reflects the performance decrement that resulted from the subject's use of a nonoptimal model. This measure captures roughly the same aspect of performance as does the matching coefficient (G) in traditional lens model analyses. Subjects receiving aggregated data performed better ($\alpha = .12$) on this criterion than did those receiving disaggregated data. The difference between the number of correct decisions that would have resulted from consistent use of the subject's decision rule and the actual number of correct decisions made by the subject reflects the decrement in performance due to inconsistency, and is analogous to the consistency measure (R_s) in multiple regression modeling. Subjects receiving disaggregated data performed significantly better ($\alpha < .05$) on this criterion. Data redundancy had no effect on either criterion.

Auditors' judgments of the reasonableness of financial forecasts were studied by Danos and Imhoff [1980]. These authors selected five cues based on interviews with 42 auditors from nine firms, and they constructed 16 cases based on these cues for each of two sets of background data. The background data pertained to corporate firms from different industries and varied along several dimensions. Forty of the 42 auditors who participated in the cue-selection process responded to the experiment.

The five cues involved the accuracy of past forecasts of both sales and net income, management's tendency toward over- or under-prediction, the sensitivity of forecasted sales to changes in industry sales and market share, and the forecasted increase in net income over the previous year's actual net income. The subjects evaluated the reasonableness of the forecasts on a ten-point scale. Analysis of variance revealed that the two cues related to past forecast accuracy typically were the most significant cues in the 80 individual judgment models (40 subjects × 2 sets of background data). On average, about 80 percent of judgment variance was explained by the five cues. Limited analyses of judgment consensus and insight suggested that both were reasonably high. The relative importance of the five cues differed slightly between the two sets of background data, but the design of the study did not allow the authors to determine the specific background items that were related to this difference.

Schultz and Gustavson [1978] studied five actuaries — one from each of five insurers in the United States that establish premiums for accountants' professional liability insurance. Each subject evaluated 32 hypothetical public accounting firms based on five cues. The evaluations were recorded on a nine-point verbally-anchored scale that represented their judgments of the probability that each firm "will incur a valid and substantial malpractice claim within the coming year" (p. 630). A valid and substantial claim was defined as "one for which you feel the expected value of the payment would exceed the deductible, were the case to go to court" (p. 634). This response scale was considered a surrogate for the premium that the insurer would set. The subjects also allocated 100 points to the five cues to reflect their relative subjective importance, and they stated, before evaluating the cases, which level of each cue (e.g., "little" versus "considerable" write-up work) they felt was more risky.

An analysis of variance applied to the responses of each actuary found that the percentage of judgment variance explained by main effects and two-cue and three-cue interactions ranged from 86.8 percent to 100 percent for the five subjects, with a median of 94.3 percent. Large individual differences existed across subjects in the relative importance of each cue. Intra-subject judgment stability based on four repeat cases was perfect, i.e., 1.00, for all subjects, but the authors suggested (p. 637) that the subjects may have compared their ratings on the two sets of cases — since they were told that repeat cases were included. Judgment insight ranged from .44 to 1.00, with a median of .92. Moreover, an analysis of cell means for main effects showed that all subjects used all cues in a manner (direction) consistent with their evaluations of the riskier level of each cue.

Consensus across actuaries was very low. Correlations between the 32 responses of all pairs of subjects ranged from -.23 to .52, with a mean of .12. The subjects' statements of the riskier level of each cue also showed considerable disagreement. To the extent that the response scale used in this study is an adequate surrogate for the liability insurance premium, these results imply that the premiums charged are sensitive to the actuary who makes the evaluation.

Eggleton [1976] had 20 student and nonstudent subjects predict the next observation in a sequence, based on a series of 12 observations that were described as monthly production cost figures. Subjects also established three credible intervals (50 percent, 75 percent, 95 percent) around their predictions, and they estimated the mean of the series. Six independent variables were manipulated: (1) sequence mean (high, low); (2) sequence variance (high, low); (3) sequence type (trend, random, alternating); (4) information reliability (high, low); (5) time (first and second viewing of the sequence); (6) scores on Pettigrew's [1958] category width test — a measure of cognitive styles (high, low).

A six-way repeated-measures analysis of variance on the predicted next observations (and a separate one on the estimated means) found highly significant effects due to the mean, variance and sequence variables. Higher means and higher variances resulted in significantly higher predictions and estimated means. Subjects seemed to differentiate the trend sequence from the random and alternating sequences, but did not differentiate the latter two sequence types from each other. An analysis of variance on the credible interval estimates found that only the variance manipulation was significant. Eggleton concluded that the results supported his expectation that subjects would abstract from the sequences a prototype consisting of mean and variance, and would pay attention to the sequence of observations.

7.9 SUMMARY COMMENTS

Irrespective of the substantive decision area, all lens studies in accounting have addressed some subset of the following topics: (1) the ability of mathematical models to represent human decision making; (2) the weighting of informational cues by individuals, and differences in cue weighting across individuals; (3) the accuracy of human predictions and the components of prediction accuracy; (4) the relative accuracy of predictions made by individuals, composites of individuals, mathematical models of individuals, and mathematical models of environmental data relationships; (5) the learning of environmental data relationships; (6) the consistency of predictions and judgments over time and across individuals; (7) the insight that an individual possesses into his or her own judgment process. In addition to these seven principal topics, some attention has been devoted to the impact on judgments of various subject and task differences.

Lens studies have demonstrated repeatedly that linear models based on a small number of cues are capable of explaining a large proportion of judgment variance, regardless of the accounting or auditing context or the type of decision maker that is studied. Policy-capturing studies have been consistent in their finding of large individual differences in cue weighting across decision makers in the same decision context. The few studies examining the stability of an individual's judgments over time generally have found stability to be high. The picture that emerges from this research is one of stable decision strategies, specific to particular individuals, that can be "captured" well by mathematical models.

The performance of individual decision makers on the other dimensions addressed in lens studies seems to differ as a function of decision context. Some of the decision contexts discussed in the chapter have generated enough studies to permit some generalizations.

In the area of internal control evaluation, the insight that individuals possess into their own idiosyncratic judgment processes typically is very high. In addition, the extent of agreement across individuals in their evaluations of internal control is also high. However, this level of consensus does not appear to extend to decisions such as allocation of audit effort and selection of sample sizes, for which internal control evaluations serve as input. Internal control studies have consistently confirmed the conventional wisdom that separation of duties is an important aspect of control. However, another type of conventional wisdom — that auditing experience is a crucial factor affecting audit judgments — has not been convincingly demonstrated in these studies. Experience is related to several dimensions of audit judgment, but the magnitude of its effect has been relatively small.

Studies of materiality judgments and related disclosure recommendations have also supported the conventional wisdom in accounting: All such studies have found that net income typically is the principal basis for making judgments of materiality. Despite this, however, the research has found sizable differences across subjects in the disclosure or other decisions that are based on materiality judgments.

Consensus among decision makers has been higher in the case of bankruptcy predictions by bank loan officers. The accuracy of bankruptcy predictions by individuals has also been relatively high. While a very large percentage of loan-officer subjects are outperformed by composite predictions, their own prediction accuracy often is virtually indistinguishable from that of their individual paramorphic models. However, recent evidence suggests that they perform much more poorly when not informed of the base rate of failure in the sample of firms being evaluated. Other recent evidence suggests that non-optimal cue selection, not processing, is the major obstacle to high predictive accuracy in this area.

While most studies of bankruptcy prediction point to high consensus and accuracy, studies of stock recommendations and price predictions point in the opposite direction. The studies reviewed in this chapter show much disagreement among subjects on cue weighting, purchase recommendations, and price predictions. The accuracy of stock price predictions was also found to be low. (This was caused, in part, by the somewhat lower environmental predictability in this area.) Composite predictions of stock prices were found to be much more accurate than the predictions of individual subjects.

A sufficient number of studies has not been conducted in other substantive decision areas to permit meaningful generalizations. However, a few studies in different areas have investigated some aspect of learning in probabilistic environments. Results have been mixed. On the one hand, studies that have supplied subjects with some form of feedback and have made clear to subjects that this feedback should be incorporated in subsequent decisions (e.g., Harrell [1977], Kessler and Ashton [1980]) have found some evidence of learning. On the other hand, studies of functional fixation have found learning to be impeded by subjects' prior experiences with the data relationships in the task. Generally, the results with respect to learning parallel those with respect to real-world experience in the decision area represented by the experimental task: Both real-world experience and experimental attempts to promote learning have produced only small effects on several measures of judgment performance.

CHAPTER EIGHT

SEU Studies in Accounting

Accounting and auditing studies related to the SEU paradigm are reviewed in this chapter. Some of these studies were conducted explicitly within the SEU framework, and the others can be interpreted within that framework. The scope and limitations of this review are the same as those mentioned in the introduction to Chapter 7. However, the organization of the SEU studies is somewhat different than that used for the lens studies. For the most part, the SEU studies are organized in terms of generic human information processing issues (e.g., global SEU maximization and probability revision) whereas the lens studies were organized via areas of application (e.g., internal control evaluation and bankruptcy prediction). While some SEU studies have addressed traditional areas of application, most have focused on very basic, sometimes abstract, judgment tasks.

The studies are organized in six categories — global SEU (or EV) maximization, conformity with axioms, subjective probability assessment, probability revision, heuristics and biases, and information evaluation. Some summary comments on SEU studies in accounting are provided in the final section of the chapter.

8.1 GLOBAL SEU (OR EV) MAXIMIZATION

The studies reviewed in this section are loosely related in that each deals with some aspect of SEU (or EV) maximization at the global level. Ronen [1971], Hirsch [1978], and Snowball and Brown [1979] examined the maximization of joint probabilities in two-stage decision processes. Schultz and Reckers [1979] and Barrett and O'Malley [1974] reported data that suggest a type of expected-value reasoning by auditors. Newton's [1977] study focused on auditors' risk attitudes and their relationship to materiality judgments. Greer [1974] attempted to determine whether certain decisions made by business executives are consistent with those prescribed by utility theory. Ward [1974, 1976] elicited auditors' loss functions for a type of income-overstatement error, and Lewis [1980] examined auditors' utilities for the outcomes that could result from a certain type of decision.

Ronen [1971], Hirsch [1978], and Snowball and Brown [1979] investigated whether subjects maximize expected values in choices involving two-stage decision processes. Expected value could be maximized in these studies by maximizing the joint probability of the occurrence of two sequential events. Ronen's study was cast in an abstract setting, but Ronen discussed several types of decisions that are structurally similar to this setting. The latter two studies involved managerial decision contexts.

Ronen [1971] presented 22 graduate business school students with two sets of two bags, each bag containing specified proportions of marbles of different colors. The objective was to choose between the two sets of bags such that a blue marble could be drawn from the first bag followed by a red marble from the second bag. The joint probability (expected value) of drawing a blue marble from Bag 1 and a red marble from Bag 2 was identical for the two sets of bags (for 16 of 20 trials), but the first-stage probabilities of drawing a blue marble from Bag 1 differed between the two sets. Therefore, subjects who follow an expected-value decision rule should be indifferent between the two sets, but subjects who employ a "discounting" strategy for second-stage probabilities should systematically prefer the set in which the first-stage probability of drawing a blue marble from Bag 1 is higher.

Seventeen of the 22 subjects chose the set in which the first-stage probability of success was higher, despite the equivalence of expected values between the two sets. Moreover, a limited amount of additional evidence suggested that subjects often preferred a set in which expected value was smaller, as long as the first-stage probability of success was greater. The results were replicated in a second experiment involving a group of 96 management-program participants. The results were not moderated by using different magnitudes of joint probabilities, but the sizes of differences between first-stage probabilities did affect choices: The sequence preference did not hold for very small differences.

Hirsch [1978] extended Ronen's study by using a manufacturing task, in addition to a "marbles" task similar to that used by Ronen, and by manipulating three independent variables: (1) the difference between the joint probabilities of the alternative choices (four levels); (2) the magnitudes of the joint probabilities (two levels); (3) the difference between the initial probabilities of the alternative choices (three levels). The subjects, 48 managers working in seven manufacturing firms, were assigned randomly to the abstract task and the manufacturing task. Each subject made 120 choices.

For the abstract task, the sequence effect (a preference for higher initial probabilities) was demonstrated, and all three independent variables were highly significant. The sequence effect was stronger at lower levels of joint-probability differences, at higher levels of joint-probability magnitudes, and at higher levels of initial-probability differences. The sequence effect was also demonstrated in the manufacturing task: All three variables again had significant effects, but the effects were weaker than in the abstract task.

Snowball and Brown [1979] devised 12 pairs of choice alternatives in which joint probabilities differed between the alternatives. Three levels of joint probability differences, and four levels of both first-stage and second-stage probability differences, were employed. The 12 pairs of choice alternatives were structured such that the researchers could determine the subjects' preference strength for four types of choice models. These models involved maximization of (1) joint probability (expected value), (2) first-stage probability, (3) second-stage probability, and (4) minimization of joint probability. The experiment was cast in an estate trust investment context, and the subjects were 37 people employed in trust banking.

Almost two-thirds of all choices displayed stronger preference for the expected value response type than for any other type. However, 18.5 percent of the choices were more consistent with maximization of the first-stage probability, and 11 percent were more consistent with maximization of the second-stage probability. Larger joint-probability differences were associated with greater preferences for the expected value response type, while larger first- or second-stage-probability differences were associated with greater preference for the sub-optimal response types.

The results of Schultz and Reckers [1979] and Barrett and O'Malley [1974] suggest the use of expected-value reasoning. Schultz and Reckers had 64 audit partners study two hypothetical cases related to loss contingencies. The auditors were required to state the minimum probability of the occurrence of loss from a contingency at which they would require footnote disclosure in the financial statements, i.e., the "remote" versus "reasonably possible" distinction required by FASB Statement No. 5 [FASB, 1975]. The materiality of the contingency was manipulated as either six percent or 14 percent of operating income. The mean probability at which subjects in the low materiality condition would require disclosure was .449, while the corresponding number for the high materiality condition was .395. The authors concluded that the auditors seemed to employ some type of expected-value reasoning — in contradiction to the (perhaps implicit) "sequential" decision model of FASB Statement No. 5. The statement appears to require an initial judgment of materiality, followed by a probability judgment for all contingencies deemed material. It does not suggest that the critical probability level be adjusted based on the degree of materiality. Note also that the subjects in this study, on average, considered probabilities less than .42 to be "remote."

Earlier, Barrett and O'Malley [1974] had produced results generally consistent with those of Schultz and Reckers. In a study conducted before FASB Statement No. 5 was issued, Barrett and O'Malley had 45 graduate and undergraduate auditing students state the minimum probability of losing a lawsuit that would be necessary to issue a qualified opinion instead of an unqualified opinion. The subjects also stated the minimum probability needed to require a disclaimer of opinion instead of a qualified opinion. Nine amounts for the lawsuit, ranging from less than one percent of total assets to more than 800 percent of total assets, were employed. Higher probabilities were required for smaller amounts, and lower probabilities for larger amounts, again implying some type of expected-value reasoning.

Newton [1977] hypothesized that materiality judgments would be influenced by the degree of uncertainty associated with the item in question, and she reported an experiment designed to assess auditors' attitudes toward risk. The subjects were 19 audit partners. Three decision cases were used, each involving three different amounts, and all subjects responded to all three cases. Case 1 was a standard gamble situation in which subjects stated the probability of winning a gamble that would make them indifferent between playing the gamble and receiving a stated amount with certainty. Case 2 involved marketable securities whose value was initially thought to have declined permanently. After the subjects specified a materiality amount, they were told that the permanence of the decline was probabilistic, and that the current value of the securities could be one of three amounts. Subjects then stated, for each of the three amounts, the minimum probability of permanent decline that would be necessary for them to qualify the audit opinion. Case 3 involved a contingent liability, of a specified maximum amount, resulting from a lawsuit that the client "fully expected to lose." After specifying a materiality amount, the subjects were told that the amount of the loss would be one of three smaller amounts. The subjects then stated the minimum probability that the loss would be reduced to each amount that would be necessary in order to issue an unqualified opinion.

Almost all the auditors were classified as risk-averse in Case 1, but the results were much more varied for the two audit-related cases. Some subjects stated that they would qualify the opinion for all amounts regardless of the probabilities involved. Others said they would issue an unqualified opinion for all amounts regardless of the probabilities. Some auditors were classified as risk-averse, and others as risk-seeking, for one or both of these cases. Ten (seven) auditors in Case 2 (Case 3) specified the same probabilities for two (or all three) of the amounts, suggesting that they did not employ expected-value reasoning for the range of amounts involved. Overall, 55 percent (34 percent) of the auditors were classified as risk-averse (risk-seeking). Newton concluded that probability seemed to be a factor that influences their materiality judgments.

Greer [1974] attempted to study the extent to which intuitive decisions made by business executives are consistent with the decisions prescribed by expected-utility models derived, in part, from estimates supplied by those same executives. Greer had "corporate decision makers" in 27 Fortune 500 firms choose between each of 20 pairs of hypothetical capital investments that were couched in a standard-gamble format. He also constructed expected-utility models based on certain data from each firm's financial statements and on the subjects' estimates of the maximum probability of total net cash flows from operations going below some minimum level that the firm is willing to accept. Typically, the expected-utility model chose the riskier of the two investments in each pair, while subjects chose the other member of the pair. In some cases, however, the opposite pattern of choices emerged, leading Greer to conclude that intuitive decisions are largely inconsistent with those prescribed by expected-utility models. Greer further suggested that the minimum possible outcome was an important factor in the subjects' decisions (cf. Libby and Fishburn [1977]).[1]

Ward [1974, 1976] reported some results that pertain to the specification of auditors' loss functions. A knowledge of loss functions is needed for the implementation of a decision-theoretic approach to auditing (e.g., Kinney [1975a, 1975b]). Ward asked eight partners and 16 managers in public accounting firms to choose one of six functional forms (e.g., linear, step, exponential) that best

---

[1] Hoskins [1975] showed that a utility function that involved defining risk as the semi-variance of outcomes (instead of the standard deviation as Greer had done) produced choices that were much more consistent with the subjects' actual choices. Greer and Skekel [1975] retorted that "after considerable trial-and-error-type conjecture" (p. 842), they had found a curvilinear utility function that was superior to Hoskins' utility function. Fishburn [1976], arguing that Greer [1974] did not test what he claimed to test, showed that the mean-standard deviation trade-off function developed by Greer was incompatible with the expected-utility model of von Neumann and Morgenstern [1947], except when the firm's utility function is linear in returns. Fishburn tried four additional utility models and found that one was superior to both Hoskins' and Greer and Skekel's models. Fishburn concluded that Greer's data provide strong support for the correspondence between intuitive decisions and those prescribed by utility models. Greer [1976] remained unconvinced.

represented the relationship between the potential negative economic consequences to the auditor from failing to detect a certain error in receivables and the percentage magnitude of income overstatement that would result. Six auditors felt that an exponential relationship was most descriptive, and more than 60 percent of the auditors thought that the potential expected loss would "level off" at some point. Six auditors thought the loss functions for income-overstatement effects and income-understatement effects were symmetrical, and these six, plus an additional six, thought the threshold amounts for the expected loss were equal for over- and understatements. However, the mean understatement threshold was about 70 percent greater than the mean overstatement threshold. Finally, 17 auditors placed dollar values on the amounts of the expected loss, while the other seven declined to do so.[2]

Lewis [1980] analyzed audit decisions within an expected utility framework. He argued that there are two sufficiency conditions for consensus among the decisions of different auditors — homogeneous probability distributions over states of nature, and homogeneous utilities for the outcomes or consequences of decisions. Lewis tested the latter condition in the context of a product liability lawsuit against a client by having subjects rate the desirability of six sets of consequences that could result from certain state/action combinations. The six combinations were formed by combining the three action choices with respect to loss contingencies allowed by FASB Statement No. 5 (require accrual; require footnote disclosure; require no disclosure) with two possible states of nature (client is held liable; client is not held liable). The subjects were 70 auditors with at least five years of experience from four Big Eight audit firms.

The materiality of the contingent loss from the lawsuit was varied, and half the subjects were assigned to low and high materiality conditions. Dependent variables were the pairwise correlations between auditors over the desirability ratings of the six sets of consequences. Lewis posited several reasons for expecting the homogeneity of utilities to differ across audit firms, and for expecting greater homogeneity within firms than between firms. The results supported both of these expectations. In addition, utilities were more homogeneous in the high materiality condition than in the low materiality condition.

8.2 CONFORMITY WITH AXIOMS

Three papers have reported studies of the SEU model conducted at the axiom level. All three focused on the irrelevance axiom. R. Ashton [1979b] investigated the extent to which choices made by 83 MBA students conformed to those required by the axiom. The classic Allais problem was couched in a hypothetical capital investment decision context, and three independent variables were manipulated: (1) the probability distribution over the potential payoffs; (2) the

---

[2] Ward [1976] also had the auditors rank 20 items, via the Q-Sort technique, in terms of their importance to the determination of materiality. The 20 items included such things as the income effect of an error, unfavorable publicity about the firm, and loss of future engagements. The auditors' rankings showed little consensus, as reflected in a Kendall W of .386. Pairwise correlations between the auditors' rankings were also computed and 91 percent of them were below .50 with 14 percent being negative.

amount of the desirable payoff; (3) the amount of the undesirable payoff, or loss. After making their initial choices, the subjects were presented with two written arguments — one consistent with the axiom, the other inconsistent with it — and were allowed to change their initial choices. The subjects also rated the two arguments on a scale from one (not compelling at all) to 11 (very compelling) and wrote a description of how they arrived at their choices.

The subjects' initial choices largely conformed to those required by the axiom, contrary to the results of prior studies. On average, only 14 percent of the subjects made choices that violated the axiom, and this number differed very little as a function of the three independent variables. Few subjects changed their initial choices after reading the two prepared arguments, although the violating argument was rated, on average, as more compelling than the conforming argument. Only 20 percent of the subjects who initially made conforming choices rated the conforming argument higher than the violating argument. The subjects' written explanations of their choices led Ashton to conclude that most subjects relied on expected-value reasoning (or calculations) — a strategy that would insure conformity with the axiom. A follow-up experiment involving 32 MBA students produced additional, though mixed, support for the expected-value hypothesis. Ashton speculated that these results were due largely to the fact that expected value is emphasized in MBA programs.

A. Ashton [1980b, 1980c] studied conformity with the irrelevance axiom by a large group of expert decision makers (439 audit partners and managers of "Big Eight" public accounting firms). She used several audit-related decision problems of a type with which these subjects should have been familiar. Ashton [1980b] focused on the original, abstract Allais problem, as well as two adaptations of the original problem to auditing contexts. One context involved bidding on one of two municipal audits, and the other involved the type of audit opinion to be issued given a technically unresolved matter. Within each of the two audit contexts, the probability of one alternative was varied across three levels — 1.00 (as in the original Allais problem), .99 and .90. The payoffs in the municipalities contexts involved net billings to the auditing firm, while those in the opinion contexts involved net billings, potential "nuisance" lawsuits and client retention.

The incidence of Allais-type violations of the axiom was significantly lower, on average, for the six problems cast in auditing contexts (violation rate = 8%) than for the original Allais problem (violation rate = 22%). The opinion problem which maintained the probabilities used by Allais produced significantly fewer violations than the original Allais problem, but the municipalities problem with the original probabilities did not. The violation rate was significantly larger, on average, for the three municipalities problems than for the three opinion problems, but the probability manipulations within the auditing contexts had no influence on violation rates. Several unsolicited comments were received from subjects in the opinion conditions. These subjects typically voiced strong objections to the notion that auditors might consider audit fees, client retention or potential lawsuits as inputs to their decision making. These comments are reproduced in Ashton [1979, Appendix B].

A. Ashton [1980c] also reported results relative to another implication of the irrelevance axiom — the "risk versus uncertainty" distinction in a problem developed by Ellsberg [1961]. Five versions of the Ellsberg problem were employed — the original, abstract problem formulated by Ellsberg, as well as three adaptations of the original problem to auditing contexts. In one of the audit-related problems, the role of the subject was varied from that of audit engagement partner or manager to majority shareholder in the client firm. The subjects were the same as those in Ashton [1980b].

Seventy percent of the subjects responding to the original Ellsberg problem made the type of risk/uncertainty violation that Ellsberg contended most subjects will make. When the original problem was recast in the auditing contexts, however, the violation rate was only nine percent, and differences among the auditing contexts were not significant. Thus, the responses to both Allais-type and Ellsberg-type problems suggest that violation rates decrease sharply when these abstract problems are cast in more familiar contexts and presented to expert decision makers.

8.3 SUBJECTIVE PROBABILITY ASSESSMENT

Assessment of subjective probabilities has been studied by Chesley [1976, 1977, 1978] (also see Chesley [1979]), Corless [1972], Crosby [1980], Felix [1976], Solomon [1981], Solomon, Krogstad, Romney, and Tomassini [1980], and Wright [1980]. The Chesley studies were conducted in abstract contexts using students as subjects. Wright's study involved a financial context. The others examined probability assessment by auditors in audit contexts.

Chesley [1976] had two groups of subjects assess subjective probabilities and subjective likelihoods, using each of two elicitation methods. The subjects were 28 undergraduate industrial engineering students and 28 undergraduate accounting students. The subjective probability elicitation task involved three variables and five probability distributions for a drill press manufacturing process. Subjects were required to assess marginal distributions as well as a joint distribution for the three variables. The subjective likelihood elicitation task was similarly structured. Subjects' performance was measured as the absolute differences between their intuitive joint distributions and the joint distributions calculated from their own marginal distributions, summed over 11 specified points of the joint distributions. The two elicitation methods used were the direct magnitude method, which requires direct estimates of the amount of the variable at particular points on the probability scale (i.e., elicitation of the independent variable of a discrete cumulative probability distribution), and the successive subdivision method, which requires repeated estimates of the amount of the variable that will bisect certain specified intervals of the probability scale. Each subject used each method in a complex experimental procedure that required repeated reconciliations of the assessments generated by the two methods.

The direct magnitude method resulted in better performance than the successive subdivision method when the probabilities or likelihoods were initially assessed. After reconciliation, the direct magnitude method was still superior, but by a smaller amount. Repeated elicitations tended to improve the successive subdivision results, but they remained inferior to those produced by the direct magnitude method. Subjects performed better when assessing probabilities than when assessing likelihoods, but the difference was not significant at the .25 level. Moreover, the performance of the two subject groups did not differ significantly. Finally, none of the two-factor interactions between the three manipulated variables was statistically significant, although Chesley had expected the engineering students to outperform the accounting students in the prior probability task, and vice versa for the likelihood task, because of differential prior experiences of the two groups. Chesley [1976, p. 46] concluded that the experimental task was "a challenge to the subjects, but well within their capabilities for the most part," and that their performance "appeared to be reasonable." He found the lack of interaction between type of task (probability versus likelihood) and type of subject encouraging, since it suggested that "minor differences in subject groups are unlikely to play a significant part in subject elicitation performance" (p. 46).

The performance superiority of the direct magnitude method over the successive subdivision method was replicated by Chesley [1977] with a different group of student subjects. The experimental context was an adapted version of the drill press manufacturing process task used in the earlier study. In addition to evaluating performance with the two response modes, Chesley [1977] employed two data modes, probabilities and odds, for displaying data to the subjects. The data mode did not have a sizable effect on performance, and did not interact with response mode.

In a similar study, Chesley [1978] compared the performance resulting from the use of five elicitation methods. All the methods were used to elicit dependent variables (e.g., odds, bids), and two of the methods also were used to elicit independent variables. The five methods involved odds, bids, lotteries, the direct magnitude method, and the "line-chart" method. Chesley [1978, pp. 227-28] described the five methods, in the case of eliciting the dependent variable, as follows: "The odds method asked for a ratio representing the cumulative odds for the specific independent variable amount. The bid method asked for the maximum bid a subject would be willing to make for a one-dollar payoff if the actual independent variable were less than or equal to the specified amount of the variable. The one-dollar amount was used to help avoid strategies caused by risk preferences or state desirabilities and to make the bid inference as easy as possible for the subject. With a one-dollar payoff, the bid should equal the cumulative probability if no risk aversion is present. The lottery method asked for the number of lottery tickets out of the one hundred in the lottery the subject would require to be indifferent between the lottery and a decision situation where the same payoff would occur if the independent variable were less than or equal to the specified level . . . . The line-chart method was similar to the direct magnitude method, in that both asked cumulative probabilities for the specified amounts of independent variables. However, it permitted subjects to draw arrows from the line of specified amounts to the line of cumulative probabilities positioned parallel to it. This approach simplifies the explanation to the subject and permits a pictorial view of the relations." When the direct magnitude and line-chart methods were used for eliciting the independent variable, the subjects were required to estimate the amount of the independent variable corresponding to nine points on the cumulative probability distribution.

Using the drill press manufacturing process task again, Chesley [1978] had subjects assess marginal and joint likelihood distributions, and their performance was measured in the same way as in Chesley [1976]. Initially, 89 subjects were chosen for the experiment — 47 student chartered accountants and 42 MBA students. However, data from 58 subjects were discarded as being "inconsistent," "unreasonable," or for other reasons, and 12 additional subjects were added. Since the performance of the student chartered accountants (n = 14) and the MBA students (n = 29) did not differ significantly, the data from both groups were pooled for the analysis.

When the five methods were used for eliciting the dependent variable, pairwise comparisons between methods revealed no performance differences ($\alpha > .20$). When the independent variable was elicited, the direct magnitude method was slightly superior to the line-chart method, but the difference was not significant at conventional alpha levels ($.125 < \alpha < .20$). The line-chart method was slightly better for estimating dependent variables than independent variables ($.05 < \alpha < .10$), but the direct magnitude method was not.

Chesley [1979] reported two experiments that focused on the relationship between numerical probabilities and several words and phrases that are used to communicate probabilistic events. Essentially, these experiments required subjects to substitute probabilities for words, and words for probabilities. The subjects in both experiments were students in undergraduate auditing classes — 29 in Experiment 1 and 23 in Experiment 2.

Both experiments revealed great disagreement across subjects concerning the words (probabilities) that were considered equivalent to particular probabilities (words). In Experiment 1, for example, the word "fair" (as in "a fair chance") received several responses, ranging from .07 to .87. Moreover, almost all subjects used the same word (probability) for more than one probability (word). For example, in Experiment 2 the probability .767 received responses that ranged from "fair" to "excellent," and .876 received responses ranging from "fair" to "certain." Some subjects who substituted probabilities for words considered "poor," "reasonable," and "excellent" to fall in the range of .16 to .20. In somewhat of an understatement, Chesley [1979, p. 141] concluded that these subjects "do not appear to have developed a refined and commonly understood language for accurately communicating uncertainty between themselves."

Wright [1980] had 22 second-year MBA students assess probability distributions for four financial variables, using each of two elicitation methods. One method (called "prob") involved the direct assignment of probabilities to seven equally-spaced intervals of values. The other method (called "bisection") involved the assignment of values to seven points on the cumulative distribution function. The subjects also rated the overall acceptability of each method, and ranked the four distributions elicited by each method in terms of expected relative accuracy. The purpose of this ranking procedure was to enable Wright to measure the subjects' self-insight concerning the relative accuracy of their distributions. Environmental relative frequencies were available for comparison purposes, and each subject's accuracy was computed, for each method, as the mean squared error (MSE) between assessed and environmental frequencies. Subjects were told that MSE would be used as the measure of accuracy.

Wright found the "prob" method to result in more accurate assessments than the "bisection" method. The former was more accurate for 15 of the 22 subjects. A slight association existed between the accuracy scores across the two methods; in other words, a subject who was relatively accurate with one method tended to be relatively accurate with the other. Eighteen subjects rated the "prob" method as more acceptable than the "bisection" method, and there was no association between the acceptability ratings of the two methods. Finally, the subjects displayed virtually no self-insight into the relative accuracy of their assessed distributions, and their level of insight did not differ across elicitation methods.

Corless [1972] studied subjective probability assessment and probability revision by a group of 88 practicing auditors who had at least three years of auditing experience. The task involved the assessment of error rates in payroll. Two hypothetical cases were used, and one reflected stronger internal controls over payroll than the other. The subjects were required to answer questions from which beta priors and discrete priors could be constructed. First, they were required to state the median and quartile error rates that they expected. Corless used this information to construct beta priors. Then the subjects estimated the probability that the error rate would fall within certain intervals. This information was used to construct discrete priors. After these subjective prior probabilities had been elicited, the subjects were shown some sampling results. Sample sizes and error rates were varied across subjects. Sample size was either 20 or 200. The "small" error rates were zero of 20 and four of 200, while the "large" error rates were ten percent of each sample size. After viewing the sampling results, the subjects answered additional questions from which the experimenter constructed judgmentally-revised probability distributions. These intuitive distributions were compared with Bayesian-revised distributions.

The results showed little consensus across auditors in either the beta or discrete prior distributions. Moreover, the beta and discrete distributions for the same auditor often were very different. The prior distributions were unrelated to the amount of experience or the statistical backgrounds of the auditors. However, auditors whose actual clients had relatively strong internal control systems tended to concentrate more probability on lower error rates than did auditors whose actual clients had weaker internal control systems. Also, the auditors who evaluated the stronger internal control case in the experiment assessed greater probability at lower error rates than did those who evaluated the weaker internal control case. Comparison of the judgmentally-revised distributions with those revised via Bayes' theorem showed greater variability across auditors in the judgmentally-revised distributions. Finally, the Bayesian-revised distributions were "tighter" than those revised via judgment: The former had more probability concentrated near the sample error rate.

Felix [1976] argued that the equivalent prior sample method should be relatively easy for auditors to understand and use, and he reported a study in which this method was compared to the quartiles method employed by Corless [1972]. Ten practicing auditors used both methods to assess the probabilities of two types of error rates in a hypothetical order-receiving/shipping/billing system. The auditors were given a brief training session in the use of the two methods before the assessments were elicited.

Felix found fewer differences between these two methods than Corless found between the two methods he studied. Both the medians and the dispersion of the two distributions elicited from each auditor were in fairly close agreement. Felix suggested that the training session could explain this consistency between the results of the two methods. However, Felix did not control for the effect of training, i.e., all subjects were given the training session. Felix reported that eight of the ten subjects considered the equivalent prior sample method "intuitively appealing,"[3] although they encountered several problems in actually using it.

The Corless and Felix studies were set in attribute sampling contexts and elicited subjective probability distributions over error rates. Solomon, Krogstad, Romney, and Tomassini [1980] extended this type of study to a more complex variables sampling context and elicited probability distributions over account balances. Based on unaudited book values and other information about the client and its internal control procedures, 26 auditors from seven Big Eight and one other national firm specified probability distributions for the population values of accounts receivable and inventory accounts. Three populations studied by Neter and Loebbecke [1975] were used, and "weak" and "strong" internal control descriptions were developed for each. All auditors estimated seven fractiles of the six cumulative distribution functions.

The study found that the auditors could understand and use this elicitation method in a variables context, and could specify probability distributions for the population values of account balances. Probability assessments for all fractiles were less variable across auditors for the strong internal control cases than for the weak ones, and intra-auditor distributions were less disperse for the strong internal control cases. Inter-auditor variability in fractile assessments was greater for the more extreme fractiles.

Using the same experimental task and elicitation method, Solomon [1981] extended this study to examine the "goodness" of subjective probability distributions assessed by individual auditors and audit teams. A total of 103 auditors from seven Big Eight and one other national firm participated, and approximately three-fourths of them were assigned to 26 audit teams. Most teams were composed of three individuals involving some combination of audit staff, seniors, and managers. The teams were distinguished by two different types of interaction patterns in formulating their assessments, but team type had only minor effects on performance. Solomon also formed "statisticized" teams by computing the simple arithmetical average of the fractile assessments of 300 randomly chosen three-person subsets of those auditors who specified probabilities on an individual basis.

The goodness of the assessed probabilities was evaluated relative to the audit values of the six Neter-Loebbecke populations by means of two criteria — cali-

---

[3] The relative "intuitive appeal" of alternative elicitation methods apparently was considered important. Felix stated: "A satisfactory assessment of the prior probability function would result when the auditor, after training, believes that the resulting distribution is a good summary of his or her qualitative evidence. A good assessment method, then, is one in which the trained assessor-auditor has confidence" (p. 801). More objective ways of evaluating the "goodness" of assessed probabilities and, indirectly, assessment methods are discussed in Chapter 5.

bration and extremeness. Calibration was described in Chapter 5. Extremeness refers to the assignment of higher probabilities near the actual population value and lower probabilities elsewhere. The team-assessed probabilities were more extreme than those assessed by individuals, but they were also more severely miscalibrated. The calibration results showed both over- and underconfidence in the probability assessments, but underconfidence seemed to predominate — especially for the audit teams. This result is inconsistent with prior calibration results in psychology. The arithmetically weighted assessments were less extreme than those specified by audit teams, were more severely miscalibrated than team assessments, and consistently revealed underconfidence. Inter-auditor variability in fractile assessments was smaller for teams than for individuals, but did not differ for teams versus arithmetically weighted assessments.

Crosby [1980] studied the effect on sample size decisions of two elicitation methods: the equivalent prior sample method and the direct assessment of fractiles on the cumulative distribution function. The subjects, 42 audit seniors, were required to (1) assess the strength of internal control in a sales/collections cycle, (2) provide subjective probabilities for error rates using the two elicitation methods, (3) plan the extent of attribute sampling by designating an expected error rate, a confidence level, and an upper precision limit, and (4) select a sample size dictated by their estimates. Classical sample size tables, as well as the auditors' judgments, were used to select sample sizes. Crosby noted that auditors often reduce the sample sizes dictated by classical techniques because of their prior beliefs concerning internal control strength.

Using the auditors' own estimates along with a beta-binomial model, Crosby computed Bayesian sample sizes for the two elicitation methods for each subject. These sample sizes were compared with the auditors' judgmental and classical sample sizes. The mean Bayesian sample sizes for the equivalent prior sample and fractiles assessment methods were 63 and 81, respectively. Both of these were much smaller than the mean judgmental (149) and classical (257) sample sizes.

8.4 PROBABILITY REVISION

Studies by Dickhaut [1973], Kennedy [1975], and Wright [1978b, 1979b] have examined probability revision by individuals. Dickhaut [1973] used two task settings — a business task in which profit was emphasized, and a more abstract task involving cubes and algebraic identities. He also used two types of information systems and two types of subjects. The information systems were referred to as "single" and "joint." In the business/profits task, the single information system associated a single profit figure, based on historical cost, with each business, while the joint information system associated two profit figures, based on historical cost and current cost, with each business. Single and joint information systems were similarly manipulated in the cubes/algebraic identities task. The subjects were 16 undergraduate business students and 16 businessmen in an executive development program.

In the business/profits task, subjects observed the profit figure(s) generated by the single or joint information system and estimated the probability that the observation came from T_1 (businesses whose stock price increased during the year) or T_2 (those whose stock price decreased). The prior probability of T_1 or T_2 was .50. The more abstract task involved a similar revision. Performance was measured as the mean absolute difference between the subject's revisions and the corresponding Bayesian revisions over 100 experimental trials.

An analysis of variance found no significant differences for either the subject or task variables. The single information system resulted in significantly better performance than the joint information system, but Dickhaut concluded that this result was probably due to measurement error (p. 77). A significant interaction occurred between type of subject and type of task: The students performed better in the cubes /algebraic identities task, and the businessmen performed better in the business/profits task. Also, the three-factor interaction among subjects, tasks and information systems was significant.

Kennedy [1975] studied probability revision by 24 experienced loan officers and credit analysts from commercial banks. The event for which probabilities were revised was bankruptcy versus nonbankruptcy for 12 business firms, half of which had actually failed. Each subject assessed a prior probability of bankruptcy for each firm, based only on the knowledge of the industry in which the firm operated. Then each subject made 60 revisions based on five cues (four financial ratios plus asset size) that represented each firm. The 60 revisions were made in an order that was random with respect to both firms and cues.

The performance of subjects was assessed in two ways. First, Kennedy computed the inferred likelihood ratio for each revision by each subject. The difference between the inferred likelihood ratio and 1.00 was defined as the impact of each cue. (A likelihood ratio of 1.00 indicates no impact.) Second, the accuracy of the direction of impact was considered. An inaccurate direction would occur, for example, when the inferred likelihood ratio favored bankruptcy (i.e., was greater than 1.00 when odds were stated in favor of bankruptcy) for a nonbankrupt firm.

All five cues had significant impacts on the probability-of-bankruptcy assessments, i.e., the inferred likelihood ratios typically deviated from 1.00. The direction of impact, however, was accurate only about half the time. The other half was split approximately equally between an inaccurate direction and no impact at all.

Wright [1978b, 1979b] reported a study in which nine MBA students and two Ph.D. students, all of whom were knowledgeable about the relationship between capital market variables and accounting information, specified probability revisions with respect to β_i, a security's systematic riskiness. Subjects were required to revise probability distributions over five categories of β_i values that would exist two years later. Fifteen such revisions were made — one for each of three levels of each of two financial variables that were used as cues, and one for each of the nine pairwise combinations of these levels (called joint cues). Thus, each subject gave 75 posterior probabilities. The experimenter had established uniform priors by dividing the distribution of β_i, based on 446 actual firms, into five equal classes. Subjects were instructed that their posterior assessments should be as close as possible to the environmental relative frequencies. After the subjects had specified the 15 posterior distributions, they were required to estimate likelihoods for the various cue values.

Wright examined both accuracy and internal consistency of the subjects' distributions. The accuracy of the group of subjects, for each of the 75 assessments, was measured as the absolute difference between the median probability estimate for the group and the relative-frequency probability. The mean of these median differences was .053 for all 75 probabilities, .045 for those based on the single cue values, and .058 for those based on the joint cue values [Wright, 1979b]. These results indicate that the assessments were fairly accurate, and that performance was better when subjects responded to single cue values instead of joint cue values.

The accuracy of *individual* assessors was also measured as the absolute differences between subjects' and environmental probabilities over the 75 assessments. The mean absolute difference for each assessment ranged from .042 to .174, and the median mean was .076. The fact that the median of the means (.076) exceeded the mean of the medians from the aggregate analysis (.053) suggests that aggregated posteriors are more accurate than individual posteriors. In fact, only two of the 11 individual subject means were less than .053.

Wright [1978b] compared the subjects' assessed posteriors with the posteriors implied by their own assessed likelihoods. The latter posteriors were calculated by applying Bayes' theorem to the subjects' likelihoods and the priors. The medians, over the 75 probabilities, of the absolute differences between the subjects' assessed posteriors and those implied by their assessed likelihoods were no larger than .06 for ten of the 11 subjects. The subjects' assessed posteriors tended to be slightly less than those implied by their assessed likelihoods, suggesting conservative probability revision.

8.5 HEURISTICS AND BIASES

Several accounting researchers have examined judgment heuristics and the information-processing biases to which they can lead. Most such studies have been motivated by the work of Kahneman and Tversky and have focused on the representativeness heuristic [Swieringa, Gibbins, Larsson and Sweeney, 1976; Gibbins, 1977; Uecker and Kinney, 1977; Joyce and Biddle, 1979a; Biddle and Joyce, 1979]. Joyce and Biddle [1979b] and Kinney and Uecker [1980] studied the anchoring-and-adjustment heuristic. Dickhaut and Eggleton [1975] and Magee and Dickhaut [1978] studied heuristics other than those suggested by Kahneman and Tversky. Review papers that discuss several implications of decision heuristics for accounting and auditing have been written by Wright [1979c] and Biddle and Joyce [1978].

Swieringa, Gibbins, Larsson, and Sweeney [1976] reported several experiments designed to investigate the representativeness heuristic. The subjects were 120 MBA students and 316 students in industrial and labor relations, 97 percent of whom were undergraduates. One set of experiments focused on the question of whether individuals ignore the prior probabilities of outcomes when making probabilistic judgments. Both a nonaccounting context and an accounting context were used. The former, used by Kahneman and Tversky [1973], involved the probability that a particular person was a lawyer versus an engineer. The other context involved the strength of internal control. The results showed that many subjects did *not* ignore prior probabilities, contrary to both the representativeness heuristic and Kahneman and Tversky's results, in either form of the problem.

The second set of experiments investigated a different implication of the representativeness heuristic — insensitivity to sample size. The subjects in the Swieringa *et al.* study were less insensitive to the impact of sample size than were those of Kahneman and Tversky [1972], for both an original Kahneman-Tversky problem and a similar problem devised by Swieringa *et al.* However, the Swieringa *et al.* subjects made many choices that were consistent with the representativeness heuristic.

A related experiment investigated the tendency for judgments of posterior probabilities to be influenced by sample proportions, instead of sample differences, in a symmetric binomial task. Two contexts were used — balls and urns, and accounts/notes receivable. Again, the Swieringa *et al.* subjects performed better than Tversky and Kahneman's [1974] subjects, and they performed better in the accounts/notes receivable problem than in the balls-and-urns problem. However, they experienced great difficulty in stating correct posterior odds.

Another experiment, involving grade-point predictions, confirmed Kahneman and Tversky's [1973] finding that subjects have greater confidence in predictions based on correlated cues than in predictions based on uncorrelated cues of equal validity. Predictive accuracy should be greater when valid cues are uncorrelated. However, the consistency of the cue values (the dispersion of the percentile scores they represented) influenced predictions more than did intercorrelation: Subjects expressed greater confidence in predictions based on less disperse cue values.

Gibbins [1977] examined reliance on the representativeness heuristic by 71 audit partners and staff from public accounting firms. To assess the impact of prior probabilities, Gibbins used the internal control problem devised by Swieringa *et al.* Gibbins concluded that his subjects were insensitive to prior probabilities (i.e., they tended to rely on the representativeness heuristic) when responding to questions about one hypothetical company, but not when considering a different hypothetical company. Sensitivity to sample size was investigated with one of the Swieringa *et al.* problems and a similar problem related to sales invoices. Thirty-one of the 71 subjects made choices consistent with the representativeness heuristic. Two additional problems, patterned after the Kahneman and Tversky [1973] grade-point prediction problem, showed that judgments were strongly affected by the consistency of cues and were not properly sensitive to cue intercorrelations.

Uecker and Kinney [1977] studied reliance on the representativeness heuristic and the "protectiveness' heuristic by 112 auditors. They hypothesized the use of the latter heuristic based on Ijiri and Kaplan's [1971] discussion of the "protection" objective of audit sampling. Each subject considered five pairs of sample results involving various sample sizes and sample error rates, and selected the member of each pair that provided better evidence that the population error rate did not exceed five percent. Each pair was constructed such that one outcome provided adequate evidence at a 95 percent confidence level, while the other outcome provided inadequate evidence at a 90 percent confidence level. Three pairs of outcomes were used to test for representativeness; in each of these pairs the better sample outcome was the one with the larger error rate. The other two pairs, used to test for the protectiveness heuristic, were constructed such that the outcome based on the smaller sample size was superior evidence. Choices based on representativeness would favor the smaller sample error rates, since these rates are more representative of the population characteristic of interest, and would be insensitive to sample size. Conversely, the protectiveness heuristic would entail selection of the outcomes based on larger sample sizes.

On average, the auditors chose the correct sample outcomes 69.1 percent of the time. Only nine (17) of the 112 auditors consistently chose the outcome with the lower error rate (larger sample size). However, 54 percent of the auditors made at least one representativeness error, and 37 percent made at least one protectiveness error. Seventy-four percent responded incorrectly in at least one of the five pairs, and 56 percent made errors in at least two pairs.

Biddle and Joyce [1979] also examined the impact of sample size on judgments. A total of 182 auditors participated in various forms of three related experiments. Consistent with the results of Gibbins's [1977] sample-size experiments, Biddle and Joyce found that many of their subjects made judgments that suggested a lack of appreciation for the relationship between sample size and sampling variability. They also found evidence for the use of a representativeness heuristic based on the sampling fraction (sample size divided by population size). In some cases, however, the subjects' judgments were inconsistent with both normative principles and representativeness.

Joyce and Biddle [1979a], using the same subjects as Biddle and Joyce [1979], investigated two additional biases associated with the representativeness heuristic: the neglect of base rates (a bias similar to the neglect of prior probabilities), and insensitivity to the reliability of information. Normative principles require that base rates remain relevant after specific additional (or "individuating") information is received. They also require that information reliability (the corresponding between the report from an information source and reality) be considered in making predictions. However, base rates and information reliability are unrelated to the representativeness of individuating information.

One experiment investigated the effect of base rates and false-positives rates on judgments of probability. The task involved estimating the probability that a client-firm manager had actually committed a fraud when his or her score on a psychological test signaled "fraud" instead of "no fraud." Two base rates of management fraud (one percent and ten percent) and two false-positives rates (four percent and 20 percent) were used. The false-positives rate is the proportion of cases in which the test signals "fraud" for an innocent manager. In all cases the positive hit rate (a "fraud" signal for a guilty manager) was held constant at 80 percent.

The results showed a statistically significant effect for the base rate but not for the false-positives rate. The subjects systematically reacted to base rates in conformance with normative principles, although the extent to which their probabilities were regressed toward the base rates was insufficient. On the other hand, the false-positives rate was considered irrelevant — in violation of normative principles. Joyce and Biddle argued that ignoring the false-positives rate could result in undue reliance on, for example, polygraph tests, with the result that innocent people could be suspected of fraud.

The sensitivity of auditors' probability assessments to base-rate information was studied in three versions of a second experiment which manipulated (1) the stated base rates of fraud, (2) the sample sizes on which these base rates were established, and (3) the individuating information (which was intended to suggest "fraud" in some cases and "no fraud" in others). For all three versions, the results showed that base rates affected the auditors' probability assessments, but that the effect of base rates was weaker than it should have been. In short, "the diagnosticity of the representative individuating information was overestimated by the subjects" (p. 23).

Another series of two experiments focused on information reliability. One experiment required subjects to estimate the probability that a particular receivable would be collected during the coming year. Some subjects were given customer information developed by the client, while others were given the same information developed by an independent credit agency. Base rates of collection were the same for both groups. Since information from the client should be considered less reliable, the probability estimates of subjects in that condition should be closer to the base rate than should estimates of subjects in the other condition. However, no differences between the two conditions were found, suggesting that the auditors were not appropriately sensitive to the reliability of the individuating information. To rule out the rival hypothesis that subjects did not regard the information from the two sources as differentially reliable, a second experiment was conducted in which each subject made a probability-of-collection estimate for both sources of information. Additionally, different subjects received different base rates of collectibility. The base rates produced marginally significant ($\alpha < .10$) results which indicated that base rates did not have as much impact on the probability estimates as they should have had. Source reliability, however, had a strong impact ($\alpha < .001$) on probability estimates, suggesting that subjects did view information reliability as relevant to their estimates — when the possibility of differential reliability was made more obvious.

Joyce and Biddle [1979b] studied the anchoring-and-adjustment heuristic in three audit-related experiments. Fifty auditors from "Big Eight" firms participated in Series 1 of each experiment, and 132 different auditors were subjects for Series 2 — which was conducted to rule out certain rival hypotheses for the Series 1 results. The subjects were the same as those in Biddle and Joyce [1979] and Joyce and Biddle [1979a]. The first experiment focused on insufficient adjustment. Subjects were supplied with an irrelevant "anchor," and were required to estimate the number of audit clients out of 1,000 that have executive-level management fraud. In Series 1, auditors given an anchor of ten estimated, on average, that 16.5 clients had fraud, while those given an anchor of 200 estimated an average of 43. Series 2 controlled for the materiality of the fraud and used four anchors (1, 10, 200 and 300 of 1,000). Insufficient adjustment from the anchor occurred again, but the strength of the anchor was not a monotonic function of its size.

The second experiment also examined adjustment from an anchor. Subjects were required to rate the extensiveness (on a scale from one to ten) of the tests they would perform to detect a particular audit error. One group made an extensiveness rating given strong internal control and then made a second rating for the same case in which two internal control features were absent, i.e., a weaker internal control case. The remaining subjects made an extensiveness rating only for the weaker case. The anchoring-and-adjustment heuristic entails that the former group would treat their responses to the strong internal control case as an anchor, and would make insufficient adjustments when rating the weaker internal control case. Thus, the mean rating for the weaker internal control case would be lower for the first group than for the second group. Contrary to the heuristic, however, the ratings of the first group were higher than those of the second. A follow-up experiment (Series 2) had some subjects respond to the stronger case first, followed by the weaker case, while a weak-then-strong sequence was used for the other subjects. The results for the strong-to-weak group were the same as in Series 1, while the weak-to-strong group did show insufficient adjustment. The anchoring-and-adjustment heuristic cannot explain both results.

The third set of experiments investigated anchoring in the evaluation of conjunctive and disjunctive events. In Series 1, some subjects were given the probabilities of five events, all of which had to occur to insure the successful introduction of a new product. Only three of these events were used for the other subjects. The subjects estimated the probability of successful product introduction. The probabilities estimated by both groups were overstated, as anchoring on the individual-event probabilities would suggest, but Joyce and Biddle could not determine whether these evaluations were "faulty" since they did not know what the subjects assumed about event independence. Some subjects in Series 2 received the three-event and five-event conjunctive formulations of the problem used in Series 1, while others received disjunctive formulations, i.e., the complements of the event probabilities for the conjunctive formulation were used and subjects were told that if any *one* of the three (or five) failures occurred then successful product introduction would be prevented. The anchoring phenomenon entails that the probability-of-success estimates would be lower in the disjunctive formulation. This did not occur. The mean probabilities in the disjunctive and conjunctive formulations were not significantly different.

Kinney and Uecker [1980] investigated the use of the anchoring-and-adjustment heuristic by 169 auditors in a compliance sampling context. Some auditors estimated a population error rate using a fractile assessment method, while others used a risk (or probability) assessment method. The use of either method had been suggested in a proposed Statement on Auditing Standards entitled "Audit Sampling." In the experiment, the auditors using the fractile assessment method responded, under one set of experimental conditions, to the following statement: "Based on a sample of 40 invoices with no errors, I believe that there is only 1 chance in 20 that the true population error rate is *greater* than ______ percent." Auditors using the risk assessment method responded to the following statement: "Based upon a sample of 40 invoices with no errors, I believe that there is a ______ (between 100% and 0%) chance that the true population error rate is greater than 8%."

Kinney and Uecker argued that a natural anchor for the fractile assessment method would be the sample error rate, and that auditors would make insufficient adjustments for sampling error in assessing the achieved upper precision limit on the population error rate. This assessment pattern would tend to result in over-reliance on internal control, underauditing, and a greater probability of Type II errors. On the other hand, a natural anchor for the risk assessment method would be even odds, and auditors would tend to make insufficient adjustments that result in an overassessment of the achieved risk that the population error rate exceeds the maximum allowable rate. This assessment pattern would tend to result in under-reliance on internal control, overauditing, and a greater probability of Type I errors.

The results confirmed these expectations. The number and percentage of Type II errors was greater with the fractile assessment method, while the number and percentage of Type I errors was greater with the risk assessment method. Note that neither method eliminated the detrimental effects of anchoring. However, since Type I errors are considered much less serious than Type II errors, the risk assessment method might be considered preferable in compliance sampling contexts. In response to Kinney and Uecker's evidence, the exposure draft on "Audit Sampling" was revised to exclude the fractile assessment method.[4]

Simplified decision strategies, or "rules of thumb," other than those identified by Kahneman and Tversky may also be used in accounting contexts. Such strategies have been found in studies by Dickhaut and Eggleton [1975] and Magee and Dickhaut [1978]. The former study concerned the notion of "just noticeable differences" (jnd's). It investigated whether jnd's in an information context follow a psychophysical law known as Weber's Law. A jnd is the magnitude by which a variable stimulus must differ from a standard stimulus before a noticeable difference from the standard is perceived. Weber's Law holds that a jnd is a constant percentage of the standard stimulus, regardless of the magnitude of the standard. For example, if two pounds must be added to (or substracted from) a ten-pound weight in order for a difference to be perceived, then six pounds must be added to (or subtracted from) a 30-pound weight. The constant, 20 percent in this case, is called the Weber Ratio, and the standard plus (minus) 20 percent is known as the upper (lower) threshold. Weber's Law entails that stimuli nearer the thresholds have a higher probability of not always being perceived consistently than do stimuli that are farther from the thresholds. For example, a 35-pound weight may sometimes be perceived as different from a 30-pound weight, and a 37-pound weight may sometimes not, but a 60-pound weight will almost certainly be perceived as different from a 30-pound weight.

Dickhaut and Eggleton's [1975] experiment investigated whether individuals' perceptions of data accord with Weber's Law, as had been found previously for perceptions of physical stimuli.[5] Using 48 graduate business school subjects, they

---

[4] In a separate experiment, Kinney and Uecker found evidence of anchoring in an analytical review context.

[5] An earlier study by Rose, Beaver, Becker, and Sorter [1970] had found that judgments of numerical stimuli could be represented by Weber's Law. In two experiments involving 75 full-time MBA students and 46 businessmen (part-time MBA students), Rose *et al.* had subjects judge whether a stock should sell for more than, less than, or the same as a series of comparison stocks, based on comparisons of earnings-per-share (EPS) figures. In both experiments, a $2.50 standard EPS figure (with comparison figures ranging from $2.00 to $3.00) and a $5.00 standard (comparisons of $4.00 to $6.00) were used. The Weber Ratios ranged from 6.6 percent to 7.0 percent of the standard stimulus across the four combinations of experiment and standard. These results were considered encouraging in an attempt to define materiality thresholds.

investigated the effects of three variables on the extent to which Weber's Law holds. Both an accounting setting and a nonconnotative numerical setting were used. The accounting setting involved comparing a budgeted figure to an actual figure. Format was varied by displaying only the standard and comparison stimuli to some subjects, but displaying these two stimuli and their difference to other subjects. The data sequence was varied by using a random ordering of two standards for some subjects and a planned ordering for others. The results showed that the stimulus size required before subjects considered it different from the standard was a constant percentage of the standard, i.e., the subjects' perceptions of the data were consistent with Weber's Law. Only the sequence variable moderated this result.

Examination of data plots for individual subjects, however, implied that the decision-making process used by subjects was different from that presumed by Weber's Law. All comparison stimuli on one side of a threshold typically were classified consistently as either different or not different from the standard. The subjects were not sensitive to the distance of a stimulus from a threshold. Dickhaut and Eggleton reported a second experiment in which 56 subjects made jnd judgments and answered several quesions (after completion of the task) designed to elicit any heuristics they employed in making these judgments. The results confirmed that almost all subjects had employed some type of simplified decision strategy in order to make the judgments. These heuristics, often a fixed percentage of the standard stimulus, typically were formulated early in the task (and sometimes prior to beginning the task), were used consistently throughout the task, and often involved handling positive and negative differences from the standard in the same way. Dickhaut and Eggleton concluded that although Weber's Law was a good representation of the subjects' judgments, the cognitive processes underlying those judgments were quite different from those believed to accompany judgments of physical stimuli.

Magee and Dickhaut [1978] suggested that decision makers have several heuristics at their disposal, and that the use of any particular heuristic will be influenced by the nature of the decision task and the incentives inherent in the task. They devised an experiment related to the cost variance investigation decision and hypothesized that the heuristic selected for making such decisions, typically drawn from the "control chart" family of heuristics, would be influenced by the type of compensation scheme used to evaluate the decision maker. Based on an earlier study by Magee [1976], they hypothesized which heuristic would be used for each of two compensation schemes. An expanded version of Dickhaut and Eggleton's "heuristics elicitation questionnaire" was used to elicit the subjects' heuristics. The subjects were 38 graduate business school students. The results strongly supported the hypotheses concerning the effect of the compensation scheme on the choice of heuristics. Moreover, additional experimental and simulation results showed that differences in heuristics were related to differences in costs to the organization that could be expected under the different compensation schemes.[6]

---

[6] (Footnote on following page.)

8.6 INFORMATION EVALUATION

Three descriptive studies couched in the framework of the two-person information evaluation model have been reported. Uecker [1978] investigated the ability of subjects (information evaluators) to learn the optimal information system for a simulated decision maker and to adapt their information system choices to different models of the decision maker. The task was a variation of problems that involve calculating the expected net gain from sampling, and was cast in a balls-and-urns context. Subjects were required to select one of ten imaginary urns and to specify the size of a sample (of black and white marbles) to be drawn from that urn. Then a computer, programmed to represent either a Bayesian or a conservative Bayesian decision maker, randomly chose an urn and displayed the sample results. The simulated decision maker then guessed the proportion of black and white marbles in the urn selected, and the subject was rewarded based on the decision maker's accuracy. Subjects were encouraged to learn the optimal sample sizes in order to maximize their earnings from the experiment. Each subject (40 undergraduate accounting students) participated in 40 experimental trials with each simulated decision maker.

The results indicated no significant convergence on the optimal sample size for either type of decision maker. It appears that the subjects were unable to learn the decision maker's decision model over a series of trials. Subjects did, however, choose systematically different sample sizes for the two decision makers. The mean chosen sample size for the Bayesian (conservative Bayesian) decision maker was 16.9 (19.4). The optimal sample sizes were 16 and 24. Thus, the mean chosen sample sizes were nearer optimal for the Bayesian than for the conservative Bayesian decision maker. Uecker suggested that additional research was needed to discover the conditions under which an evaluator can learn a decision maker's model and to develop techniques to facilitate learning. He also noted that his study did not permit "identification of the major impediment to improved performance over successive replications — learning the user's model or learning to apply this knowledge in making information system choices." (p. 182).

R. Ashton [1980c] reported a study that used the lens model equation to measure both the acquisition of knowledge about a simulated decision-maker's model and the application of that knowledge to the evaluator's own decision making. Acquisition of knowledge was measured by the matching coefficient (G), and application of that knowledge by the consistency coefficient (R_s). Three groups of subjects (undergraduates, MBAs, Ph.D.s[7]) attempted to learn the mul-

[6] This section has focused on the use of probabilistic information in decision making, and several accounting contexts that involve the use of probabilistic information were considered. An additional context that may be relevant here is that of "probabilistic financial statements." Such statements would explicitly display the uncertainty inherent in (at least some) amounts that appear on traditional financial statements. Confidence-interval financial statements may be considered a "first step" toward more refined probabilistic statements. While no studies of users' reactions to probabilistic financial statements have been reported, three studies related to confidence-interval statements have appeared. Oliver [1972] and Keys [1978] investigated loan decisions by bankers who were given either traditional "point-estimate" or confidence-interval financial statements, while Birnberg and Slevin [1976] studied the impact of confidence intervals in a nonaccounting setting involving MBA students. None of these studies found significant differences between decisions based on traditional versus confidence-interval financial statements.

[7] The Ph.D. students were participants in the 1976 AAA Doctoral Consortium.

tiple regression model of a simulated decision maker. The experimental task, involving the relationship between product selling prices and three variables on which those prices were based, was similar to that used by Ashton [1976a] and Swieringa, Dyckman, and Hoskin [1979] to study functional fixation.

Three simulated decision makers of differential predictability were used. The decision makers' predictability (R_s) represented "environmental" predictability (R_e) for the evaluator. The three levels of predictability were .01, .82, and .98. Subjects were required to (1) study a set of 30 pricing decisions made by the simulated decision maker, (2) infer the decision maker's model from this set of decisions, and (3) implement the inferred model in establishing prices for a series of 30 new products. Subjects were then supplied with one of two types of feedback information, and the three steps described above were repeated. One type of feedback was very specific, telling the subjects that the three variables should be weighted equally in their decision making. The other type of feedback was much more general. The three types of subjects ($n = 138$) were assigned randomly to the six combinations of predictability level and feedback type.

The results showed that acquisition of decision-model knowledge was slightly superior to application of that knowledge: The median matching coefficient was .94 and the median consistency coefficient .88 on the first set of decisions. Both acquisition and application of knowledge were positively related to the level of predictability of the decision maker. The Ph.D. students, who were assumed to be more familiar with probability, statistics and formal notions of decision making, tended to outperform the other two subject groups, especially in terms of consistency. The post-feedback results differed very little from the pre-feedback results. Neither type of feedback had a consistent effect on performance. Ashton's results were consistent with Uecker's in their implication that individuals have great difficulty improving their performance after feedback.

Uecker [1980] used a modified version of his [1978] expected-net-gain-from-sampling task to investigate the ability of information evaluators to use knowledge of the decision maker's model in *simplified* information evaluation. It was pointed out in Chapter 6 that because of resource and information-processing constraints information evaluators, as well as decision makers, are likely to use simplified decision strategies (e.g., heuristics) instead of the complete decision formulation of the information evaluation paradigm. Uecker suggested several reasons that knowledge of the decision maker's model might be of little or no benefit to the evaluator in the context of simplified information evaluation.

The decision maker's model, a lexicographic model employing sample proportion and prior probabilities, was communicated to 20 of the 39 undergraduate accounting students who served as subjects. The other 19 subjects received no information about the model. All subjects were given an "anchor," prior to beginning a series of 50 sample size choices, in an effort to induce them to employ a simplified information evaluation strategy. The subjects were told that their anchors were chosen at random by a computer. Actually, half were given the number four and half the number 40, which were equidistant from the optimal sample size of 22. Subjects were required to estimate, prior to undertaking the main part of the task, whether the optimal sample size needed to maximize expected value was greater than, less than, or equal to the anchor, and to specifically estimate the optimal sample size. The estimate of optimal sample size was made again at the completion of the experimental task. Performance was measured by the expected values of the subjects' chosen sample sizes and by the absolute deviations of chosen sample sizes from the optimal sample size. Generally, these two measures produced consistent results.

The anchoring manipulation was effective. Subjects anchored at four (40) made, on average, initial optimal-sample-size estimates of 24 (35.8). Moreover, the effect of anchoring was strong throughout the 50 trials and in the final estimates of the optimal sample size. Further, there were no significant differences in either the initial or second optimal-sample-size estimates for the subjects who were given information about the decision maker's model versus those who were not. In addition, several analyses of chosen sample sizes across successive trials found no significant differences in the performance of the knowledge and no-knowledge groups. Further study of the 19 subjects who were not told the decision maker's model found that 18 of them could predict the decision maker's choices in at least seven of ten trials, and 13 of these 18 reported that they had learned the decision maker's model after 11 to 13 of the 50 trials. However, the performance of these 18 subjects did not improve over successive trials. Uecker concluded that knowledge of the decision maker's model did not help subjects improve their performance. Moreover, he suggested, the success of the anchoring attempt provides a possible explanation for this result, i.e., the subjects (information evaluators) were using a simplified model.

8.7 SUMMARY COMMENTS

Accounting studies that have been conducted within the SEU framework — or can be interpreted within that framework — typically have addressed the subjective assessment or use of probabilistic information. Normative criteria have been employed in many studies as standards for evaluating the quality of probabilistic judgments. Other studies have focused on the agreement of subjective probabilities and probabilistic judgments across individuals and across methods of probability elicitation.

The results have been mixed. For example, the diverse set of studies related to the global SEU or expected value decision criterion, as well as studies conducted at the axiom level, have identified several examples of decision-making behavior that seems to be consistent with SEU maximization. However, some behavior that is not consistent with this criterion has also been found. The preference for initial-stage probabilities in two-stage decision processes is one example.

Much of the research activity, especially in recent years, has concentrated on the assessment of subjective probabilities and the impact of judgment heuristics on the interpretation and use of probabilistic information. With respect to subjective probability assessment, several elicitation methods have been employed. The principal methods have been the bisection, fractiles, fixed interval, and equivalent prior sample methods. The probabilities elicited by these and other methods have been evaluated with reference to at least five types of criteria: (1) understandability or intuitive appeal; (2) the agreement of probabilities elicited by different methods; (3) performance criteria involving correspondence between marginal and joint distributions, and correspondence between subjective probabilities and environmental relative frequency information; (4) other criteria of "goodness" such as calibration and extremeness; (5) the impact of the elicited probabilities on decisions.

The probability assessment research conducted in accounting contexts has not yet identified the preferable elicitation method(s) vis-à-vis any of these five criteria. This is not unlike the situation in psychology and other disciplines (see Chapter 5). In accounting, the fractiles and bisection elicitation methods have been popular, and some researchers have reported that subjects find these methods understandable and usable. However, little research has been done on the *relative* understandability of the various methods. Other researchers in accounting have argued for the intuitive appeal of the equivalent prior sample method, but some recent work by Solomon, Romney, Krogstad, and Tomassini [1980] indicates that practicing auditors find this method counterintuitive in a variables sampling context.

The early probability assessment studies in accounting found a great deal of intra-subject disagreement in probabilities assessed by different methods, as well as inter-subject disagreement in probabilities assessed by the same method. Some recent work has begun to examine how inter-subject disagreement is affected by certain requirements of the elicitation task (e.g., the fractiles assessed), but more work of this type is needed before conclusions are possible.

Studies evaluating the quality of assessed probabilities relative to performance criteria, other measures of "goodness," and decision impact sometimes have found one elicitation method superior to another and sometimes have not. In addition, different studies have compared different combinations of methods. Thus, generalizations about the quality of assessed probabilities in accounting contexts seem unwarranted. Moreover, the findings reported by Solomon [1981] suggest that generalizing the results of studies based on individual probability assessment to the team assessment context may be less than straightforward.

In addition to the work on probability assessment and the studies of SEU-related behavior at the global and axiom levels, another major subset of studies has examined the apparent reliance on judgment heuristics in the interpretation and use of probabilistic information. Almost all of this research has followed closely the original work of Kahneman and Tversky, and much of it has focused on the representativeness heuristic. Several potentially detrimental judgment biases may result from using this heuristic. The principal biases studied by accounting researchers are insensitivity to sample size and information reliability, and the tendency to ignore base rates and prior probabilities. The results in this area are consistent across studies: Auditors and other subjects are not properly sensitive to several dimensions of probabilistic information. While the evidence from accounting studies suggests greater sensitivity than that from non-accounting studies, auditors and other subjects nevertheless deviate from normative principles of decision making in ways that are consistent with the use of the representativeness heuristic. The use of other heuristics — primarily anchoring and adjustment — also has been strongly suggested by the results of accounting-related studies.

Recent work in the heuristics area has begun to examine ways of helping individuals avoid biases that are associated with judgment heuristics. One possibility is training in the tenets of good judgment. The mixed success of training efforts in lens studies was noted at the end of Chapter 7. The "information evaluation" studies reviewed in the present chapter noted the apparent inability of subjects to benefit from certain types of feedback information. This evidence suggests that improving human judgment via training will not be easy, but it may be the only feasible judgment-improvement option in many contexts.

CHAPTER NINE

Conclusion

Three topics are discussed in this final chapter. First, some general comments are offered about the first ten years of human information processing research in accounting. More specific conclusions may be found in the report of the Committee on Human Information Processing [1977], Libby and Lewis [1977, 1981], Einhorn [1976], and the summary comments at the end of Chapters 7 and 8. Second, some recent research trends are noted. Particular attention is devoted to the use of verbal protocol analysis as a research tool. Finally, some comments are offered on the real-world implementation of the results of human information processing studies.

9.1 THE FIRST DECADE

Human information processing research in accounting is approaching the end of its first decade. In many ways this has been a period of education — in the models, methodologies and literature that have guided this type of research in psychology. The accounting research has followed the psychology research in terms of the generic human information processing issues addressed and the methodologies employed.

The accounting research has also followed the psychology research in terms of *results*. For the most part, the psychologists' findings have been replicated when human information processing studies have employed decision tasks and subjects relevant to accounting. Examples of consistent results between the two areas are the ability of linear models to paramorphically represent judgment strategies; the relatively poor levels of judgment accuracy; the moderate effectiveness of feedback information; the disagreement among implied cue weights, overall judgments and subjective probability assessments of different individuals; the mixed success of the expected value model in predicting actual choices; and the generally poor understanding and utilization of statistical and probabilistic concepts.

On the other hand, the research in accounting has produced a few results that conflict with those found by psychologists: Judgment insight often is very high in accounting studies, and inter-subject consensus in overall judgments has sometimes exceeded that found in other areas; The accuracy of individual judgments has been found to equal or exceed that of individuals' judgment models in some cases; Individuals' performance in the use of statistical and probabilistic concepts, and in following the irrelevance axiom, has been found superior to that in non-accounting settings.

Accounting researchers tend to find the differences between accounting and non-accounting results very interesting, and some interest has been shown in tracing these differences in results to differences between the subjects and/or tasks studied in accounting and those studied in other contexts. However, if one considers the entire body of human information processing results produced in accounting, it is clear that three critically important features of individuals and tasks are common to both the accounting and non-accounting research: (1) Individuals' judgments do not adequately reflect formal notions of statistics or probability; (2) Individuals make inconsistent judgments; (3) Judgment tasks entail several formal or statistical characteristics that influence both individuals' judgments and the usefulness of decision aids. In combination, these three features account for many of the basic results of human information processing research in accounting as in other areas.

9.2 RECENT RESEARCH TRENDS

Some recent trends in human information processing research in accounting are discussed in this section. It seems likely that the amount of research conducted in each area mentioned below will increase in the future. The replication, extension and refinement of existing work, including some research that raises questions about the typical application of the lens and SEU paradigms, is considered first. Next, the increased motivation for human information processing research provided by both normative paradigms and by descriptive paradigms other than lens or SEU is considered briefly. The increased emphasis on description of human information processing, including the use of process-tracing research techniques, is discussed at more length. Another trend, the growing concern for the "real world," is discussed in Section 9.3.

9.2.1 Replication, Extension and Refinement

One trend in recent research is that toward replication, extension and refinement of earlier work. Examples of this trend include the series of studies on internal control evaluation and on heuristics and biases. Some work in these and other areas involves relatively modest departures from earlier studies, while other work involves more substantial changes in focus. Of course, almost all "later" studies can be viewed as involving replication, extension or refinement of studies that preceded them. Sets of related empirical studies are necessary for the advancement of knowledge in this area.

Most of the accounting- and auditing-related work in human information processing has emphasized the *internal* validity of the experimental tasks employed. This is true of both the original studies in the various substantive and methodological areas and the replications, extensions and refinements that have followed. The future probably will see a greater concern for the *external* validity of human information processing research. This type of refinement will involve questioning some of the basic aspects of the lens and SEU paradigms as they typically are applied. Some research of this nature has already begun, and additional work should be encouraged as long as a requisite degree of internal validity is not sacrificed.

In lens studies, for example, the experimental tasks typically employed have involved a number of simplificatons, including the use of a small cue set, the absence of realistic cue intercorrelations, and simplified response scales for recording the subjects' judgments. Similar task simplifications have been employed in SEU studies. The performance criterion employed in many lens studies has been correlational, with its implied squared-error loss function. Little attention has been given to the robustness of lens results to different performance criteria. (See Kessler [1977] for an exception.) Normative criteria such as expected value maximization and Bayesian revision have been employed in many SEU-paradigm studies, but the appropriateness of such criteria can be questioned (see Einhorn and Hogarth [1981]).

Many of the early lens and SEU studies in accounting and auditing investigated only a small portion of the total decision environment faced by decision makers in the real world. For example, internal control evaluations by auditors were studied in isolation from time-allocation decisions or sample-size decisions for which these evaluations should serve as inputs. Similarly, subjective probability assessments and the apparent reliance on judgment heuristics by auditors were studied in isolation from their effects on other audit decisions. Some of the more recent research has begun to investigate the impact of judgments and judgment biases on decision making; other recent research has focused on team, instead of individual, decision making, and on cue selection as well as processing. While these studies, like their predecessors, necessarily abstracted from many features of "real" decision making, they do represent important attempts to mirror realistic decision environments. Efforts to structure human information processing research so that its relevance to real-world decision making is more apparent are likely to intensify in the future.

9.2.2. Relation to Other Paradigms

Another recent trend has been an attempt by human information processing researchers to explicitly tie their studies to *normative* research paradigms. The normative information evaluation model and, more generally, the expected utility model are the primary examples. Relying on normative paradigms as bases for descriptive research offers many of the same advantages ascribed in Chapter 1 to reliance on the lens and SEU paradigms of human information processing research.

Accounting researchers whose work derives primarily from a normative orientation appear to be increasingly recognizing the descriptive counterparts of their research. Recent papers by Hilton [1980], Newman [1978], and Sundem [1979] are examples. This may be indicative of a more general trend in the economics literature (see, e.g., Grether and Plott [1979] and other recent papers in the *American Economic Review*).

Some recent human information processing research in accounting has employed psychological research paradigms other than lens or SEU. For example, Brown [1980] has employed signal detection theory,[1] and Shields, Birnberg, and

---

[1] See, for example, Green and Swets [1974] and Pastore and Scheirer [1974] for discussions of signal detection theory.

Frieze [1979] and Birnberg and Shields [1979] have relied on attribution theory,[2] in studies concerning variance investigation decisions. While these two paradigms are similar in some respects to the lens and SEU paradigms, they involve somewhat different orientations.

9.2.3 Emphasis on Process Descriptions

Both the lens and SEU paradigms of human information processing research involve significant reliance on representational models of decision making. The SEU model represents decision making *as if* an individual multiplies the probabilities and utilities of outcomes and sums these products to make a choice. Similarly, the multiple regression formulation of the lens paradigm represents decision making *as if* an individual multiplies regression coefficients by cue values and sums these products to reach a judgment or decision.

In recent years several important attempts have been made to study decision making and human information processing at more descriptive levels of analysis. Such studies have resulted in significant insights into human information processing. Examples include the research on judgment heuristics and descriptive alternatives to expectation models of risky decision making, e.g., risk dimensions and elimination-by-aspects models. Some of the results of studies in these areas may provide a basis for a descriptive alternative to the SEU model. An example is Kahneman and Tversky's [1979] exposition of a "prospect theory" model of risky choice. In any event, the emphasis on description of human information processing has increased recently, and that emphasis seems likely to continue.

One component of the growing concern for description is the use of process-tracing research techniques, including verbal protocol analysis and the analysis of information acquisition or search behavior. The use of process-tracing techniques is motivated, in part, by a recognition that "input-output analyses . . . are not fully adequate to develop and test process models of decision behavior" [Payne, Braunstein, and Carroll, 1978, p. 19]. The most prominent process-tracing technique, verbal protocol analysis, requires that subjects "think aloud" when analyzing a decision task, searching for information, or evaluating and choosing among alternatives. The collection of verbal protocols is intended to provide information on the sequential, step-by-step processes that subjects employ en route to formulating a judgment or decision. A subject's verbalizations are interpreted, or "coded," by the researcher in order to construct a description, and often a model, of the subject's judgment process.[3]

The descriptions and models that result from verbal protocol analyses may seem closer to underlying decision processes than the results of input-output

---

[2] Kelley [1967, 1973] provides a good description of attribution theory. Nisbett and Borgida [1975] and Fischhoff [1976] discuss similarities and differences between judgment research and attribution theory research; Fischhoff observes: "The former deals primarily with predictive inferences about unknown events — typically set in the future. The latter deals with how people attribute causes to or explain events which have already transpired" (p. 421). Birnberg, Frieze, and Shields [1977] discuss the role of attribution theory in the management control process.

[3] Some typical (non-accounting) studies that have employed verbal protocol analysis are Carroll and Payne [1977], Clarkson [1962], Kleinmuntz [1968], Newell and Simon [1972], Payne [1976], and Svenson [1979].

analyses such as linear regression models. In other words, the "face validity" of verbal protocol analyses may be high. Step-by-step models constructed from verbal protocols may agree with people's intuitive notions of how they make decisions, whereas the structure of most input-output models, e.g., multiple regression, may not.

Face validity and intuition can be misleading, however. Einhorn, Kleinmuntz, and Kleinmuntz [1979] argue that both process-tracing models *and* linear regression models capture the basic nature of the judgment process as seen by Brunswik [1943, 1952, 1956] — but at different levels of detail. In their words,

> . . . the process-tracing model is the result of an attempt to find general rules by looking at responses made on many specific cases, whereas the regression model is an attempt to capture a general strategy embedded in a theory of judgment (Brunswik's). This difference in starting points can account for the feeling that the process model is more firmly rooted in the observable than the statistical model. However, two cautions are necessary. First, although process-tracing data may be more specific with respect to process, this does not imply an isomorphism . . . . Therefore, one should be careful not to overstate what process-tracing data mean. Second, any type of model is no less (or more) a process model because of the level of detail of the variables it considers. Moreover, processes are neither more nor less true or real as a function of a particular level of analysis. Rather, regression and process-tracing models both deal with underlying psychological process, but at a different level of generality (p. 470).

These researchers further argue that linear additive regression models are not devoid of psychological content and that process-tracing protocols can be generated via a general additive rule. Viewed in this way, verbal protocol analysis and input-output modeling can be considered compatible and complementary methodologies for human information processing research.

Payne, Braunstein, and Carroll [1978] discuss four possible uses of data derived from verbal protocol analysis. First, the collection of verbal protocols may be useful in an *exploratory* sense, i.e., in the early stages of research that searches for regularities in behavior. Second, such data may be useful in a *supplementary* way — "to confirm and extend the interpretations of data collected by other methods" (Payne, Braunstein, and Carroll, 1978, p. 29). Third, verbal protocol data may be useful for *testing hypotheses* about information search and information utilization.[4] Finally, such data may be used for *building and testing models* of decision making. The verbal protocol technique, like regression modeling, re-

---

[4] Some researchers have used verbal protocol analysis to examine the "underlying process assumptions" of various judgment models, including the linear additive model frequently operationalized via multiple regression analysis. While choosing to view this model as having underlying information processing assumptions may facilitate insights into decision making, it must be remembered that such a model is intended to be a representation, not a description, of judgment processes. As noted in Chapter 2, Hoffman [1960] addressed this issue at length. More recently, the point has been emphasized by Einhorn, Kleinmuntz, and Kleinmuntz [1979]: " . . . criticisms that LRMs [Linear Regression Models] of judgment are too simplistic to capture the highly interactive and contingent methods that are believed to be used in judgment rest on the erroneous belief that the mathematical form of a model is isomorphic with the process it is supposed to represent . . . . Experts shown a linear model of their judgments may claim that they do not multiply cues by weights and then add up the products to form their judgment . . . . An analogy might be that a quarterback does not compute a set of differential equations in throwing a touchdown pass, although one might model that activity in such a way" (p. 469).

sults in representational models of decision making; however, verbal protocol modeling begins with self-report process descriptions provided by decision makers, instead of inferring decision models from the relationships between inputs and outputs.

To be of maximum usefulness in any of the four ways mentioned above, verbal protocol results should be "validated" in some way. One type of validity that relates to the exploratory, supplementary and hypothesis-testing uses of verbal protocol data involves comparing the results of verbal protocol analysis with results obtained via other types of analyses. Agreement of the results produced by different types of analyses will enhance the credibility of each type. However, the disagreement of such results will not necessarily indicate which analysis is superior.

When verbal protocol data are used for building and testing models of decision making, two types of validation tests can be performed. One is a *process* test: Does the model generate the behavior of interest in the same step-by-step fashion that was followed by the subject? Payne, Braunstein, and Carroll [1978, p. 32] point out that most process validations of models constructed from verbal protocol analyses have been based on "eyeball" comparisons between the models and actual decision behavior. The second type of validaton test is based on *output* instead of process: Does the model make the same final decisions as the subject who is being modeled? This type of test, used routinely in input-output modeling, is more rigorous than an eyeball test of process.

The success of verbal protocol models vis-à-vis an output criterion has been mixed. Payne, Braunstein, and Carroll [1978, p. 32] mentioned four studies that found "a high degree of correspondence" between the models' outputs and actual decisions. In contrast, Einhorn, Kleinmuntz, and Kleinmuntz [1979] reported results that are less encouraging for verbal protocol analysis. These researchers conducted an experiment that compared, on an output criterion, a verbal protocol model and a linear regression model of an experienced decision maker. The verbal protocol model made 26 errors in the prediction of 96 actual binary decisions, whereas the linear regression model made nine errors. Moreover, the correlation between actual and predicted decisions was .46 for the verbal protocol model and .82 for the linear regression model.

To explain this result, Einhorn, Kleinmuntz, and Kleinmuntz considered what are perhaps the two most significant problems of the verbal protocol analysis technique: "(a) the degree to which verbal reports access cognitive processes . . . and (b) the ability of the experimenter to adequately translate the verbal reports into a computer model" (pp. 475-76). With respect to the first problem, Nisbett and Wilson [1977] reviewed a great deal of evidence which they interpreted as "consistent with the most pessimistic view concerning people's ability to report accurately about their cognitive processes" (p. 247). Ericsson and Simon [1978, 1979] and others have pointed out that Nisbett and Wilson's evidence relates to retrospective verbal reports provided after the completion of decision tasks, instead of concurrent verbal reports provided during the performance of the tasks. Concurrent verbal reports upon which protocol analysis is based should be less suspect than retrospective verbal reports. On the other hand, Smith and Miller [1978] noted that in decision tasks involving routine skills, mental processes will likely function "automatically" and be inaccessible, thereby preventing accurate self-reports. Since the decision maker studied by Einhorn, Kleinmuntz, and Kleinmuntz [1979] was very experienced in the task, lack of access to mental processes is a possible explanation for their results.[5]

The second explanation considered for the relatively poor predictive ability of this protocol model focused on "the experimenter's ability to infer correctly the rules and strategies of the judge from the protocol and to build the computer model to incorporate these rules" [Einhorn, Kleinmuntz, and Kleinmuntz, 1979, p. 476]. The reliability with which verbal protocols can be interpreted has been raised frequently, and the evidence is mixed [Payne, Braunstein, and Carroll, 1978, p. 28]. In addition, the efforts of readers of verbal protocol reports to evaluate the reliability of protocol interpretations are sometimes frustrated by sketchy discussions of coding procedures and reliability checks presented in published articles. Moreover, some researchers do not attempt to assess in any formal way the reliability of protocol interpretations, relying instead on "the persuasiveness of the web of inference" from a protocol [Payne, Braunstein, and Carroll, 1978, p. 28]. In any event, the critical importance of human judgment in the interpretation of verbal protocols should be recognized.

Other process-tracing techniques involve the monitoring of information acquisition or search behavior. By structuring the decision task to facilitate such monitoring, the researcher can collect data on the information sought, the order in which it is acquired, the total amount of information sought, the duration for which it is examined, and other aspects of information search behavior [Payne, Braunstein, and Carroll, 1978]. One explicit monitoring technique involves the use of "information boards." This monitoring tool might list m choice alternatives across the top and n attributes that characterize each alternative along the sides, and contain the values of the m x n alternative/attribute combinations in the cells of the display. Payne [1976] provides a good example of the use of this technique. Other information search techniques (e.g., the recording of eye movements) have been used also.

Some accounting researchers have employed process-tracing techniques. Within the general theoretical framework of attribution theory, Shields [1979] used both information boards and verbal protocol analysis to study the information search and utilization behavior of 12 corporate managers as they analyzed performance reports. Biggs and Mock [1980] conducted a verbal protocol study of four auditors, using an adaptation of the Mock and Turner (forthcoming) task. Biggs [1979, 1980] used verbal protocol analysis to study both the information search [1980] and choice [1979] behavior of 11 financial analysts as they made earning-power evaluations of five companies. While the Biggs [1980], Biggs and Mock [1980] and Shields [1979] studies may be considered exploratory, Biggs [1979] was concerned with testing hypotheses about information utilization

[5] This possibility was supported by a second experiment in which a nonexpert decision maker performed an unfamiliar task. A model based on verbal protocol analysis was slightly more successful than a linear regression model in predicting actual decisions on a cross-validation sample. However, Einhorn, Kleinmuntz, and Kleinmuntz stressed that the two models yielded very similar predictions.

behavior. Another protocol study [Bhaskar and Dillard, 1979] had two subjects verbalize as they worked an intermediate-level financial accounting problem.

Verbal protocol analysis can play a positive role in accounting research as in other areas, especially in the exploratory stages of research and as a supplement to other research methods. A multi-method approach that recognizes the complementary nature of different research methodologies can be useful. Both Payne, Braunstein, and Carroll [1978] and Einhorn, Kleinmuntz, and Kleinmuntz [1979] argued for the use of multi-method approaches — the former for verbal protocol analysis combined with information search techniques, and the latter for process-tracing techniques combined with input-output modeling. When applied rigorously in these ways and reported in sufficient detail, the use of verbal protocol analysis may lead to important insights into human information processing.

9.3 THE REAL WORLD

Behavioral decision making research in accounting has always had a "practical" flavor. Both proponents and critics have emphasized the desirability of focusing on real decision makers, employing realistic decision tasks, and considering the real-world implications of the research. It was noted in Section 9.2.1 that recent research in this area has shown increased concern for the realistic representation of decision environments. In addition, much of the recent research has involved real decision makers. In fact, most of the studies reviewed in Chapters 7 and 8 used primary decision makers as subjects, e.g., auditors, managers, and financial analysts. The remainder used graduate or undergraduate students. More than 80 percent of the studies concerned with auditing employed practicing auditors as subjects. This emphasis on primary decision makers is a positive feature of human information processing research in accounting.

It would be a mistake, however, to conclude that studies employing student subjects are necessarily irrelevant, or of lower quality, than those employing decision makers of more direct interest to the research questions posed. Consider, for example, Zelditch and Evan's [1962] analogy of the use of student subjects by behavioral researchers and the use of fruit-flies by geneticists:

> The geneticist finds the fruit-fly a strategic and convenient research subject because the relevant process is run through so rapidly, there are so many replicates, and they are so readily confined and observed. But what is so important about the fruit-fly is that its genetic process is not fundamentally different from the human genetic process. Neither its size nor its structure is correlated with the process investigated . . . . (p. 59).

Likewise, the extent to which differences between student subjects and primary decision makers are likely to affect research results must be explicitly considered before any firm conclusions can be drawn.

In this regard, Ashton and Kramer [1980] analyzed several studies in accounting, business, psychology, and consumer behavior that had employed both students and primary decision makers as subjects. They concluded that studies of *attitudes* had found large differences between students and other groups, but that studies of *decision making* had found the decisions and the underlying information processing behavior of students and primary decision makers to be very similar. More recent studies by Hamilton and Wright [1980] and Zimmer [1980] found results based on students to be virtually indistinguishable from those based on primary decision makers. Such results are positive indicators of the potential ability to extrapolate human information processing results from the laboratory to practice.

In addition to their concern for the *subjects* used in human information processing research, several researchers in accounting have shown a growing concern for the decision *tasks* that are used. The importance of task characteristics was recognized in the psychology literature a few years ago, and is reflected in the comments of Edwards [1971] and Dawes [1975]. Edwards [1971] argued that

> . . . psychology is not only about people who emit behavior — it is also, perhaps more importantly, about the tasks that elicit that behaior . . . . [M]any deeply sophisticated psychological theorists fail to recognize how much effort they spend in modelling the task, and how little effort they spend in modelling the behavior of the subject in the task . . . . My own guess is that most successful models now available are successful exactly because of their success in describing tasks, not people (pp. 640-41).

Similarly, Dawes [1971] suggested that judgment models

> . . . are primarily models of the task, and that they represent the subjects' behavior only because the subjects have acquired certain (simple) abilities that allow them to behave appropriately (not necessarily optimally) in the task situation (p. 119).

For relatively structured judgment tasks, Brehmer [1976a, 1976b] has argued that the formal (statistical) characteristics of the tasks are more important determinants of the resulting decisions than are either the substantive (content) characteristics of the tasks or the particular subjects in the tasks. Judgment tasks can be described by their formal characteristics regardless of their content. Formal task characteristics include task predictability, the number of cues, the intercorrelations of the cues, the distribution of cue validities, and several other characteristics.

While some accounting researchers have noted the importance of formal task characteristics, others have been concerned with the distinction between "simple" and "complex" tasks. Although "simple" and "complex" typically are not explicitly defined, they seem to relate more to the content of tasks than to formal task characteristics. For example, questions are sometimes raised as to whether the simplified tasks used in much human information processing research are sufficiently representative of actual decision situations faced by decision makers.

Certainly, complex tasks have more face validity than simple tasks, and the use of complex tasks probably increases the confidence that some observers have in the results of human information processing research. However, the extent to which the use of complex tasks increases our knowledge of human information processing, or provides a better basis than simple tasks for extrapolating from the laboratory to practice, is an unanswered question. One view, exemplified by Winkler and Murphy [1973], holds that the simplified, well-structured nature of many experimental tasks does not adequately capture subjects' judgment processes that have been developed in a complex, ill-structured world. As a result, Winkler and Murphy argue, decision makers may perform more poorly in experimental tasks than in real-world settings. A different view, exemplified by Slovic, Fischhoff, and Lichtenstein [1977], maintains that many experimental tasks may show decision makers at their best. That is, such tasks often abstract from substantive issues that may prejudice decision makers' performance, and they often provide all the information needed for optimal responses and exclude information that is ambiguous or irrelevant. Of course, perceptions, as well as facts, about the subjects and tasks used in human information processing research are important in efforts to implement the results of such research.

The early psychological research on human information processing typically placed student subjects in basic tasks for which they had no particular expertise, and the reports of such research were addressed almost exclusively to other researchers in the same or allied fields. Later work in psychology has shown more concern for expert decision makers responding to realistic tasks, and many of the results have been communicated through channels designed to reach users who potentially can put such results into practice. The review by Slovic, Fischhoff, and Lichtenstein [1977] indicates that real-world decision makers in several disciplines have begun to pay attention to psychological research on human information processing.[6]

It is too early to know whether the practitioner groups who comprise the accounting researcher's audience (managers, auditors, bankers, financial analysts, etc.) will attempt to use the results of human information processing research in their fields. Typically, several years have elapsed before other types of accounting research have produced (even moderate) impacts on practice. Examples are the adoption of statistical sampling techniques in auditing, some acceptance of market efficiency, and the recognition that accounting standard-setting is, in part at least, a political process. As noted in Chapter 1, human information processing research in accounting is still fairly new. Thus far, it has been communicated almost entirely via "academic" journals and small working-paper networks. Few attempts have been made to reach practitioner groups who might use the results of this research in a practical way.

An exception to this general statement is human information processing research in auditing. Some efforts have been made to communicate, through both formal and informal means, the results and potential implications of this research to auditing practitioners. The auditing profession is a highly identifiable, organized group (as opposed to corporate managers, for example). It has a set of relatively well-defined decision problems for which human information processing research appears very useful. Equally important, some auditors and auditing

---

[6] The recent literature in psychology and in several applied fields reflects the growing concern for the practical usefulness of human information processing research. This concern is also reflected in recent lists of reprints and working papers available from certain organizations or institutes devoted to behavioral decision research. Examples are Paul Slovic's "Decision Research" group in Eugene, Oregon; Kenneth Hammond's "Center for Research on Judgment and Policy" group in the Institute of Behavioral Science at the University of Colorado; and Hillel Einhorn's "Center for Decision Research" group at the Graduate School of Business, University of Chicago.

firms have shown a willingness to consider the potential implications of this research, as well as to support research that they consider useful through financial grants, the provision of subjects and data, and comments on research papers or ideas.

Efforts are needed to "translate" the results and potential implications of human information processing research into a form usable by practitioners. Of course, such efforts require the translator to be knowledgeable about issues faced by practitioners, to be able to distinguish good research from poor research, and to match the implications of good research with his or her knowledge of practical issues. Implementing the results of human information processing research in practice is an important issue, and the future will likely see more attention being devoted to it.

A complementary need at this point is additional research. This should include interpretations of research conducted in other disciplines, as well as rigorous empirical research in accounting guided by the lens and SEU paradigms and by the additional perspectives mentioned earlier. Quality control issues should continue to be emphasized, since poor research will not be useful to either practitioners as a basis for implementation efforts nor to researchers as a basis for additional study. Good human information processing research has the potential for being useful to both groups.

References

Abdel-khalik, A.R., and K. El-Sheshai, "Information Choice and Utilization in an Experiment on Default Prediction," *Journal of Accounting Research* (Autumn 1980), pp. 325-42.

———, and T.F. Keller, *Earnings or Cash Flows: An Experiment on Functional Fixation and the Valuation of the Firm* (American Accounting Association, 1979).

Accounting Principles Board, "Interim Financial Reporting," *APB Opinion No. 28* (AICPA, 1973).

Adelman, L., T.R. Stewart, and K.R. Hammond, "A Case History of the Application of Social Judgment Theory to Policy Formulation," *Policy Sciences* (June 1975), pp. 137-59.

Alberoni, F. "Contribution to the Study of Subjective Probability. I," *Journal of General Psychology* (April 1962), pp. 241-64.

Alker, H.A., and M.G. Hermann, "Are Bayesian Decisions Artifically Intelligent? The Effect of Task and Personality on Conservatism in Processing Information," *Journal of Personality and Social Psychology* (July 1971), pp. 31-41.

Allais, M., "Le Comportement de L'Homme Rationnel Devant le Risque: Critique des Postulates et Axioms de L'Ecole Americaine," *Econometrica* (October 1953), pp. 503-46. (English summary, pp. 503-05).

Allport, F.H., *Theories of Perception and the Concept of Structure* (Wiley, 1955).

Altman, E.I., "Financial Ratios, Discriminant Analysis and the Prediction of Corporate Bankruptcy," *Journal of Finance* (September 1968), pp. 589-609.

———, and T.P. McGough, "Evaluation of a Company as a Going Concern," *The Journal of Accountancy* (December 1974), pp. 50-57.

American Institute of Certified Public Accountants, *Objectives of Financial Statements,* Vols. 1 and 2 (AICPA, 1974).

———, *AICPA Professional Standards,* Vol. 1 (AICPA, 1979).

Anderson, N.H., "Functional Measurement and Psychophysical Judgment," *Psychological Review* (May 1970), pp. 153-70.

———, "Integration Theory and Attitude Change," *Psychological Review* (May 1971), pp. 171-206.

———, "Information Integration Theory: A Brief Survey," in D.H. Krantz, R.C. Atkinson and P. Suppes, eds., *Contemporary Developments in Mathematical Psychology,* Vol. 2 (Freeman, 1974), pp. 236-305.

Anthony, R.N., "Distinguishing Good From Not-So-Good Accounting Research," *Proceedings of the 22nd Annual Institute on Accounting* (Ohio State University, 1960), pp. 65-75.

———, *Planning and Control Systems: A Framework for Analysis* (Harvard University, 1965).

Arditti, F., "Risk and the Required Return on Equity," *Journal of Finance* (March 1967), pp. 19-36.

———, "Another Look at Mutual Fund Performance," *Journal of Financial and Quantitative Analysis* (June 1971), pp. 909-12.

Argyris, C., *The Impact of Budgets on People* (Controllership Foundation, 1952).

Armstrong, W.E., "The Determinateness of the Utility Function," *Economic Journal* (September 1939), pp. 453-67.

———, "Uncertainty and the Utility Function," *Economic Journal* (March 1948), pp. 1-10.

———, "A Note on the Theory of Consumer's Behaviour," *Oxford Economic Papers* (January 1950), pp. 119-22.

———, "Utility and the Theory of Welfare," *Oxford Economic Papers* (October 1951), pp. 259-71.

Arrow, K.J., *Social Choice and Individual Values* (Yale University, 1963).

———, *Essays in the Theory of Risk-Bearing* (Markham, 1971).

Ashton, A.H., "Human Behavior and the Requirements of Normative Decision Theory," unpublished manuscript, University of Texas, 1977.

_________, "The Descriptive Validity of Normative Decision Theory in Auditing Contexts," unpublished Ph.D. dissertation, University of Texas, 1979.

_________, "An Empirical Study of Budget-Related Predictions of Corporate Executives" unpublished manuscript, New York University, 1980. (a) (Forthcoming in *Journal of Accounting Research*.)

_________, "The Descriptive Validity of Normative Decision Theory in Auditing Contexts," unpublished manuscript, New York University, 1980. (b) (Forthcoming in *Journal of Accounting Research*.)

_________, "The Distinction Between Risk and Uncertainty in Real World Decision Settings," unpublished manuscript, New York University, 1980. (c)

Ashton, R.H., "Judgment Formation in the Evaluation of Internal Control: An Application of Brunswik's Lens Model," unpublished Ph.D. dissertation, University of Minnesota, 1973.

_________, "An Experimental Study of Internal Control Judgments," *Journal of Accounting Research* (Spring 1974), pp. 143-57. (a)

_________, "Cue Utilization and Expert Judgments: A Comparison of Independent Auditors with Other Judges," *Journal of Applied Psychology* (August 1974), pp. 437-44. (b)

_________, "The Predictive-Ability Criterion and User Prediction Models," *The Accounting Review* (October 1974), pp. 719-32. (c)

_________, "User Prediction Models in Accounting: An Alternative Use," *The Accounting Review* (October 1975), pp. 710-22. (a)

_________, "Assessing Perceived Similiarity of Judgmental Cues with Hierarchical Cluster Analysis," *Midwest AIDS Proceedings* (1975), pp. 48-51. (b)

_________, "Cognitive Changes Induced by Accounting Changes: Experimental Evidence on the Functional Fixation Hypothesis," *Studies on Human Information Processing in Accounting*, Supplement to *Journal of Accounting Research* (1976), pp. 1-17. (a)

_________, "The Predictive-Ability Criterion and User Prediction Models: A Reply," *The Accounting Review* (July 1976), pp. 680-82. (b)

_________, "The Robustness of Linear Models for Decision Making," *OMEGA, The International Journal of Management Science* (October 1976), pp. 609-15. (c)

_________, "Objectivity of Accounting Measures: A Multirule-Multimeasurer Approach," *The Accounting Review* (July 1977), pp. 567-75.

_________, "Some Implications of Parameter Sensitivity Research for Judgment Modeling in Accounting," *The Accounting Review* (January 1979), pp. 170-79. (a)

_________, "Behavioral Assumptions of Normative Decision Theory: An Experimental Test of the Independence Axiom in an Accounting/Business Context," in T.H. Burns, ed., *Behavioral Experiments in Accounting II* (Ohio State University, 1979), pp. 175-204. (b)

_________, "Comment: Some Observations on Auditors' Evaluations of Internal Accounting Controls," *Journal of Accounting, Auditing and Finance* (Fall 1979), pp. 56-66. (c)

_________, "Review of *Earnings or Cash Flows: An Experiment on Functional Fixation and the Valuation of the Firm,* by A.R. Abdel-khalik and T.F. Keller, *The Accounting Review* (January 1980), pp. 196-97. (a)

_________, "Sensitivity of Multi-Attribute Decision Models to Alternative Specifications of Weighting Parameters," *Journal of Business Research* (September 1980), pp. 341-59. (b)

_________, "A Descriptive Study of Information Evaluation," unpublished manuscript, New York University, 1980. (c) (Forthcoming in *Journal of Accounting Research*.)

_________, and P.R. Brown, "Descriptive Modeling of Auditors' Internal Control Judgments: Replication and Extension," *Journal of Accounting Research* (Spring 1980), pp. 269-77.

_________, and S.S. Kramer, "Students as Surrogates in Behavioral Accounting Research: Some Evidence," *Journal of Accounting Research* (Spring 1980), pp. 1-15.

Atkinson, J.W., "Motivational Determinants of Risk-Taking Behavior," *Psychological Review* (November 1957), pp. 359-72.

Balke, W.W., K.R. Hammond, and G.D. Meyer, "An Alternative Approach to Labor-Management Relations," *Administrative Science Quarterly* (September 1973), pp. 311-26.

Barclay, S., and L.R. Beach, "Combinatorial Properties of Personal Probabilities," *Organizational Behavior and Human Performance* (August 1972), pp. 176-83.

————, L.R. Beach, and W.P. Braithwaite, "Normative Models in the Study of Cognition," *Organizational Behavior and Human Performance* (July 1971), pp. 389-413.

Barefield, R.M., "The Effect of Aggregation on Decision Making Success: A Laboratory Study," *Journal of Accounting Research* (Autumn 1972), pp. 229-42.

Bar-Hillel, M., "On the Subjective Probability of Compound Events," *Organizational Behavior and Human Performance* (June 1973), pp. 396-406.

Barrett, M.J., and J. O'Malley, "Choice-Shifts and Auditor Opinions," *Symposium on Auditing Research* (University of Illinois, 1974), pp. 187-204.

Barron, F.H., "Axiomatic Conjoint Measurement," *Decision Sciences* (July 1977), pp. 548-59.

Beach, B.H., "Expert Judgment About Uncertainty: Bayesian Decision Making in Realistic Settings," *Organizational Behavior and Human Performance* (August 1975), pp. 10-59.

Beach, L.R., "Multiple Regression as a Model for Human Information Utilization," *Organizational Behavior and Human Performance* (August 1967), pp. 276-89.

————, and C.R. Peterson, "Subjective Probabilities for Unions of Events," *Psychonomic Science* (July 15, 1966), pp. 307-08.

————, and T.S. Scopp, "Intuitive Statistical Inferences About Variances," *Organizational Behavior and Human Performance* (May 1968), pp. 109-23.

————, and J.A. Wise, "Subjective Probability and Decision Strategy," *Journal of Experimental Psychology* (January 1969), pp. 133-38.

Beaver, W.H., "Financial Ratios as Predictors of Failure," *Empirical Research in Accounting: Selected Studies, 1966*, Supplement to *Journal of Accounting Research* (1966), pp. 71-111.

————, "Alternative Accounting Measures as Predictors of Failure," *The Accounting Review* (January 1968), pp. 113-22. (a)

————, "The Information Content of Annual Earnings Announcements," in *Empirical Research in Accounting: Selected Studies, 1968*, Supplement to *Journal of Accounting Research* (1968), pp. 67-92. (b)

————, "The Behavior of Security Prices and Its Implications for Accounting Research (Methods)," Supplement to *The Accounting Review* (1972), pp. 407-37.

————, "What Should be the FASB's Objectives?" *The Journal of Accountancy* (August 1973), pp. 49-56.

————, "Implications of Security Price Research for Accounting: A Reply to Bierman," *The Accounting Review* (July 1974), pp. 563-71.

————, *Financial Reporting: An Accounting Revolution* (Prentice-Hall, 1981). (a)

————, "Market Efficiency," *The Accounting Review* (January 1981), pp. 23-37. (b)

————, J.W. Kennelly and W.M. Voss, "Predictive Ability as a Criterion for the Evaluation of Accounting Data," *The Accounting Review* (October 1968), pp. 675-83.

————, P. Kettler and M. Scholes, "The Association Between Market Determined and Accounting Determined Risk Measures," *The Accounting Review* (October 1970), pp. 654-82.

Becker, G.M., and C.G. McClintock, "Value: Behavioral Decision Theory," *Annual Review of Psychology* (1967), pp. 239-86.

Becker, S., "The Behavior of 'Behavioral' Accountants," in R.R. Sterling and W.F. Bentz, eds., *Accounting in Perspective: Contributions to Accounting Thought by Other Disciplines* (South-Western, 1971), pp. 69-78.

Becker, S.W., and F.O. Brownson, "What Price Ambiguity? Or the Role of Ambiguity in Decision-Making," *Journal of Political Economy* (February 1964), pp. 62-73.

Beckwith, N.E., and D.R. Lehmann, "The Importance of Differential Weights in Multiple Attribute Models of Consumer Attitude," *Journal of Marketing Research* (May 1973), pp. 141-45.

Bhaskar, R., and J.F. Dillard, "Human Cognition in Accounting: A Preliminary Analysis," in T.H. Burns, ed., *Behavioral Experiments in Accounting II* (Ohio State University, 1979), pp. 323-85.

Biddle, G.C., and E.J. Joyce, "Heuristics and Biases: Their Implications for Probabilistic Inference in Auditing," unpublished manuscript, University of Chicago, 1978.

————, "The Role of Sample Size in Probabilistic Inference in Auditing," unpublished manuscript, University of Chicago, 1979.

Biggs, S.F., "An Empirical Investigation of the Information Processes Underlying Four Models of Choice Behavior," in T.H. Burns, ed., *Behavioral Experiments in Accounting II* (Ohio State University, 1979), pp. 35-81.

__________, "Financial Analysts' Information Search in the Assessment of Corporate Earning Power," unpublished manuscript, University of Wisconsin, 1980.

__________, and T.J. Mock, "An Investigation of Auditor Decision Processes in the Evaluation of Internal Controls and Audit Scope Decisions," unpublished manuscript, University of Wisconsin, 1980.

Birnbaum, M.H., "The Devil Rides Again: Correlation as an Index of Fit," *Psychological Bulletin* (April 1973), pp. 239-42.

Birnberg, J.G., "Comments on a Paper by David Green," in N. Dopuch and L. Revsine, eds., *Accounting Research 1960-1970: A Critical Evaluation* (University of Illinois, 1973), pp. 126-32.

__________, I.H. Frieze, and M.D. Shields, "The Role of Attribution Theory in Control Systems," *Accounting, Organizations and Society,* Vol. 2, No. 3 (1977), pp. 189-200.

__________, and M.D. Shields, "An Attribution Theory Analysis of Performance Expectation and Variance Investigation Decisions," unpublished manuscript, University of Pittsburgh, 1979.

__________, and D.P. Slevin, "A Note on the Use of Confidence Interval Statements in Financial Reporting," *Journal of Accounting Research* (Spring 1976), pp. 153-57.

Bjorkman, M., "Feedforward and Feedback as Determiners of Knowledge and Policy: Notes on a Neglected Issue," *Scandinavian Journal of Psychology* (Second Quarter 1972), pp. 152-58.

__________, "Inference Behavior in Nonmetric Ecologies," in L. Rappoport and D.A. Summers, eds., *Human Judgment and Social Interaction* (Holt, Rinehart and Winston, 1973).

Blevins, D.E., "Claimed Versus Calculated Cue-Weighting Systems for Screening Employee Applicants," *Journal of Vocational Behavior* (December 1975), pp. 327-36.

Blood, M.R., "The Validity of Importance," *Journal of Applied Psychology* (October 1971), pp. 487-88.

Blum, M.L., and J.C. Naylor, *Industrial Psychology: Its Theoretical and Social Foundations* (Harper and Row, 1968).

Boatsman, J.R., and J.C. Robertson, "Policy-Capturing on Selected Materiality Judgments," *The Accounting Review* (April 1974), pp. 342-52.

Bogartz, R.S., and J.H. Wackwitz, "Polynomial Response Scaling and Functional Measurement," *Journal of Mathematical Psychology* (August 1971), pp. 418-43.

Borch, K., "The Allais Paradox: A Comment," *Behavioral Science* (November 1968), pp. 488-89.

Bowman, E.H., "Consistency and Optimality in Managerial Decision Making," *Management Science* (January 1963), pp. 310-21.

Brehmer, B., "Effects of Communication and Feedback on Cognitive Conflict," *Scandinavian Journal of Psychology* (Third Quarter 1971), pp. 205-16.

__________, "Note on Clinical Judgment and the Formal Characteristics of Clinical Tasks," *Psychological Bulletin* (September 1976), pp. 778-82. (a)

__________, "Social Judgment Theory and the Analysis of Interpersonal Conflict," *Psychological Bulletin* (November 1976), pp. 985-1003. (b)

Brier, G.W., "Verification of Forecasts Expressed in Terms of Probability," *Monthly Weather Review* (1950), pp. 1-3.

Brown, C., "Human Information Processing for Decisions to Investigate Cost Variances," unpublished manuscript, University of Illinois, 1980.

Bruns, W.J., "Inventory Valuation and Management Decisions," *The Accounting Review* (April 1965), pp. 345-57.

__________, "The Accounting Period Concept and Its Effect on Management Decisions," *Empirical Research in Accounting: Selected Studies, 1966,* Supplement to *Journal of Accounting Research* (1966), pp. 1-14.

__________, "Comments on a Paper by David Green," in N. Dopuch and L. Revsine, eds., *Accounting Research 1960-1970: A Critical Evaluation* (University of Illinois, 1973), pp. 116-25.

Brunswik, E., "Thing Constancy as Measured by Correlation Coefficients," *Psychological Review* (January 1940), pp. 69-78.
__________, "Organismic Achievement and Environmental Probability," *Psychological Review* (March 1943), pp. 255-72.
__________, *The Conceptual Framework of Psychology* (University of Chicago, 1952).
__________, "Representative Design and Probabilistic Theory in a Functional Psychology," *Psychological Review* (May 1955), pp. 193-217. (a)
__________, "In Defense of Probabilistic Functionalism: A Reply," *Psychological Review* (May 1955), pp. 236-42. (b)
__________, *Perception and the Representative Design of Psychological Experiments* (University of California, 1956).
Campbell, D.T., "Systematic Error on the Part of Human Links in Communication Systems," *Information and Control* (December 1958), pp. 334-69.
__________, and D.W. Fiske, "Convergent and Discriminant Validation by the Multitrait-Multimethod Matrix," *Psychological Bulletin* (March 1959), pp. 81-105.
__________, and J.C. Stanley, *Experimental and Quasi-Experimental Designs for Research* (Rand-McNally, 1963).
Caplan, E.H., "Accounting Research as an Information Source for Theory Construction," Supplement to *The Accounting Review* (1972), pp. 437-44.
Carroll, J.D., and J.J. Chang, "Analysis of Individual Differences in Multi-Dimensional Scaling via an N-way Generalization of 'Eckart-Young' Decomposition," *Psychometrika* (September 1970), pp. 283-319.
Carroll, J.S., and J.W. Payne, "Judgments About Crime and the Criminal: A Model and a Method for Investigating Parole Decisions," in B.D. Sales, ed., *Perspectives in Law and Psychology: The Criminal Justice System,* Vol. 1 (Plenum, 1977), pp. 191-239.
Casey, C.J., "The Predictive-Ability Criterion and User Prediction Models: A Comment," *The Accounting Review* (July 1976), pp. 677-79.
__________, "Variation in Accounting Information Load: The Effect on Loan Officers' Predictions of Bankruptcy," *The Accounting Review* (January 1980), pp. 36-49. (a)
__________, "The Usefulness of Accounting Ratios for Subjects' Predictions of Corporate Failure: Replication and Extensions," *Journal of Accounting Research* (Autumn 1980), pp. 603-13. (b)
Castellan, N.J., "The Analysis of Multiple Criteria in Multiple-Cue Judgment Tasks," *Organizational Behavior and Human Performance* (October 1972), pp. 242-61.
__________, "Comments on the 'Lens Model' Equation and the Analysis of Multiple-Cue Judgment Tasks," *Psychometrika* (March 1973), pp. 87-100.
__________, "The Effect of Different Types of Feedback in Multiple-Cue Probability Learning," *Organizational Behavior and Human Performance* (February 1974), pp. 44-64.
Cattin, P., "A Predictive-Validity-Based Procedure for Choosing Between Regression and Equal Weights," *Organizational Behavior and Human Performance* (August 1978), pp. 93-102.
Chandler, M.J., "Self-Awareness and Its Relation to Other Parameters of the Clinical Inference Process," *Journal of Consulting and Clinical Psychology* (October 1970), pp. 258-64.
Chang, D.L., and J.G. Birnberg, "Functional Fixity in Accounting Research: Perspective and New Data," *Journal of Accounting Research* (Autumn 1977), pp. 300-12.
Chapman, L.J., "Illusory Correlation in Observational Report," *Journal of Verbal Learning and Verbal Behavior* (February 1967), pp. 151-55.
__________, and J.P. Chapman, "Genesis of Popular but Erroneous Psychodiagnostic Observations," *Journal of Abnormal Psychology* (June 1967), pp. 193-204.
__________, "Illusory Correlation as an Obstacle to the Use of Valid Psychodiagnostic Signs," *Journal of Abnormal Psychology* (June 1969), pp. 271-80.
Charters, W.W., "Constructing a Language and Grammar Scale," *Journal of Educational Research* (April 1920), pp. 249-57.
Chase, C.I., "Computation of Variance Accounted for in Multiple Correlation," *Journal of Experimental Education* (March 1960), pp. 265-66.
Chernoff, H., and M.H. Rizvi, "Effect of Classification Errors on Random Permutations of

Features in Representing Multi-variate Data by Faces," *Journal of the American Statistical Association* (September 1975), pp. 548-54.

Chesley, G.R., "Elicitation of Subjective Probabilities: A Review," *The Accounting Review* (April 1975), pp. 325-37.

————, "The Elicitation of Subjective Probabilities: A Laboratory Study in an Accounting Context," *Journal of Accounting Research* (Spring 1976), pp. 27-48.

————, "Subjective Probability Elicitation: The Effect of Congruity of Datum and Response Mode on Performance," *Journal of Accounting Research* (Spring 1977), pp. 1-11.

————, "Subjective Probability Elicitation Techniques: A Performance Comparison," *Journal of Accounting Research* (Autumn 1978), pp. 225-41.

————, "Procedures for the Communication of Uncertainty in Auditor's Working Papers," in T.H. Burns, ed., *Behavioral Experiments in Accounting II* (Ohio State University, 1979), pp. 115-49.

Chow, G.C., "Tests of Equality Between Sets of Coefficients in Two Linear Regressions," *Econometrica* (October 1960), pp. 591-605.

Christal, R.E., "JAN: A Technique for Analyzing Group Judgment," *Journal of Experimental Education* (Summer 1968), pp. 24-27.

Clarkson, G.P.E., *Portfolio Selection: A Simulation of Trust Investment* (Prentice-Hall, 1962).

Claudy, J.G., "A Comparison of Five Variable Weighting Procedures," *Educational and Psychological Measurement* (Summer 1972), pp. 311-22.

Cochran, W.G., and G.M. Cox, *Experimental Designs* (Wiley, 1957).

Cohen, J., and E.I. Chesnik, "The Doctrine of Psychological Chances," *British Journal of Psychology* (August 1970), pp. 323-34.

————, E.J. Dearnaley, and C.E.M. Hansel, "Skill With Chance: Variations in Estimates of Skill With an Increasing Element of Chance," *British Journal of Psychology* (November 1958), pp. 319-23.

————, and C.E.M. Hansel, "The Idea of a Distribution," *British Journal of Psychology* (May 1955), pp. 111-21. (a)

————, "The Idea of Independence," *British Journal of Psychology* (August 1955), pp. 178-90. (b)

Committee on Accounting Valuation Bases, "Report of the Committee on Accounting Valuation Bases," Supplement to *The Accounting Review* (1972), pp. 535-73.

Committee on Behavioral Science Content of The Accounting Curriculum, "Report of the Committee on Behavioral Science Content of the Accounting Curriculum," Supplement to *The Accounting Review* (1971), pp. 247-85.

Committee on Concepts and Standards for External Financial Reports, *Statement on Accounting Theory and Theory Acceptance* (American Accounting Association, 1977).

Committee on Human Information Processing, "Report of the 1976-77 Committee on Human Information Processing," *American Accounting Association Committee Reports Vol. 78-2* (August 1977).

Committee on the Relationship of Behavioral Science and Accounting, "Report of the Committee on the Relationship of Behavioral Science and Accounting," Supplement to *The Accounting Review* (1974), pp. 127-39.

Conrath, D.W., "From Statistical Decision Theory to Practice: Some Problems With the Transition," *Management Science* (April 1973), pp. 873-83.

Cook, R.L. and T.R. Stewart, "A Comparison of Seven Methods for Obtaining Subjective Descriptions of Judgmental Policy," *Organizational Behavior and Human Performance* (February 1975), pp. 31-45.

Cooke, J.K., "Clinicians' Decisions as a Basis for Deriving Actuarial Formulae," *Journal of Clinical Psychology* (April 1967), pp. 232-33. (a)

————, "MMPI in Actuarial Diagnosis of Psychological Disturbance Among College Males," *Journal of Counseling Psychology* (September 1967), pp. 474-77. (b)

Coombs, C.H., T.G. Bezembinder and F.M. Goode, "Testing Expectation Theories of Decision Making Without Measuring Utility or Subjective Probability," *Journal of Mathematical Psychology* (February 1967), pp. 72-103.

_________ and J.N. Bowen, "A Test of VE-Theories of Risk and the Effect of the Central Limit Theorem," *Acta Psychologica* (January 1971), pp. 15-28.

_________, R.M. Dawes and A. Tversky, *Mathematical Psychology* (Prentice-Hall, 1970).

_________ and L. Huang, "Polynomial Psychophysics of Risk," *Journal of Mathematical Psychology* (June 1970), pp. 317-38.

_________ and D.G. Pruitt, "Components of Risk in Decision Making: Probability and Variance Preferences," *Journal of Experimental Psychology* (November 1960), pp. 265-77.

Corless, J.C., "Assessing Prior Distributions for Applying Bayesian Statistics in Auditing," *The Accounting Review* (July 1972), pp. 556-66.

Cox, D.R., *Planning of Experiments* (Wiley, 1958).

Crandall, V.J., D. Solomon and R. Kellaway, "Expectancy Statements and Decision Times as Functions of Objective Probabilities and Reinforcement Values," *Journal of Personality* (December 1955), pp. 192-203.

_________, D. Solomon, and R. Kellaway, "The Value of Anticipated Events as a Determinant of Probability Learning and Extinction," *Journal of General Psychology* (January 1958), pp. 3-10.

Crosby, M.A., "Implications of Prior Probability Elicitation on Auditor Sample Size Decisions," *Journal of Accounting Research* (Autumn 1980), pp. 585-93.

Cvetkovich, G., "Small Group Dynamics in Extended Judgment Situations," in L. Rappoport and D. Summers, eds., *Human Judgment and Social Interaction* (Holt, Rinehart and Winston, 1973).

Dalkey, N.C., "The Delphi Method: An Experimental Study of Group Opinion," RAND Corporation Report No. RM-5888-PR (1969).

_________, and O. Helmer, "An Experimental Application of the Delphi Method to the Use of Experts," *Management Science* (April 1963), pp. 458-67.

Danos, P., and E.A. Imhoff, Jr., "Auditor Review of Financial Forecasts: An Analysis of Factors Affecting Reasonableness Judgments," unpublished manuscript, University of Michigan, 1980. (Forthcoming in *The Accounting Review).*

Darlington, R.B., "Multiple Regression in Psychological Research and Practice," *Psychological Bulletin* (March 1968), pp. 161-82.

Davenport, W.G., and M.A. Middleton, "Expectation Theories of Decision Making for Duplex Gambles," *Acta Psychologica* (June 1973), pp. 155-72.

Davidson, D., and J. Marschak, "Experimental Tests of a Stochastic Decision Theory," in C.W. Churchman and P. Ratoosh, eds., *Measurement: Definitions and Theories* (Wiley, 1959), pp. 233-69.

Davis, J.M., "The Transitivity of Preferences," *Behavioral Science* (January 1958), pp. 26-33.

Dawes, R.M., "A Case Study of Graduate Admissions: Application of Three Principles of Human Decision Making," *American Psychologist* (February 1971), pp. 180-88.

_________, "The Mind, the Model, and the Task," in F. Restle, R.M. Shiffrin, N.J. Castellan, H.R. Lindman and D.B. Pisoni, eds., *Cognitive Theory*, Vol. 1 (Erlbaum, 1975), pp. 119-29.

_________ and B. Corrigan, "Linear Models in Decision Making," *Psychological Bulletin* (February 1974), pp. 95-106.

Deakin, E.B., "A Discriminant Analysis of Predictors of Business Failure," *Journal of Accounting Research* (Spring 1972), pp. 167-79.

Deane, D.H., K.R. Hammond, and D.A. Summers, "Acquisition and Application of Knowledge in Complex Inference Tasks," *Journal of Experimental Psychology* (January 1972), pp. 20-26.

Demski, J.S., *Information Analysis* (Addison-Wesley, 1972).

_________, "Choice Among Financial Reporting Alternatives," *The Accounting Review* (April 1974), pp. 221-32.

_________, *Information Analysis*, 2nd ed. (Addison-Wesley, 1980).

_________, and G.A. Feltham, *Cost Determination: A Conceptual Approach* (Iowa State University, 1976).

Dermer, J.D., "Cognitive Characteristics and the Perceived Importance of Information," *The Ac-*

counting Review (July 1973), pp. 511-19.

Devine, C.T., "Research Methodology and Accounting Theory Formation," *The Accounting Review* (July 1960), pp. 387-99.

———, "Some Behavioral Aspects of Accounting," *Essays in Accounting Theory,* Vol. 1 (1962), pp. 70-85.

Dickhaut, J.W., "Alternative Information Structures and Probability Revisions," *The Accounting Review* (January 1973), pp. 61-79.

———, and I.R.C. Eggleton, "An Examination of the Processes Underlying Comparative Judgments of Numerical Stimuli," *Journal of Accounting Research* (Spring 1975), pp. 38-72.

Digman, J.M., "Interaction and Non-Linearity in Multivariate Experiment," in R.B. Cattell, ed., *Handbook of Multivariate Experimental Psychology* (Rand-McNally, 1966), pp. 459-75.

Domas, P.A., and C.R. Peterson, "Probabilistic Information Processing Systems: Evaluation with Conditionally Dependent Data," *Organizational Behavior and Human Performance* (February 1972), pp. 77-85.

Douglass, H.R., and P.L. Spencer, "Is It Necessary to Weight Exercises in Standard Tests?," *Journal of Educational Psychology* (February 1923), pp. 109-12.

Driver, M.J., and T.J. Mock, "Human Information Processing, Decision Style Theory, and Accounting Information Systems," *The Accounting Review* (July 1975), pp. 490-508.

DuCharme, W.M., "A Response Bias Explanation of Conservative Human Inference," *Journal of Experimental Psychology* (July 1970), pp. 66-74.

———, and M.L. Donnell, "Intrasubject Comparison of Four Response Modes for 'Subjective Probability' Assessment," *Organizational Behavior and Human Performance* (August 1973), pp. 108-17.

———, and C.R. Peterson, "Intuitive Inference about Normally Distributed Populations," *Journal of Experimental Psychology* (October 1968), pp. 269-75.

Dudycha, A.L., "A Monte Carlo Evaluation of JAN: A Technique for Capturing and Clustering Raters' Policies," *Organizational Behavior and Human Performance* (September 1970), pp. 501-16.

Dudycha, L.W. and J.C. Naylor, "Characteristics of the Human Inference Process in Complex Choice Behavior Situations," *Organizational Behavior and Human Performance* (September 1966), pp. 110-28.

Dyckman, T.R., "On the Investment Decision," *The Accounting Review* (April 1964), pp. 285-95. (a)

———, "The Effects of Alternative Accounting Techniques on Certain Management Decisions," *Journal of Accounting Research* (Spring 1964), pp. 91-107. (b)

———, "On the Effects of Earnings-trend, Size, and Inventory Valuation Procedures in Evaluating a Business Firm," in R.K. Jaedicke, Y. Ijiri, and O. Nielsen, eds., *Research in Accounting Measurement* (American Accounting Association, 1966), pp. 175-85.

———, D.H. Downes, and R.P. Magee, *Efficient Capital Markets and Accounting: A Critical Analysis* (Prentice-Hall, 1975).

———, M. Gibbins, and R.J. Swieringa, "Experimental and Survey Research in Financial Accounting: A Review and Evaluation," in A.R. Abdel-khalik and T.F. Keller, eds., *The Impact of Accounting Research on Practice and Disclosure* (Duke University, 1978), pp. 48-105.

Edmister, R.O., "An Empirical Test of Financial Ratio Analysis for Small Business Failure Prediction," *Journal of Financial and Quantitative Analysis* (March 1972), pp. 1477-93.

Edwards, W., "Probability-Preferences in Gambling," *American Journal of Psychology* (July 1953), pp. 349-64.

———, "Probability-Preferences Among Bets With Differing Expected Values," *American Journal of Psychology* (March 1954), pp. 56-67. (a)

———, "The Reliability of Probability Preferences," *American Journal of Psychology* (March 1954), pp. 68-95. (b)

———, "The Theory of Decision Making," *Psychological Bulletin* (July 1954), pp. 380-417. (c)

__________, "Variance Preferences in Gambling," *American Journal of Psychology* (September 1954), pp. 441-52. (d)

__________, "The Prediction of Decisions Among Bets," *Journal of Experimental Psychology* (September 1955), pp. 201-14.

__________, "Reward Probability, Amount, and Information as Determiners of Sequential Two-Alternative Decisions," *Journal of Experimental Psychology* (September 1956), pp. 177-88.

__________, "Behavioral Decision Theory," *Annual Review of Psychology* (1961), pp. 473-98.

__________, "Utility, Subjective Probability, Their Interaction, and Variance Preferences," *Journal of Conflict Resolution* (March 1962), pp. 42-51. (a)

__________, "Dynamic Decision Theory and Probabilistic Information Processing," *Human Factors* (April 1962), pp. 59-73. (b)

__________, "Conservatism in Human Information Processing," in B. Kleinmuntz, ed., *Formal Representation of Human Judgment* (Wiley, 1968).

__________, "Bayesian and Regression Models of Human Information Processing — A Myopic Perspective," *Organizational Behavior and Human Performance* (November 1971), pp. 639-48.

__________, H. Lindman, and L.D. Phillips, "Emerging Technologies for Making Decisions," *New Directions in Psychology II* (Holt, Rinehart, and Winston, 1965), pp. 261-325.

__________, and L.J. Savage, "Bayesian Statistical Inference for Psychological Research," *Psychological Review* (May 1963), pp. 193-242.

__________, and L.D. Phillips, "Man as Transducer for Probabilities in Bayesian Command and Control Systems," in M.W. Shelly and G.L. Bryan, eds., *Human Judgments and Optimality* (Wiley, 1964).

__________, W.L. Hays, and B.C. Goodman, "Probabilistic Information Processing Systems: Design and Evaluation," *IEEE Transactions on Systems Science and Cybernetics* (September 1968), pp. 248-65.

Eggleton, I.R.C., "Patterns, Prototypes, and Predictions: An Exploratory Study," *Studies on Human Information Processing in Accounting,* Supplement to *Journal of Accounting Research* (1976), pp. 68-131.

Einhorn, H.J., "The Use of Nonlinear, Noncompensatory Models in Decision Making," *Psychological Bulletin* (March 1970), pp. 221-30.

__________, "Use of Nonlinear, Noncompensatory Models as a Function of Task and Amount of Information," *Organizational Behavior and Human Performance* (January 1971), pp. 1-27.

__________, "Expert Measurement and Mechanical Combination," *Organizational Behavior and Human Performance* (February 1972), pp. 86-106.

__________, "Expert Judgment: Some Necessary Conditions and an Example," *Journal of Applied Psychology* (October 1974), pp. 562-71.

__________, "A Synthesis: Accounting and Behavioral Science," *Studies on Human Information Processing in Accounting*, Supplement to *Journal of Accounting Research* (1976), pp. 196-206.

__________, and R.M. Hogarth, "Unit Weighting Schemes for Decision Making," *Organizational Behavior and Human Performance* (April 1975), pp. 171-92.

__________, "Behavioral Decision Theory: Processes of Judgment and Choice," *Annual Review of Psychology* (1981), pp. 53-88.

__________, and E. Klempner, "Quality of Group Judgment," *Psychological Bulletin* (January 1977), pp. 158-72.

__________, D.N. Kleinmuntz, and B. Kleinmuntz, "Linear Regression *and* Process-Tracing Models of Judgment," *Psychological Review* (September 1979), pp. 465-85.

Elgers, P.T., "Accounting-Based Risk Predictions: A Re-examination," *The Accounting Review* (July 1980), pp. 389-408.

Ellsberg, D., "Risk, Ambiguity, and the Savage Axioms," *Quarterly Journal of Economics* (November 1961), pp. 643-69.

__________, "Reply," *Quarterly Journal of Economics* (May 1963), pp 336-42.

Emery, D.R., "DIST: A Numerical Conjoint Measurement Program Designed to Scale Data to a

Distributive Model in Three Dimensions," *Journal of Marketing Research* (August 1977), pp. 413-14. (a)

———, "DULDST: A Numerical Conjoint Measurement Program Designed to Scale Data to a Dual-Distributive Model in Three Dimensions," *Journal of Marketing Research* (November 1977), pp. 558-59. (b)

———, and F.H. Barron, "Axiomatic and Numerical Conjoint Measurement: An Evaluation of Diagnostic Efficacy," *Psychometrika* (June 1979), pp. 195-210.

Englehart, M.D., "The Technique of Path Coefficients," *Psychometrika* (December 1936), pp. 287-93.

Epstein, E.S., "A Bayesian Approach to Decision Making in Applied Meteorology," *Journal of Applied Meteorology* (1962), pp. 169-77.

Ericsson, K.A. and H.A. Simon, "Retrospective Verbal Reports as Data," unpublished manuscript, Carnegie-Mellon University, 1978.

———, "Thinking-Aloud Protocols as Data: Effects of Verbalization," unpublished manuscript, Carnegie-Mellon University, 1979.

Eskew, R.K., "The Forecasting Ability of Accounting Risk Measures: Some Additional Evidence," *The Accounting Review* (January 1979), pp. 107-18.

Ewen, R.B., "Weighting Components of Job Satisfaction," *Journal of Applied Psychology* (February 1967), pp. 68-73.

Fama, E.F., and M.H. Miller, *The Theory of Finance* (Dryden, 1972).

Feather, N.T., "Subjective Probability and Decision Under Uncertainty," *Psychological Review* (May 1959), pp. 150-64.

Federer, W.T., *Experimental Design* (Macmillan, 1955).

Felix, W.L., "Evidence on Alternative Means of Assessing Prior Probability Distributions for Audit Decision Making," *The Accounting Review* (October 1976), pp. 800-07.

Feltham, G.A., *Information Evaluation* (American Accounting Association, 1972).

———, and J.S. Demski, "The Use of Models in Information Evaluation," *The Accounting Review* (October 1970), pp. 623-40.

Financial Accounting Standards Board, "Accounting for Contingencies," *FASB Statement No. 5* (FASB, 1975).

———, *Conceptual Framework for Financial Accounting and Reporting: Elements of Financial Statements and Their Measurement* (FASB, 1976).

———, "Objectives of Financial Reporting by Business Enterprises," *Statement of Financial Accounting Concepts No. 1* (FASB, 1978).

Firth, M., "Consensus Views and Judgment Models in Materiality Decisions," *Accounting, Organizations and Society*, Vol. 4, No. 4 (1979), pp. 283-95.

Fischer, G.W., "Multidimensional Utility Models for Risky and Riskless Choice," *Organizational Behavior and Human Performance* (October 1976), pp. 127-46.

Fischhoff, B., "Hindsight†Foresight: The Effect of Outcome Knowledge on Judgment Under Uncertainty," *Journal of Experimental Psychology: Human Perception and Performance* (May 1975), pp. 288-99.

———, "Attribution Theory and Judgment Under Uncertainty," in J.H. Harvey, W.J. Ickes, and R.F. Kidd, eds., *New Directions in Attribution Research* (Erlbaum, 1976), pp. 421-52.

———, "Perceived Informativeness of Facts," *Journal of Experimental Psychology: Human Perception and Performance* (May 1977), pp. 349-58.

———, and R. Beyth, "'I Knew It Would Happen' — Remembered Probabilities of Once-Future Things," *Organizational Behavior and Human Performance* (February 1975), pp. 1-16.

Fishburn, P.C., "Theory Versus Practice in Risk Analysis: An Empirical Study: A Comment," *The Accounting Review* (July 1976), pp. 657-62.

Ford, D., G. Huber, and D. Gustafson, "Predicting Job Choices with Models that Contain Subjective Probability Judgments: An Empirical Comparison of Five Models," *Organizational Behavior and Human Performance* (June 1972), pp. 397-416.

Friedman, M., "The Methodology of Positive Economics," in M. Friedman, ed., *Essays in Positive Economics* (University of Chicago, 1953), pp. 3-43.

Gaumnitz, B.R., T.R. Nunamaker, J.J. Surdick, and M.F. Thomas, "Auditor Consensus in Internal Control Evaluation and Audit Program Planning," unpublished manuscript, University of Wisconsin, 1980. (Forthcoming in *Journal of Accounting Research.*)

Gettys, C., and T.A. Willke, "The Application of Bayes' Theorem When the True Data State is Uncertain," *Organizational Behavior and Human Performance* (May 1969), pp. 125-41.

Ghiselli, E.E., *Theory of Psychological Measurement* (McGraw-Hill, 1964).

Gibbins, M., "Human Inference, Heuristics and Auditors' Judgment Processes," *CICA Auditing Research Symposium*, 1977.

Glass, G.V., and A.R. Hakstian, "Measures of Association in Comparative Experiments: Their Development and Interpretation," *American Educational Research Journal* (May 1969), pp. 403-14.

Goldberg, L.R., "Simple Models or Simple Processes? Some Research on Clinical Judgments," *American Psychologist* (July 1968), pp. 483-96.

_________, "Man Versus Model of Man: A Rationale, Plus Some Evidence, for a Method of Improving on Clinical Inferences," *Psychological Bulletin* (June 1970), pp. 422-32.

_________, "Five Models of Clinical Judgment: An Empirical Comparison Between Linear and Nonlinear Representations of the Human Inference Process," *Organizational Behavior and Human Performance* (July 1971), pp. 458-79.

_________, "Man Versus Model of Man: Just How Conflicting is That Evidence?," *Organizational Behavior and Human Performance* (June 1976), pp. 13-22.

_________, and C.E. Werts, "The Reliability of Clinicians' Judgments: A Multitrait-Multimethod Approach," *Journal of Consulting Psychology* (June 1966), pp. 199-206.

Golding, S.L., and L.G. Rorer, "Illusory Correlation and Subjective Judgment," *Journal of Abnormal Psychology* (June 1972), pp. 249-60.

Gonedes, N.J., and N. Dopuch, "Capital Market Equilibrium, Information Production, and Selecting Accounting Techniques: Theoretical Framework and Review of Empirical Work," *Studies on Financial Accounting Objectives,* Supplement to *Journal of Accounting Research* (1974), pp. 48-129. (a)

_________, and N. Dopuch, "A Reply," *Studies on Financial Accounting Objectives*, Supplement to *Journal of Accounting Research* (1974), pp. 158-69. (b)

_________, and Y. Ijiri, "Improving Subjective Probability Assessment for Planning and Control in Team-Like Organizations," *Journal of Accounting Research* (Autumn 1974), pp. 251-69.

Grant, D.L., and D.W. Bray, "Validation of Employment Tests for Telephone Company Installation and Repair Occupations," *Journal of Applied Psychology* (February 1970), pp. 7-14.

Green, D.M., and J.A. Swets, *Signal Detection Theory and Psychophysics* (Krieger, 1974).

Green, D.O., "Behavioral Science and Accounting Research," in N. Dopuch and L. Revsine, eds., *Accounting Research 1960-1970: A Critical Evaluation* (University of Illinois, 1973), pp. 93-104.

Green, P.E., "On the Robustness of Multidimensional Scaling Techniques," *Journal of Marketing Research* (February 1975), pp. 73-81.

_________, F.J. Carmone, and Y. Wind, "Subjective Evaluation Models and Conjoint Measurement," *Behavioral Science* (May 1972), pp. 288-99.

_________, and V.R. Rao, "Conjoint Measurement for Quantifying Judgmental Data," *Journal of Marketing Research* (August 1971), pp. 355-63.

_________, and D.S. Tull, *Research for Marketing Decisions* (Prentice-Hall, 1975).

Greer, W.R., "Theory Versus Practice in Risk Analysis: An Empirical Study," *The Accounting Review* (July 1974), pp. 496-505.

_________, "Theory Versus Practice in Risk Analysis: An Empirical Study: A Reply," *The Accounting Review* (July 1976), p. 663.

_________, and T.D. Skekel, "Theory Versus Practice in Risk Analysis: A Reply," *The Accounting Review* (October 1975), pp. 839-43.

Grether, D.M., and C.R. Plott, "Economic Theory of Choice and the Preference Reversal Phenomenon," *American Economic Review* (September 1979), pp. 623-38.

Griswold, B.J., and R.D. Luce, "Choices Among Uncertain Outcomes: A Test of a Decomposition

and Two Assumptions of Transitivity," *American Journal of Psychology* (March 1962), pp. 35-44.
Gulliksen, H., *Theory of Mental Tests* (Wiley, 1950).
Gustafson, D.H., "Evaluation of Probabilistic Information Processing in Medical Decision Making," *Organizational Behavior and Human Performance* (February 1969), pp. 20-34.
Hamilton, R.E., and W.F. Wright, "The Evaluation of Internal Controls Over Payroll," unpublished manuscript, Stanford University, 1977.
_________, "Empirical Analysis of Internal Control Judgments," unpublished manuscript, University of Minnesota, 1980.
Hammond, K.R., "Probabilistic Functioning and the Clinical Method," *Psychological Review* (July 1955), pp. 255-62.
_________, "New Directions in Research on Conflict Resolution," *Journal of Social Issues* (July 1965), pp. 44-66.
_________, ed., *The Psychology of Egon Brunswik* (Holt, Rinehart, and Winston, 1966).
_________, "Computer Graphics as an Aid to Learning," *Science* (May 1971), pp. 903-08.
_________, "The Cognitive Conflict Paradigm," in L. Rappoport and D.A. Summers, eds., *Human Judgment and Social Interaction* (Holt, Rinehart and Winston, 1973), pp. 188-205.
_________, and B. Brehmer, "Quasi-Rationality and Distrust: Implications for International Conflict," in L. Rappoport and D.A. Summers, eds., *Human Judgment and Social Interaction* (Holt, Rinehart, and Winston, 1973), pp. 338-91.
_________, C.J. Hursch, and F.J. Todd, "Analyzing the Components of Clinical Inference," *Psychological Review* (November 1964), pp. 438-56.
_________, T.R. Stewart, B. Brehmer, and D.O. Steinmann, "Social Judgment Theory," in M. Kaplan and S. Schwartz, eds., *Human Judgments and Decision Processes* (Academic Press, 1975), pp. 271-312.
_________ and D.A. Summers, "Cognitive Dependence on Linear and Nonlinear Cues," *Psychological Review* (May 1965), pp. 215-24.
_________, "Cognitive Control," *Psychological Review* (January 1972), pp. 58-67.
_________, and D.H. Deane, "Negative Effects of Outcome Feedback in Multiple-Cue Probability Learning," *Organizational Behavior and Human Performance* (February 1973), pp. 30-34.
_________, F.J. Todd, M.M. Wilkins, and T.O. Mitchell, "Cognitive Conflict Between Persons: Application of the 'Lens Model' Paradigm," *Journal of Experimental Social Psychology* (October 1966), pp. 343-60.
Hampton, J.M., P.G. Moore, and H. Thomas, "Subjective Probability and Its Measurement," *Journal of the Royal Statistical Society*, Series A, Part I (1973), pp. 21-42.
Harrell, A.M., "The Decision-Making Behavior of Air Force Officers and the Management Control Process," *The Accounting Review* (October 1977), pp. 833-41.
Hayes, J.R., "Strategies in Judgmental Research," in B. Kleinmuntz, ed., *Formal Representation of Human Judgment* (Wiley, 1968).
Hays, W.L., *Statistics* (Holt, Rinehart and Winston, 1973).
Herman, L.M., and H.P. Bahrick, "Information Encoding and Decision Time as Variables in Human Choice Behavior," *Journal of Experimental Psychology* (May 1966), pp. 718-24.
Hilton, R.W., "Integrating Normative and Descriptive Theories of Information Processing," *Journal of Accounting Research* (Autumn 1980), pp. 477-505.
Hirsch, M.L., "Disaggregated Probabilistic Accounting Information: The Effect of Sequential Events on Expected Value Maximization Decisions," *Journal of Accounting Research* (Autumn 1978), pp. 254-69.
Hodges, B.H., "Adding and Averaging Models for Information Integration," *Psychological Review*, (January 1973), pp. 80-84.
Hoepfl, R.T., and G.P. Huber, "A Study of Self-Explicated Utility Models," *Behavioral Science* (September 1970), pp. 408-14.
Hoffman, P.J., "The Paramorphic Representation of Clinical Judgment," *Psychological Bulletin* (March 1960), pp. 116-31.
_________, "Assessment of the Independent Contributions of Predictors," *Psychological Bulletin* (January 1962), pp. 77-80.

————, "Cue-Consistency and Configurality in Human Judgment," in B. Kleinmuntz, ed., *Formal Representation of Human Judgment* (Wiley, 1968).

————, P. Slovic and L.G. Rorer, "An Analysis-of-Variance Model for the Assessment of Configural Cue Utilization in Clinical Judgment," *Psychological Bulletin* (May 1968), pp. 338-49.

Hofstedt, T.R., "A State-of-the-Art Analysis of Behavioral Accounting Research," *Journal of Contemporary Business* (Autumn 1975), pp. 27-49.

————, and G.D. Hughes, "An Experimental Study of the Judgment Element in Disclosure Decisions," *The Accounting Review* (April 1977), pp. 379-95.

————, and J.C. Kinard, "A Strategy for Behavioral Accounting Research," *The Accounting Review* (January 1970), pp. 38-54.

Hogarth, R.M., "Cognitive Processes and the Assessment of Subjective Probability Distributions," *Journal of the American Statistical Association* (June 1975), pp. 271-89.

————, "Functional and Dysfunctional Aspects of Judgmental Heuristics: A Dynamic Perspective," unpublished manuscript, University of Chicago, 1979.

————, *Judgement and Choice: The Psychology of Decision* (Wiley, 1980).

Holt, J.O., and T.S. Wallsten, "A User's Manual for CONJOINT: A Computer Program for Evaluating Certain Conjoint-Measurement Axioms," *Research Memorandum No. 42*, L.L. Thurstone Psychometric Laboratory, University of North Carolina, 1974.

Holt, R.R., "Clinical *and* Statistical Prediction: A Reformulation and Some New Data," *Journal of Abnormal and Social Psychology* (January 1958), pp. 1-12.

————, "Yet Another Look at Clinical and Statistical Prediction: Or, is Clinical Psychology Worthwhile?" *American Psychologist* (April 1970), pp. 337-49.

Hoskins, C.G., "Theory Versus Practice in Risk Analysis: An Empirical Study: A Comment," *The Accounting Review* (October 1975), pp. 835-38.

Huber, G.P., "Multi-Attribute Utility Models: A Review of Field and Field-Like Studies," *Management Science* (June 1974), pp. 1393-1402. (a)

————, "Methods for Quantifying Subjective Probabilities and Multi-Attribute Utilities," *Decision Sciences* (July 1974), pp. 430-58. (b)

————, V.K. Sahney, and D.L. Ford, "A Study of Subjective Evaluation Models," *Behavioral Science* (November 1969), pp. 483-89.

Hull, J., P.G. Moore, and H. Thomas, "Utility and Its Measurement," *Journal of the Royal Statistical Society*, Series A, Part 2 (1973), pp. 226-47.

Hursch, C.J., K.R. Hammond, and J.L. Hursch, "Some Methodological Considerations in Multiple Cue Probability Studies," *Psychological Review* (January 1964), pp. 42-60.

Ijiri, Y., *Theory of Accounting Measurement* (American Accounting Association, 1975).

————, and R.S. Kaplan, "A Model for Integrating Sampling Objectives in Auditing," *Journal of Accounting Research* (Spring 1971), pp. 73-87.

Irwin, F.W., "The Realism of Expectations," *Psychological Review* (March 1944), pp. 120-26.

————, "Stated Expectations as Functions of Probability and Desirability of Outcomes," *Journal of Personality* (March 1953), pp. 329-35.

————, and C.N. Graae, "Tests of the Discontinuity Hypothesis of the Effects of Independent Outcome Values Upon Bets," *Journal of Experimental Psychology* (March 1968), pp. 444-49.

————, and M.J. Metzger, "Effects of Probabilistic Independent Outcomes Upon Prediction," *Psychonomic Science* (May 15, 1966), pp. 79-80.

————, "Effects of Independent Outcome-Values of Past Events Upon Subsequent Choices," *Psychonomic Science* (December 25, 1967), pp. 613-14.

————, and W.A.S. Smith, "Value, Cost, and Information as Determiners of Decision," *Journal of Experimental Psychology* (September 1957), pp. 229-32.

————, and J.G. Snodgrass, "Effects of Independent and Dependent Outcome Values Upon Bets," *Journal of Experimental Psychology* (February 1966), pp. 282-85.

Jenkins, H.M. and W.C. Ward, "Judgment of Contingency Between Responses and Outcomes," *Psychological Monographs: General and Applied* (1965). (Whole No. 594)

Jensen, M.C., "Capital Markets: Theory and Evidence" *Bell Journal of Economics and Management Science* (Autumn 1972), pp. 357-98.

Jensen, R.E., "An Experimental Design for Study of Effects of Accounting Variations in Decision Making," *Journal of Accounting Research* (Autumn 1966), pp. 224-38.

Jessor, R., and J. Readio, "The Influence of the Value of an Event Upon the Expectancy of its Occurrence," *Journal of General Psychology* (January 1957), pp. 219-28.

Jiambalvo, J., "Prediction Achievement and Simulated Decision Makers as an Extension of the Predictive Ability Criterion: Some Comments," *The Accounting Review* (July 1976), pp. 667-71.

Johnson, S.C., "Hierarchical Clustering Schemes," *Psychometrika* (September 1967), pp. 241-54.

Joyce, E.J., "Expert Judgment in Audit Program Planning," *Studies on Human Information Processing in Accounting,* Supplement to *Journal of Accounting Research* (1976), pp. 29-60.

__________, and G.C. Biddle, "Are Auditors' Judgments Sufficiently Regressive?," unpublished manuscript, University of Chicago, 1979. (a) (Forthcoming in *Journal of Accounting Research.*)

__________, "Anchoring and Adjustment in Probabilistic Inference in Auditing," unpublished manuscript, University of Chicago, 1979. (b) (Forthcoming in *Journal of Accounting Research.*)

Kahneman, D., and A. Tversky, "Subjective Probability: A Judgment of Representativeness," *Cognitive Psychology* (July 1972), pp. 430-54.

__________, "On the Psychology of Prediction," *Psychological Review* (July 1973), pp. 237-51.

__________, "Prospect Theory: An Analysis of Decision Under Risk," *Econometrica* (March 1979), pp. 263-91.

Kaplan, R.J., and J.R. Newman, "Studies in Probabilistic Information Processing," *IEEE Transactions on Human Factors in Electronics* (1966), pp. 49-63.

Kelley, H.H., "Attribution Theory in Social Psychology," in D. Levine, ed., *Nebraska Symposium on Motivation* (University of Nebraska Press, 1967), pp. 192-240.

__________, "The Process of Causal Attribution," *American Psychologist* (February 1973), pp. 107-28.

Kempthorne, O., *The Design and Analysis of Experiments* (Wiley, 1952).

__________, and L. Folks, *Probability, Statistics, and Data Analysis* (Iowa State University Press, 1971).

Kennedy, H.A., "A Behavioral Study of the Usefulness of Four Financial Ratios," *Journal of Accounting Research* (Spring 1975), pp. 97-116.

__________, "Human Information Processing in Auditing: The Lens Model and Auditors' Judgments," *CICA Auditing Research Symposium,* 1977.

Kessler, L., and R.H. Ashton, "Feedback and Prediction Achievement in Financial Analysis," unpublished manuscript, Duke University, 1980. (Forthcoming in *Journal of Accounting Research.*)

Keys, D.E., "Confidence Interval Financial Statements: An Empirical Investigation," *Journal of Accounting Research* (Autumn 1978), pp. 389-99.

Kida, T., "An Investigation Into Auditors' Continuity and Related Qualification Judgments," *Journal of Accounting Research* (Autumn 1980), pp. 506-23.

Kiger, J.E., "An Empirical Investigation of NYSE Volume and Price Reactions to the Announcement of Quarterly Earnings," *Journal of Accounting Research* (Spring 1972), pp. 113-28.

King, B., "Stepwise Clustering Procedures," *Journal of the American Statistical Association* (March 1967), pp. 86-101.

Kinney, W.R., "A Decision Theory Approach to the Sampling Problem in Auditing," *Journal of Accounting Research* (Spring 1975), pp. 117-32. (a)

__________, "Decision Theory Aspects of Internal Control System Design/Compliance and Substantive Tests," *Studies on Statistical Methodology in Auditing,* Supplement to *Journal of Accounting Research* (1975), pp. 14-29. (b)

__________, and W.C. Uecker, "Mitigating the Consequences of Anchoring in Auditor Judgments," unpublished manuscript, University of Iowa, 1980.

Kleinmuntz, B., "The Processing of Clinical Information by Man and Machine," in B. Kleinmuntz, ed., *Formal Representation of Human Judgment* (Wiley, 1968), pp. 149-88.

Kogan, N., and M.A. Wallach, *Risk Taking: A Study in Cognition and Personality* (Holt, Rinehart and Winston, 1964).

__________, "Risk Taking as a Function of the Situation, the Person, and the Group," *New Directions in Psychology III* (Holt, Rinehart, and Winston, 1967).

Koopmans, T.C., "The Construction of Economic Knowledge," in T.C. Koopmans, ed., *Three Essays on the State of Economic Science* (McGraw-Hill, 1957), pp. 127-66.

Korman, A.K., "The Prediction of Managerial Performance: A Review," *Personnel Psychology* (Autumn 1968), pp. 295-322.

Kort, F., "A Nonlinear Model for the Analysis of Judicial Decisions," *American Political Science Review* (June 1968), pp. 546-55.

Krantz, D.H., R.D. Luce, P. Suppes and A. Tversky, *Foundations of Measurement*, Vol. 1 (Academic Press, 1971).

__________, and A. Tversky, "Conjoint-Measurement Analysis of Composition Rules in Psychology," *Psychological Review* (March 1971), pp. 151-69.

Kraus, A., and R.H. Litzenberger, "Skewness Preference and the Valuation of Risk Assets," *Journal of Finance* (September 1976), pp. 1085-1100.

Kruskal, J.B., "Analysis of Factorial Experiments by Estimating Monotone Transformations of the Data," *Journal of the Royal Statistical Society*, Series B (1965), pp. 251-63.

Kuhn, T.S., *The Structure of Scientific Revolutions* (University of Chicago, 1962).

Kunreuther, H., "Extensions of Bowman's Theory on Managerial Decision Making," *Management Science* (April 1969), pp. 415-39.

Lathrop, R.G., "Perceived Variability," *Journal of Experimental Psychology* (April 1967), pp. 498-502.

Lawshe, C.H., and R.E. Schucker, "The Relative Efficiency of Four Test Weighting Methods in Multiple Prediction," *Educational and Psychological Measurement* (Spring 1959), pp. 103-14.

Lee, J.C., and R.B. Tucker, "An Investigation of Clinical Judgment: A Study in Method," *Journal of Abnormal and Social Psychology* (April 1962), pp. 272-80.

Lee, W., "Preference Strength, Expected Value Difference, and Expected Regret Ratio," *Psychological Bulletin* (March 1971), pp. 186-91. (a)

__________, "The Effects of Expected Value Difference and Expected Regret Ratio on Preference Strength," *American Journal of Psychology* (June 1971), pp. 194-204. (b)

__________, *Decision Theory and Human Behavior* (Wiley, 1971). (c)

Lewis, B.L., "Expert Judgment in Auditing: An Expected Utility Approach," *Journal of Accounting Research* (Autumn 1980), pp. 594-602.

Libby, R., "Accounting Ratios and the Prediction of Failure: Some Behavioral Evidence," *Journal of Accounting Research* (Spring 1975), pp. 150-61. (a)

__________, "The Use of Simulated Decision Makers in Information Evaluation," *The Accounting Review* (July 1975), pp. 475-89. (b)

__________, "Man Versus Model of Man: Some Conflicting Evidence," *Organizational Behavior and Human Performance* (June 1976), pp. 1-12. (a)

__________, "Man Versus Model of Man: The Need for a Nonlinear Model," *Organizational Behavior and Human Performance* (June 1976), pp. 23-26. (b)

__________, "Prediction Achievement as an Extension of the Predictive Ability Criterion: A Reply," *The Accounting Review* (July 1976), pp. 672-76. (c)

__________, "Discussion of Cognitive Changes Induced by Accounting Changes: Experimental Evidence on the Functional Fixation Hypothesis," *Studies on Human Information Processing in Accounting,* Supplement to *Journal of Accounting Research* (1976), pp. 18-24. (d)

__________, "Bankers' and Auditors' Perceptions of the Message Communicated by the Audit Report," *Journal of Accounting Research* (Spring 1979), pp. 99-122. (a)

__________, "The Impact of Uncertainty Reporting on the Loan Decision," *Selections from the Research Opportunities in Auditing Program,* Supplement to *Journal of Accounting Research* (1979), pp. 35-57. (b)

__________, *Accounting and Human Information Processing: Theory and Applications* (Prentice-Hall, 1981).

__________, and R.K. Blashfield, "Performance of a Composite as a Function of the Number of Judges," *Organizational Behavior and Human Performance* (April 1978), pp. 121-29.

__________, and P.C. Fishburn, "Behavioral Models of Risk Taking in Business Decisions: A Survey and Evaluation," *Journal of Accounting Research* (Autumn 1977), pp. 272-92.

__________, and B.L. Lewis, "Human Information Processing Research in Accounting: The State of the Art," *Accounting, Organizations and Society*, Vol. 2, No. 3 (1977), pp. 245-68.

__________, "Human Information Processing Research in Accounting: The State of the Art in 1981," unpublished manuscript, University of Michigan, 1981.

Lichtenstein, S., "Bases for Preferences Among Three-Outcome Bets," *Journal of Experimental Psychology* (February 1965), pp. 162-69.

__________, and B. Fischhoff, "Do Those Who Know More Also Know More About How Much They Know?," *Organizational Behavior and Human Performance* (December 1977), pp. 159-83.

__________, and L.D. Phillips, "Calibration of Probabilities: The State of the Art," in H. Jungermann and G. deZeeuw, eds., *Decision Making and Change in Human Affairs* (Reidel, 1977), pp. 275-324.

Lichtenstein, S., and P. Slovic, "Reversals of Preference Between Bids and Choices in Gambling Decisions," *Journal of Experimental Psychology* (July 1971), pp. 46-55.

__________, "Response-Induced Reversals of Preference in Gambling: An Extended Replication in Las Vegas," *Journal of Experimental Psychology* (November 1973), pp. 16-20.

__________, and D. Zink, "Effect of Instruction in Expected Value on Optimality of Gambling Decisions," *Journal of Experimental Psychology* (February 1969), pp. 236-40.

Lindell, M.K., "Cognitive and Outcome Feedback in Multiple-Cue Probability Learning Tasks," *Journal of Experimental Psychology: Human Learning and Memory* (November 1976), pp. 739-45.

Lindman, H.R., "Inconsistent Preferences Among Gambles," *Journal of Experimental Psychology* (August 1971), pp. 390-97.

Lingoes, J.C., "An IBM-7090 Program for Guttman-Lingoes Conjoint Measurement, I," *Behavioral Science* (November 1967), pp. 501-02.

Linn, R.L., and C.E. Werts, "Assumptions in Making Causal Inferences from Part Correlations, Partial Correlations, and Partial Regression Coefficients," *Psychological Bulletin* (November 1969), pp. 307-10.

Lintner, J., "The Aggregation of Investors' Diverse Judgments and Preferences in Purely Competitive Security Markets," *Journal of Financial and Quantitative Analysis* (December 1969), pp. 347-400.

Littig, L.W., "Effects of Skill and Chance Orientations on Probability Preferences," *Psychological Reports* (February 1962), pp. 67-70.

Lodwick, G.S., "Computer-aided Diagnosis in Radiology: A Research Plan," *Investigative Radiology* (January - February 1966), pp. 72-80.

__________, A.H. Turner, L.B. Lusted, and A.W. Templeton, "Computer-aided Analysis of Radiographic Images," *Journal of Chronic Diseases* (1966), pp. 485-96.

Luce, R.D., "Semiorders and a Theory of Utility Discrimination," *Econometrica* (April 1956), pp. 178-91.

__________, and P. Suppes, "Preferences, Utility and Subjective Probability," in R.D. Luce, R.R. Bush, and E. Galanter, eds., *Handbook of Mathematical Psychology* (Wiley, 1965), pp. 249-410.

__________, and J.W. Tukey, "Simultaneous Conjoint Measurement: A New Type of Fundamental Measurement," *Journal of Mathematical Psychology* (February 1964), pp. 1-27.

MacCrimmon, K.R., "An Experimental Study of the Decision Making Behavior of Business Executives," unpublished Ph.D. dissertation, University of California at Los Angeles, 1965.

__________, "Descriptive and Normative Implications of the Decision-Theory Postulates," in K. Borch and J. Mossin, eds., *Risk and Uncertainty* (Macmillan, 1968), pp. 3-23.

__________, and S. Larsson, "Utility Theory: Axioms Versus 'Paradoxes'," University of British Columbia Working Paper No. 311 (May 1975), forthcoming in M. Allais and O. Hagen, eds., *Rational Decisions Under Uncertainty*, special volume of *Theory and Decision*.

Magee, R.P., "A Simulation Analysis of Alternative Cost Variance Investigation Models," *The Accounting Review* (July 1976), pp. 529-44.

__________, and J.W. Dickhaut, "Effects of Compensation Plans on Heuristics in Cost Variance

Investigations," *Journal of Accounting Research* (Autumn 1978), pp. 294-314.

Maguire, T.O., and G.V. Glass, "Component Profile Analysis (COPAN) — An Alternative to PROF," *Educational and Psychological Measurement* (Winter 1968), pp. 1021-33.

Mao, J.C.T., "Survey of Capital Budgeting: Theory and Practice," *Journal of Finance* (May 1970), pp. 349-60.

Markowitz, H., "Portfolio Selection," *Journal of Finance* (March 1952), pp. 77-91.

Marks, D.F., and J.K. Clarkson, "An Explanation of Conservatism in the Bookbag-and-Poker-chip Situation," *Acta Psychologica* (April 1972), pp. 145-60.

Marks, R.W., "The Effect of Probability, Desirability and 'Privilege' on the Stated Expectations of Children," *Journal of Personality* (March 1951), pp. 332-51.

Marschak, J., "Decision Making: Economic Aspects," in D.L. Sills, ed., *International Encyclopedia of the Social Sciences* (Macmillan, 1968), pp. 42-55.

_________, *Economic Information, Decision, and Prediction* (Reidel, 1974).

_________, and R. Radner, *Economic Theory of Teams* (Yale University Press, 1972).

Marschak, T.A., "Economic Theories of Organization," in J.G. March, ed., *Handbook of Organizations* (Rand-McNally, 1965), pp. 423-50.

Martin, D.W., and C.F. Gettys, "Feedback and Response Mode in Performing a Bayesian Decision Task," *Journal of Applied Psychology* (October 1969), pp. 413-18.

May, K.O., "Intransitivity, Utility, and the Aggregation of Preference Patterns," *Econometrica* (January 1954), pp. 1-13.

May, R.G., and G.L. Sundem, "Cost of Information and Security Prices: Market Association Tests for Accounting Policy Decisions," *The Accounting Review* (January 1973), pp. 80-94.

_________, "Research for Accounting Policy: An Overview," *The Accounting Review* (October 1976), pp. 747-63.

Mayer-Sommer, A.P., "Understanding and Acceptance of the Efficient Markets Hypothesis and Its Accounting Implications," *The Accounting Review* (January 1979), pp. 88-106.

McGhee, W., M.D. Shields, and J.G. Birnberg, "The Effects of Personality on a Subject's Information Processing," *The Accounting Review* (July 1978), pp. 681-97.

Meehl, P.E., *Clinical Versus Statistical Prediction: A Theoretical Analysis and Review of the Literature* (University of Minnesota Press, 1954).

_________, "A Comparison of Clinicians with Five Statistical Methods of Identifying Psychotic MMPI Profiles," *Journal of Counseling Psychology* (Summer 1959), pp. 102-09.

Merton, R.K., "On Sociological Theories of the Middle Range," in R.K. Merton, ed., *On Theoretical Sociology* (Free Press, 1967), pp. 39-72.

Messier, W.F., "An Analysis of Expert Judgment in the Materiality/Disclosure Decision," unpublished manuscript, University of Florida, 1979.

Miller, H., "Environmental Complexity and Financial Reports," *The Accounting Review* (January 1972), pp. 31-37.

Miller, L., and J.T. Lanzetta, "Choice Among Four-Alternative Gambles as a Function of Monetary Level of Play," *Psychological Reports* (December 1962), pp. 869-94.

Miller, M.J., "Interpersonal Understanding: Laboratory and Field Investigations," in L. Rappoport and D.A. Summers, eds., *Human Judgment and Social Interaction* (Holt, Rinehart and Winston, 1973), pp. 267-94.

Mock, T.J., T.L. Estrin, and M.A. Vasarhelyi, "Learning Patterns, Decision Approach, and Value of Information," *Journal of Accounting Research* (Spring 1972), pp. 129-53.

_________, and J.L. Turner, "The Effect of Changes in Internal Controls on Audit Programs," in T.H. Burns, ed., *Behavioral Experiments in Accounting II* (Ohio State University, 1979), pp. 277-302.

_________, *Internal Accounting Control Evaluation and Auditor Judgment,* Audit Research Monograph No. 3 (American Institute of Certified Public Accountants, forthcoming).

Mock, T.J., and M.A. Vasarhelyi, "A Synthesis of the Information Economics and Lens Models," *Journal of Accounting Research* (Autumn 1978), pp. 414-23.

Mood, A.M., "Macro-Analysis of the American Educational System," *Operations Research* (October 1969), pp. 770-84.

_________, "Partitioning Variance in Multiple Regression Analyses as a Tool for Developing

Learning Models," *American Educational Research Journal* (March 1971), pp. 191-202.

Moriarity, S., "Communicating Financial Information Through Multidimensional Graphics," *Journal of Accounting Research* (Spring 1979), pp. 205-24.

__________, and F.H. Barron, "Modeling the Materiality Judgments of Audit Partners," *Journal of Accounting Research* (Autumn 1976), pp. 320-41.

__________, "Judgment Based Definition of Materiality," *Selections from the Research Opportunities in Auditing Program,* Supplement to *Journal of Accounting Research* (1979), pp. 114-35.

__________, and W. Roach, "Chernoff Faces as an Aid to Analytical Review," unpublished manuscript, University of Oklahoma, 1977.

Morlock, H.C., and K.J. Hertz, "Effect of the Desirability of Outcomes on Decision Making," *Psychological Reports* (February 1964), pp. 11-17.

Morrison, H.W., "Testable Conditions for Triads of Paired Comparison Choices," *Psychometrika* (December 1963), pp. 369-90.

Moscovici, S., E. Lage, and M. Naffrechoux, "Conflict in Three-Person Groups: The Relationship Between Social Influence and Cognitive Style," in L. Rappoport and D. Summers, eds., *Human Judgment and Social Interaction* (Holt, Rinehart and Winston, 1973).

Moskowitz, H., "Effects of Problem Representation and Feedback on Rational Behavior in Allais and Morlat-Type Problems," *Decision Sciences* (April 1974), pp. 225-42.

__________, and J.G. Miller, "Man, Models of Man, or Mathematical Models for Managerial Decision Making?," *Proceedings of the Fourth Annual Meeting of the American Institute for Decision Sciences* (1972), pp. 849-56.

Mosteller, F., and P. Nogee, "An Experimental Measurement of Utility," *Journal of Political Economy* (October 1951), pp. 371-404.

Murphy, A.H., "Scalar and Vector Partitions of the Probability Score: Part I. Two-State Situation," *Journal of Applied Meterology* (1972), p. 273-82.

__________, "A New Vector Partition of the Probability Score," *Journal of Applied Meteorology* (1973), pp. 595-600.

__________, "A Sample Skill Score for Probability Forecasts," *Monthly Weather Review* (January 1974), pp. 48-55.

__________, and R.L. Winkler, "Scoring Rules in Probability Assessment and Evaluation," *Acta Psychologica* (December 1970), pp. 273-86.

__________, "Forecasters and Probability Forecasts: Some Current Problems," *Bulletin of the American Meteorological Society* (April 1971), pp. 239-47.

__________, "Subjective Probability Forecasting of Temperature: Some Experimental Results," *Proceedings of the Third Conference on Probability and Statistics in Atmospheric Science,* American Meteorological Society, Boulder, Colorado, June, 1973.

Myers, J.L., R.E. Reilly, and H.A. Taub, "Differential Cost, Gain, and Relative Frequency of Reward in a Sequential Choice Situation," *Journal of Experimental Psychology* (October 1961), pp. 357-60.

__________, M.M. Suydam and B. Gambino, "Contingent Gains and Losses in a Risk-Taking Situation," *Journal of Mathematical Psychology* (July 1965), pp. 363-70.

Nagel, E., "Assumptions in Economic Theory," *American Economic Review* (May 1963), pp. 211-19.

Naylor, J.C., and E.A. Schenck, "The Influence of Cue Redundancy Upon the Human Inference Process for Tasks of Varying Degrees of Predictability," *Organizational Behavior and Human Performance* (January 1968), pp. 47-61.

__________, and R.J. Wherry, "The Use of Simulated Stimuli and the 'JAN' Technique to Capture and Cluster the Policies of Raters," *Educational and Psychological Measurement* (Winter 1965), pp. 969-86.

Neter, J., and J.K. Loebbecke, *Behavior of Major Statistical Estimators in Sampling Accounting Populations,* Audit Research Monograph No. 2 (American Institute of Certified Public Accountants, 1975).

Newell, A., and H.A. Simon, *Human Problem Solving* (Prentice-Hall, 1972).

Newman, D.P., "Prospect Theory: Implications for Information Evaluation," unpublished manuscript, University of Texas, 1978. (Forthcoming in *Accounting, Organizations and Society.*)

Newman, J.R., "Differential Weighting in Multiattribute Utility Measurement: When It Should Not and When It Does Make a Difference," *Organizational Behavior and Human Performance* (December 1977), pp. 312-25.
Newton, J.R., "Judgment and Feedback in a Quasi-Clinical Situation," *Journal of Personality and Social Psychology* (April 1965), pp. 336-42.
Newton, L.K., "The Risk Factor in Materiality Decisions," *The Accounting Review* (January 1977), pp. 97-108.
Ng, D.S., "An Information Economics Analysis of Financial Reporting and External Auditing," *The Accounting Review* (October 1978), pp. 910-20.
Nickerson, R.S., and C.E. Feehrer, "Decision Making and Training: A Review of Theoretical and Empirical Studies of Decision Making and Their Implications for the Training of Decision Makers," *Naval Training and Equipment Center Technical Report No. 73-C-0128-1* (Orlando, Florida, 1975).
Nisbett, R.E., and E. Borgida, "Attribution and the Psychology of Prediction," *Journal of Personality and Social Psychology* (November 1975), pp. 932-43.
________, and L. Ross, *Human Inference: Strategies and Shortcomings of Social Judgment* (Prentice-Hall, 1980).
Nisbett, R.E. and T.D. Wilson, "Telling More Than We Can Know: Verbal Reports on Mental Processes," *Psychological Review* (May 1977), pp. 231-59.
Nunnally, J.C., *Psychometric Theory* (McGraw-Hill, 1967).
Nystedt, L., "Consensus Among Judges as a Function of Amount of Information," *Educational and Psychological Measurement* (Spring 1974), pp. 91-101.
________, and D. Magnusson, "Cue Relevance and Feedback in a Clinical Prediction Task," *Organizational Behavior and Human Performance* (February 1973), pp. 100-109.
________, "Integration of Information in a Clinical Judgment Task, An Empirical Comparison of Six Models," *Perceptual and Motor Skills* (April 1975), pp. 343-56.
________, and E. Aronowitsch, "Generalization of Ratings Based on Projective Tests," *Scandinavian Journal of Psychology* (First Quarter 1975), pp. 72-78.
Oliver, B.L., "A Study of Confidence Interval Financial Statements," *Journal of Accounting Research* (Spring 1972), pp. 154-66.
Oskamp, S., "Clinical Judgment From the MMPI: Simple or Complex?," *Journal of Clinical Psychology* (October 1967), pp. 411-15.
Pankoff, L.D., and H.V. Roberts, "Bayesian Synthesis of Clinical and Statistical Prediction," *Psychological Bulletin* (December 1968), pp. 762-73.
Papandreou, A.G., O.H. Sauerlander, O.H. Brownlee, L. Hurwicz and W. Franklin, "A Test of a Stochastic Theory of Choice," *University of California Publications in Economics* (1957), pp. 1-18.
Pastore, R.E., and C.J. Scheirer, "Signal Detection Theory: Considerations for General Application," *Psychological Bulletin* (November 1974), pp. 945-58.
Payne, J.W., "Alternative Approaches to Decision Making Under Risk: Moments Versus Risk Dimensions," *Psychological Bulletin* (December 1973), pp. 439-53.
________, "Task Complexity and Contingent Processing in Decision Making: An Information Search and Protocol Analysis," *Organizational Behavior and Human Performance* (August 1976), pp. 366-87.
________, and M.L. Braunstein, "Preferences Among Gambles With Equal Underlying Distributions," *Journal of Experimental Psychology* (January 1971), pp. 13-18.
________, and J.S. Carroll, "Exploring Pre-decisional Behavior: An Alternative Approach to Decision Research," *Organizational Behavior and Human Performance* (August 1978), p. 17-44.
Permut, S.E., "Cue-Utilization Patterns in Student-Faculty Evaluations," *The Journal of Psychology* (January 1973), pp. 41-48.
Person, H.B., "SCJM: A Stochastic Conjoint Measurement Diagnosis Program," *Journal of Marketing Research* (February 1977), pp. 98-99.
________, "Cross-Comparison of ANOVA and SCJM: A New Approach to Axiomatic Conjoint Measurement for Noisy Data," *Decision Sciences* (April 1979), pp. 177-94.

Peterson, C.R., and L.R. Beach, "Man as an Intuitive Statistician," *Psychological Bulletin* (January 1967), pp. 29-46.

_________, K.R. Hammond and D.A. Summers, "Optimal Responding in Multiple-Cue Probability Learning," *Journal of Experimental Psychology* (October 1965), pp. 270-76. (a)

_________, "Multiple Probability Learning with Shifting Weights of Cues," *American Journal of Psychology* (December 1965), pp. 660-63. (b)

Peterson, C.R., and A. Miller, "Mode, Median, and Mean as Optimal Strategies," *Journal of Experimental Psychology* (October 1964), pp. 363-67.

_________, R.J. Schneider, and A. Miller, "Sample Size and the Revision of Subjective Probabilities," *Journal of Experimental Psychology* (May 1965), pp. 522-27.

_________, Z.J. Ulehla, A.J. Miller, L.E. Bourne, and D.W. Stilson, "Internal Consistency of Subjective Probabilities," *Journal of Experimental Psychology* (November 1965), pp. 526-33.

Pettigrew, T.F., "The Measurement and Correlates of Category Width as a Cognitive Variable," *Journal of Personality* (1958), pp. 532-44.

Phillips, L.D., and W. Edwards, "Conservatism in a Simple Probability Inference Task," *Journal of Experimental Psychology* (September 1966), pp. 346-54.

_________, W.L. Hays, and W. Edwards, "Conservatism in Complex Probability Inference," *IEEE Transactions on Human Factors in Electronics* (1966), pp. 7-18.

Pitz, G.F., "Subjective Probability Distributions for Imperfectly Known Quantities," in L.W. Gregg, ed., *Knowledge and Cognition* (Wiley, 1974), pp. 29-41.

_________, and L. Downing, "Optimality of Decision Making as a Function of Payoffs and Instructions," *Journal of Experimental Psychology* (April 1967), pp. 549-55.

_________, and H. Reinhold, "Sequential Effects in the Revision of Subjective Probabilities," *Canadian Journal of Psychology* (October 1967), pp. 381-93.

Pruitt, D.G., and R.D. Hoge, "Strength of the Relationship Between the Value of an Event and its Subjective Probability as a Function of Method of Measurement," *Journal of Experimental Psychology* (May 1965), pp. 483-89.

Pugh, R.C., "The Partitioning of Criterion Score Variance Accounted for in Multiple Correlation," *American Educational Research Journal* (November 1968), pp. 639-46.

Quandt, R.E., "A Probabilistic Theory of Consumer Behavior," *Quarterly Journal of Economics* (November 1956), pp. 507-36.

Raiffa, H., "Risk, Ambiguity, and the Savage Axioms: Comment," *Quarterly Journal of Economics* (November 1961), pp. 690-94.

_________, *Decision Analysis* (Addison-Wesley, 1968).

Ramsey, F.P., "Truth and Probability," in R.B. Braithwaite, ed., *The Foundations of Mathematics and Other Logical Essays* (Harcourt Brace, 1931).

Rapoport, A., "Research Paradigms for Studying Dynamic Decision Behavior," in D. Wendt and C.A.J. Vlek, eds., *Utility, Probability, and Human Decision Making* (Reidel, 1975), pp. 349-69.

_________, and T.S. Wallsten, "Individual Decision Behavior," *Annual Review of Psychology* (1972), pp. 131-76.

Reckers, P.M.J., and M.E. Taylor, "Consistency in Auditors' Evaluations of Internal Accounting Controls," *Journal of Accounting, Auditing and Finance* (Fall 1979), pp. 42-55.

Reynolds, P.D., *A Primer in Theory Construction* (Bobbs-Merrill, 1971).

Revsine, L., "Change in Budget Pressure and Its Impact on Supervisor Behavior," *Journal of Accounting Research* (Autumn 1970), pp. 290-92. (a)

_________, "Data Expansion and Conceptual Structure," *The Accounting Review* (October 1970), pp. 704-11. (b)

Roberts, H.V., "Risk, Ambiguity, and the Savage Axioms: Comment," *Quarterly Journal of Economics* (May 1963), pp. 327-36.

Rokeach, M., *The Open and Closed Mind* (Basic Books, 1960).

Ronen, J., "Some Effects of Sequential Aggregation in Accounting on Decision Making," *Journal of Accounting Research* (Autumn 1971), pp. 307-32.

_________, and S. Sadan, "Smoothing Income Numbers: Objectives, Means, and Implications," unpublished manuscript, New York University, 1978.

Root, H.E., "Probability Statements in Weather Forecasting," *Journal of Applied Meteorology* (1962), pp. 163-67.

Rorer, L.G., "A Circuitous Route to Bootstrapping Selection Procedures," *Oregon Research Institute Research Bulletin,* Vol. 12, No. 9 (1973); revised version of "A Circuitous Route to Bootstrapping," in H.B. Haley, A.G. D'Costa, and A.M. Schafer, eds., *Conference on Personality Measurement in Medical Education* (Association of American Medical Colleges, 1971).

_________, P.J. Hoffman, H.R. Dickman, and P. Slovic, "Configural Judgments Revealed," *Proceedings of the 75th Annual Convention of the American Psychological Association* (1967), pp. 95-96.

Rose, A.M., "Conditions for Irrational Choices," *Social Research* (Summer 1963), pp. 143-56.

Rose, J., W. Beaver, S. Becker, and G. Sorter, "Toward An Empirical Measure of Materiality," *Empirical Research in Accounting: Selected Studies, 1970,* Supplement to *Journal of Accounting Research* (1970), pp. 138-56.

Rotwein, E., "On 'The Methodology of Positive Economics'," *Quarterly Journal of Economics* (November 1959), pp. 554-75.

Royden, H.L., P. Suppes, and K. Walsh, "A Model for the Experimental Measurement of the Utility of Gambling," *Behavioral Science* (January 1959), pp. 11-18.

Ruesch, J., "The Observer and the Observed: Human Communication Theory," in R.R. Grinaker, ed., *Toward a Unified Theory of Human Behavior* (Basic Books, 1967), pp. 36-54.

Ryans, D.G., "An Analysis and Comparison of Certain Techniques for Weighting Criterion Data," *Educational and Psychological Measurement* (Autumn 1954), pp. 449-57.

Salamon, G.L., W.C. Uecker, and R. Simmons, "Prediction Achievement and Simulated Decision Makers as an Extension of the Predictive Ability Criterion: Some Comments," *The Accounting Review* (July 1976), pp. 664-66.

Samuelson, P.A., "Probability, Utility, and the Independence Axiom," *Econometrica* (October 1952), pp. 670-78.

_________, "Discussion," *American Economic Review* (May 1963), pp. 231-36.

Sanders, F., "On Subjective Probability Forecasting," *Journal of Applied Meteorology* (April 1963), pp. 191-201.

_________, "Skill in Forecasting Daily Temperature and Precipitation: Some Experimental Results," *Bulletin of the American Meteorological Society* (November 1973), pp. 1171-79.

San Miguel, J.G., "Human Information Processing and its Relevance to Accounting: A Laboratory Study," *Accounting, Organizations and Society,* Vol. 1, No. 4 (1976), pp. 357-73.

Savage, L.J., *The Foundations of Statistics* (Wiley, 1954).

_________, "Elicitation of Personal Probabilities and Expectations," *Journal of the American Statistical Association* (December 1971), pp. 783-801.

Savich, R.S., "The Use of Accounting Information in Decision Making," *The Accounting Review* (July 1977), pp. 642-52.

Sawyer, J., "Measurement *and* Prediction, Clinical *and* Statistical," *Psychological Bulletin* (September 1966), pp. 178-200.

Schaefer, R.E., and K. Borcherding, "The Assessment of Subjective Probability Distributions: A Training Experiment," *Acta Psychologica* (April 1973), pp. 117-29.

Scheibe, J.E., "The Effect of Value on Statements of Expectancy Under Four Experimental Conditions," *Psychological Record* (April 1964), pp. 137-44.

Schmidt, F.L., "The Relative Efficiency of Regression and Simple Unit Predictor Weights in Applied Differential Psychology," *Educational and Psychological Measurement* (Autumn 1971), pp. 699-714.

_________, "The Reliability of Differences Between Linear Regression Weights in Applied Differential Psychology," *Educational and Psychological Measurement* (Winter 1972), pp. 879-86.

Schmitt, N., B.W. Coyle, and L. King, "Feedback and Task Predictability as Determinants of Performance in Multiple Cue Probability Learning Tasks," *Organizational Behavior and Human Performance* (August 1976), pp. 388-402.

_________, B.W. Coyle, and B.B. Saari, "Types of Task Information Feedback in Multiple-Cue

Probability Learning," *Organizational Behavior and Human Performance* (April 1977), pp. 316-28.

———, and R.L. Levine, "Statistical and Subjective Weights: Some Problems and Proposals," *Organizational Behavior and Human Performance* (October 1977), pp. 15-30.

Schönemann, P.H., T. Cafferty, and J. Rotton, "A Note on Additive Functional Measurement," *Psychological Review* (January 1973), pp. 85-87.

Schroder, H.M., M.J. Driver and S. Streufert, *Human Information Processing* (Holt, Rinehart and Winston, 1967).

Schultz, J.J., and S.G. Gustavson, "Actuaries' Perceptions of Variables Affecting the Independent Auditors' Legal Liability," *The Accounting Review* (July 1978), pp. 626-41.

———, and P.M.J. Reckers, "Choice-Shift Impact Between Individual and Group Audit Decisions," unpublished manuscript, University of Illinois, 1979.

Schum, D.A., "Inferences on the Basis of Conditionally Non-Independent Data," *Journal of Experimental Psychology* (September 1966), pp. 401-09.

Scodel, A., P. Ratoosh, and J.S. Minas, "Some Personality Correlates of Decision Making Under Conditions of Risk," *Behavioral Science* (January 1959), pp. 19-28.

Sharpe, W., "A Simplified Model for Portfolio Analysis," *Management Science* (January 1963), pp. 277-93.

———, "Capital Asset Prices: A Theory of Market Equilibrium Under Conditions of Risk," *Journal of Finance* (September 1964), pp. 425-42.

Shields, M.D., "On the Use of an Accounting Information System: A Behavioral Approach," unpublished manuscript, University of North Carolina, 1979.

———, J.G. Birnberg, and I.H. Frieze, "Information Seeking and Causal Attribution Utilization to Explain Performance in a Management Control Process," unpublished manuscript, University of North Carolina, 1979.

Shuford, E., and T.A. Brown, "Elicitation of Personal Probabilities and Their Assessment," *Instructional Science* (1975), pp. 137-88.

Simon, H.A., "A Behavioral Model of Rational Choice," *Quarterly Journal of Economics* (February 1955), pp. 99-118.

———, "Discussion," *American Economic Review* (May 1963), pp. 229-31.

———, H. Guetzkow, G. Kozmetsky, and G. Tyndall, *Centralization vs. Decentralization in Organizing the Controller's Department* (Controllership Foundation, 1954).

Slovic, P., "Value as a Determiner of Subjective Probability," *IEEE Transactions on Human Factors in Electronics* (March 1966), pp. 22-28.

———, "The Relative Influence of Probabilities and Payoffs Upon Perceived Risk of a Gamble," *Psychonomic Science* (October 1967), pp. 223-24.

———, "Analyzing the Expert Judge: A Descriptive Study of a Stockbroker's Decision Processes," *Journal of Applied Psychology* (August 1969), pp. 255-63.

———, B. Fischhoff, and S. Lichtenstein, "Behavioral Decision Theory," *Annual Review of Psychology* (1977), pp. 1-39.

———, D. Fleissner, and W.S. Bauman, "Analyzing the Use of Information in Investment Decision Making: A Methodological Proposal," *Journal of Business* (April 1972), pp. 283-301.

Slovic, P., and S. Lichtenstein, "Relative Importance of Probabilities and Payoffs in Risk Taking," *Journal of Experimental Psychology Monograph* (November 1968). (a)

———, "Importance of Variance Preferences in Gambling Decisions," *Journal of Experimental Psychology* (December 1968), pp. 646-54. (b)

———, "Comparison of Bayesian and Regression Approaches to the Study of Information Processing in Judgment," *Organizational Behavior and Human Performance* (November 1971), pp. 649-744.

———, and A. Tversky, "Who Accepts Savage's Axiom?," *Behavioral Science* (November 1974), pp. 368-73.

Smedslund, J., "The Concept of Correlation in Adults," *Scandinavian Journal of Psychology* (Third Quarter 1963), pp. 165-73.

———, "Note on Learning, Contingency, and Clinical Experience," *Scandinavian Journal of Psychology* (Fourth Quarter 1966), pp. 265-66.

Smith, E.R., and F.D. Miller, "Limits on Perception of Cognitive Processes: A Reply to Nisbett and Wilson," *Psychological Review* (July 1978), pp. 355-62.

Smith, V.L., "Measuring Nonmonetary Utilities in Uncertain Choices: The Ellsburg Urn," *Quarterly Journal of Economics* (May 1969), pp. 324-29.

Snapper, K.J., W. Edwards, and C.R. Peterson, "Information Purchase Strategies of Gamblers and Students," *Journal of Experimental Psychology* (November 1972), pp. 211-13.

Snowball, D., "Human Information Processing and Accounting Research," unpublished manuscript, University of Florida, 1976.

_________, and C. Brown, "Decision Making Involving Sequential Events: Some Effects of Disaggregated Data and Dispositions Toward Risk," *Decision Sciences* (October 1979), pp. 527-46.

Solomon, I., "Probability Assessment by Individual Auditors and Audit Teams: An Empirical Investigation," unpublished manuscript, University of Arizona, 1981.

_________, J.L. Krogstad, M.B. Romney, and L.A. Tomassini, "Auditors' Prior Probability Distributions for Account Balances," unpublished manuscript, University of Arizona, 1980. (Forthcoming in *Accounting, Organizations and Society*.)

_________, "On the Use of the Equivalent Prior Sample Elicitation Method by Auditors," unpublished manuscript, University of Arizona, 1980.

Spetzler, C.S. and C.-A.S. Staël von Holstein, "Probability Encoding in Decision Analysis," *Management Science* (November 1975), pp. 340-58.

Srinivasan, V., "A Theoretical Comparison of the Predictive Power of the Multiple Regression and Equal Weighting Procedures," unpublished manuscript, Stanford University, 1977.

Staël von Holstein, C.-A.S., "Measurement of Subjective Probability," *Acta Psychologica* (December 1970), pp. 146-59.

_________, "An Experiment in Probabilistic Weather Forecasting," *Journal of Applied Meteorology* (August 1971), pp. 635-45.

_________, "Probabilistic Forecasting: An Experiment Related to the Stock Market," *Organizational Behavior and Human Performance* (August 1972), pp. 139-58.

Stalnaker, J.M., "Weighting Questions in the Essay-Type Examination," *Journal of Educational Psychology* (October 1938), pp. 481-90.

Starr, J., and E.S. Katkin, "The Clinician as an Aberrant Actuary: Illusory Correlation and the Incomplete Sentences Blank," *Journal of Abnormal Psychology* (December 1969), pp. 670-75.

Steiger, J.H., and C.F. Gettys, "Best-Guess Errors in Multistage Inference," *Journal of Experimental Psychology* (January 1972), pp. 1-7.

Steinmann, D.O., "Transfer of Lens Model Training," *Organizational Behavior and Human Performance* (August 1974), pp. 1-16.

_________, "The Effects of Cognitive Feedback and Task Complexity in Multiple-Cue Probability Learning," *Organizational Behavior and Human Performance* (April 1976), pp. 168-79.

Stenson, H.H., "The Lens Model With Unknown Cue Structure," *Psychological Review* (May 1974), pp. 257-64.

Stewart, T.R., "Components of Correlation and Extensions of the Lens Model Equation," *Psychometrika* (March 1976), pp. 101-20.

Summers, D.A., "Rule Versus Cue Learning in Multiple Probability Tasks," *Proceedings of the 75th Annual Convention of the American Psychological Association* (1967), pp. 43-44.

_________, "Adaptation to Change in Multiple Probability Tasks," *American Journal of Psychology* (June 1969), pp. 235-40.

_________, and K.R. Hammond, "Inference Behavior in Multiple-Cue Tasks Involving Both Linear and Nonlinear Relations," *Journal of Experimental Psychology* (May 1966), pp. 751-57.

_________, and T.R. Stewart, "Regression Models of Foreign Policy Judgments," *Proceedings of the 76th Annual Convention of the American Psychological Association* (1968), pp. 195-96.

_________, J.D. Taliaferro, and D.J. Fletcher, "Subjective vs. Objective Description of Judgment Policy," *Psychonomic Science* (February 1970), pp. 249-50. (a)

———, "Judgment Policy and Interpersonal Learning," *Behavioral Science* (November 1970), pp. 514-21. (b)

Summers, S.A., "The Learning of Responses to Multiple Weighted Cues," *Journal of Experimental Psychology* (July 1962), pp. 29-34.

———, R.C. Summers, and V.T. Karkau, "Judgments Based on Different Functional Relationships Between Interacting Cues and a Criterion," *American Journal of Psychology* (June 1969), pp. 203-11.

Sundem, G.L., "A Game Theory Model of the Information Evaluator and the Decision Maker," *Journal of Accounting Research* (Spring 1979), pp. 243-61.

Suydam, M.M., "Effects of Cost and Gain Ratios, and Probability of Outcome on Ratings of Alternative Choices," *Journal of Mathematical Psychology* (February 1965), pp. 171-79.

Svenson, O., "Process Descriptions of Decision Making," *Organizational Behavior and Human Performance* (February 1979), pp. 86-112.

Swieringa, R.J., T.R. Dyckman, and R.E. Hoskin, "Empirical Evidence About the Effects of an Accounting Change on Information Processing," in T.H. Burns, eds., *Behavioral Experiments in Accounting II* (Ohio State University, 1979), pp. 225-59.

———, M. Gibbins, J. Lawson, and J. Sweeney, "Experiments in the Heuristics of Information Processing," *Studies on Human Information Processing in Accounting,* Supplement to *Journal of Accounting Research* (1976), pp. 159-87.

Taub, H.A., and J.L. Myers, "Differential Monetary Gains in a Two-Choice Situation," *Journal of Experimental Psychology* (February 1961), pp. 157-62.

Teigen, K.H., "Subjective Sampling Distributions and the Additivity of Estimates," *Scandinavian Journal of Psychology* (First Quarter 1974), pp. 50-55.

Todd, F.J., and K.R. Hammond, "Differential Feedback in Two Multiple-Cue Probability Learning Tasks," *Behavioral Science* (October 1965), pp. 429-35.

Trattner, M.H., "Comparison of Three Methods for Assembling Aptitude Test Batteries," *Personnel Psychology* (Autumn 1963), pp. 221-32.

Tucker, L.R., "A Suggested Alternative Formulation in the Developments by Hursch, Hammond, and Hursch, and by Hammond, Hursch, and Todd," *Psychological Review* (November 1964), pp. 528-30.

Tullock, G., "The Irrationality of Intransitivity," *Oxford Economic Papers* (November 1964), pp. 401-06.

Tversky, A., "A General Theory of Polynomial Conjoint Measurement," *Journal of Mathematical Psychology* (February 1967), pp. 1-20. (a)

———, "Additivity, Utility, and Subjective Probability," *Journal of Mathematical Psychology* (June 1967), pp. 175-202. (b)

———, "Utility Theory and Additivity Analysis of Risky Choices," *Journal of Experimental Psychology* (September 1967), pp. 27-36. (c)

———, "Intransitivity of Preferences," *Psychological Review* (January 1969), pp. 31-48.

———, "Elimination by Aspects: A Theory of Choice," *Psychological Review* (July 1972), pp. 281-99.

———, and D. Kahneman, "Belief in the Law of Small Numbers," *Psychological Bulletin* (August 1971), pp. 105-10.

———, "Availability: A Heuristic for Judging Frequency and Probability," *Cognitive Psychology* (September 1973), pp. 207-32.

———, "Judgment Under Uncertainty: Heuristics and Biases," *Science* (September 1974), pp. 1124-31.

Tversky, A., and A.A. Zivian, "A Computer Program for Additivity Analysis," *Behavioral Science* (January 1966), pp. 78-79.

Uecker, W.C., "A Behavioral Study of Information System Choice," *Journal of Accounting Research* (Spring 1978), pp. 169-89.

———, "The Effects of Knowledge of the User's Decision Model in Simplified Information Evaluation," *Journal of Accounting Research* (Spring 1980), pp. 191-213.

———, and W.R. Kinney, "Judgmental Evaluation of Sample Results: A Study of the Type and Severity of Errors Made by Practicing CPAs," *Accounting, Organizations and Society,* Vol. 2, No. 3 (1977), pp. 269-75.

Uhl, C., "Learning of Interval Concepts. I. Effects of Differences in Stimulus Weights," *Journal of Experimental Psychology* (September 1963), pp. 264-73.

Ullrich, J.R., and D.E. Cummins, "PCJM: A Program for Conjoint Measurement Analysis of Polynomial Composition Rules," *Behavioral Science* (May 1973), pp. 226-27.

_________, and J.R. Painter, "A Conjoint Measurement Analysis of Human Judgment," *Organizational Behavior and Human Performance* (August 1974), pp. 50-61.

Van der Meer, H.C., "Decision Making: The Influence of Probability Preference, Variance Preference and Expected Value on Strategy in Gambling," *Acta Psychologica* (1963), pp. 231-59.

Vasarhelyi, M.A., "Man-Machine Planning Systems: A Cognitive Style Examination of Interactive Decision Making," *Journal of Accounting Research* (Spring 1977), pp. 138-53.

von Neumann, J., and D. Morgenstern, *Theory of Games and Economic Behavior* (Princeton University Press, 1947).

Wagenaar, W.A., "Appreciation of Conditional Probabilities in Binary Sequences," *Acta Psychologica* (December 1970), pp. 348-56.

_________, "Generation of Random Sequences by Human Subjects: A Critical Survey of Literature," *Psychological Bulletin* (January 1972), pp. 65-72.

Wainer, H., "Estimating Coefficients in Linear Models: It Don't Make No Nevermind," *Psychological Bulletin* (March 1976), pp. 213-17.

_________, and D. Thissen, "Three Steps Toward Robust Regression," *Psychometrika* (March 1976), pp. 9-34.

Wallsten, T.S., "Subjects' Probability Estimates and Subjectively Expected Utility Theory: Their Relationship and Some Limitations," Psychometric Laboratory Technical Report No. 85, University of North Carolina, 1970.

_________, "Subjectively Expected Utility Theory and Subjects' Probability Estimates: Use of Measurement-Free Techniques," *Journal of Experimental Psychology* (April 1971), pp. 31-40.

Ward, B.H., "An Investigation of Auditors' Perceptions of the Severity of Error in Audited Financial Statements," *Symposium on Auditing Research* (University of Illinois, 1974), pp. 23-39.

_________, "An Investigation of the Materiality Construct in Auditing," *Journal of Accounting Research* (Spring 1976), pp. 138-52.

Ward, J.H., "Comments on 'The Paramorphic Representation of Clinical Judgment'," *Psychological Bulletin* (January 1962), pp. 74-76.

_________, "Hierarchical Grouping to Optimize an Objective Function," *Journal of the American Statistical Association* (March 1963), pp. 236-44.

_________, "Partitioning of Variance and Contribution or Importance of a Variable: A Visit to a Graduate Seminar," *American Educational Research Journal* (May 1969), pp. 467-74.

_________, and K. Davis, "Teaching a Digital Computer to Assist in Making Decisions," in L.J. Cronbach and G.C. Gleser, *Psychological Tests and Personnel Decisions* (University of Illinois, 1965), pp. 268-72.

_________, and M.E. Hook, "Application of an Hierarchical Grouping Procedure to a Problem of Grouping Profiles," *Educational and Psychological Measurement* (Spring 1963), pp. 69-81.

Ward, W.C., and H.M. Jenkins, "The Display of Information and the Judgment of Contingency," *Canadian Journal of Psychology* (September 1965), pp. 231-41.

Watts, R., "Corporate Financial Statements: Product of the Market and Political Processes," *Australian Journal of Management* (April 1977), pp. 53-75.

_________, and J.L. Zimmerman, "Towards a Positive Theory of the Determination of Accounting Standards," *The Accounting Review* (January 1978), pp. 112-34.

Webb, E.J., "Individual and Organizational Forces Influencing the Interpretation of Indicators," Research Paper P-488 (Institute for Defense Analyses, 1969).

Weber, R., "Auditor Decision Making on Overall System Reliability: Accuracy, Consensus, and the Usefulness of a Simulated Decision Aid," *Journal of Accounting Research* (Autumn 1978), pp. 368-88.

Weick, K.E., "Middle Range Theories of Social Systems," *Behavioral Science* (November 1974), pp. 357-67.

Weinstein, A.A., "Individual Preference Intransitivity," *Southern Economic Journal* (January 1968), pp. 335-43.

Werts, C.E., "The Partitioning of Variance in School Effects Studies," *American Educational Research Journal* (May 1968), pp. 311-18.

__________, "The Partitioning of Variance in School Effects Studies: A Reconsideration," *American Educational Research Journal* (January 1970), pp. 127-32.

Wesman, A.G., and G.K. Bennett, "Multiple Regression vs. Simple Addition of Scores in Prediction of College Grades," *Educational and Psychological Measurement* (Summer 1959), pp. 243-46.

West, P.V., "The Significance of Weighted Scores," *Journal of Educational Psychology* (April 1924), pp. 302-08.

Wherry, R.J., "A New Formula for Predicting the Shrinkage of the Multiple Correlation Coefficient," *Annals of Mathematical Statistics* (November 1931), pp. 440-57.

__________, "Underprediction from Overfitting: 45 Years of Shrinkage," *Personnel Psychology* (Spring 1975), pp. 1-18.

__________, and J.C. Naylor, "Comparison of Two Approaches — JAN and PROF — for Capturing Rater Strategies," *Educational and Psychological Measurement* (Summer 1966), pp. 267-86.

Wiggins, N., and P.J. Hoffman, "Three Models of Clinical Judgment," *Journal of Abnormal Psychology* (February 1968), pp. 70-77.

__________, and E.S. Kohen, "Man Versus Model of Man Revisited: The Forecasting of Graduate School Success," *Journal of Personality and Social Psychology* (July 1971), pp. 100-06.

Wilks, S.S., "Weighting Systems for Linear Functions of Correlated Variables When There Is No Dependent Variable," *Psychometrika* (March 1938), pp. 23-40.

Williams, J.D., S.D. Harlow, A. Lindem, and D.A. Gab, "A Judgment Analysis Program for Clustering Similar Judgmental Systems," *Educational and Psychological Measurement* (Spring 1970), pp. 171-73.

Wilson, D.A., "A Note on 'Environmental Complexity and Financial Reports'," *The Accounting Review* (July 1973), pp. 586-88.

Winkler, R.L., "The Assessment of Prior Distributions in Bayesian Analysis," *Journal of the American Statistical Association* (September 1967), pp. 776-800. (a)

__________, "The Quantification of Judgment: Some Methodological Suggestions," *Journal of the American Statistical Association* (December 1967), pp. 1105-20. (b)

__________, "The Consensus of Subjective Probability Distributions," *Management Science* (October 1968), pp. 61-75.

__________, "Probabilistic Prediction: Some Experimental Results," *Journal of the American Statistical Association* (December 1971), pp. 675-85.

__________, *Introduction to Bayesian Inference and Decision* (Holt, Rinehart and Winston, 1972).

__________, and L.L. Cummings, "On the Choice of a Consensus Distribution in Bayesian Analysis," *Organizational Behavior and Human Performance* (February 1972), pp. 63-76.

__________, and A.H. Murphy, " 'Good' Probability Assessors," *Journal of Applied Meteorology* (October 1968), pp. 751-58. (a)

__________, "Evaluation of Subjective Precipitation Probability Forecasts," *Proceedings of the First National Conference on Statistical Meteorology* (American Meteorological Society, 1968), pp. 148-57. (b)

__________, "Experiments in the Laboratory and the Real World," *Organizational Behavior and Human Performance* (October 1973), pp. 252-70.

Worell, L., "The Effect of Goal Value Upon Expectancy," *Journal of Abnormal and Social Psychology* (July 1956), pp. 48-53.

Wright, W.F., "Financial Information Processing Models: An Empirical Study," *The Accounting Review* (July 1977), pp. 676-89. (a)

__________, "Self-Insight Into the Cognitive Processing of Financial Information," *Accounting, Organizations and Society,* Vol. 2, No. 4 (1977), pp. 323-31. (b)

__________, "Analysis and Comparison of the Lens and Subjective Probability Information Processing Paradigms,'' unpublished manuscript, Stanford University, 1978. (a) (Forthcoming in *Accounting,Organizations and Society*.)

__________, ''An Empirical Study of Subjective Probability Revision in a Financial Context,'' unpublished manuscript, Stanford University, 1978. (b)

__________, ''Properties of Judgment Models in a Financial Setting,'' *Organizational Behavior and Human Performance* (February 1979), pp. 73-85. (a)

__________, ''Accuracy of Subjective Probabilities for a Financial Variable,'' in T.H. Burns, ed., *Behavioral Experiments in Accounting II* (Ohio State University, 1979), pp. 1-13. (b)

__________, ''Cognitive Information Processing Biases: Implications for Producers and Users of Financial Information,'' unpublished manuscript, Stanford University, 1979. (c) (Forthcoming in *Decision Sciences*.)

__________, ''Empirical Comparison of Subjective Probability Encoding Methods,'' unpublished manuscript, Stanford University, 1980.

Yerkes, R.M., ed., ''Psychological Examining in the United States Army,'' *Memoirs of the National Academy of Sciences*, Vol. 15, 1921.

Yntema, D.B., and W.S. Torgerson, ''Man-Computer Cooperation in Decisions Requiring Common Sense,'' *IRE Transactions on Human Factors in Electronics* (1961), pp. 20-26.

Youssef, I., and C.R. Peterson, ''Intuitive Cascaded Inferences,'' *Organizational Behavior and Human Performance* (December 1973), pp. 349-58.

Zelditch, M., and W.M. Evan, ''Simulated Bureaucracies: A Methodological Analysis,'' in H. Guetzkow, ed., *Simulation in Social Science: Readings* (Prentice-Hall, 1962), pp. 48-60.

Zimmer, I., ''A Lens Study of the Prediction of Corporate Failure by Bank Loan Officers,'' *Journal of Accounting Research* (Autumn 1980), pp. 629-36.

__________, ''A Comparison of the Prediction Accuracy of Loan Officers and Their Linear-Additive Models,'' *Organizational Behavior and Human Performance* (February 1981), pp. 69-74.

Zimmerman, J.L., ''Positive Research in Accounting,'' in R.D. Nair and T.H. Williams, eds., *Perspectives on Research: Proceedings of the 1980 Beyer Consortium* (University of Wisconsin, 1980), pp. 107-28.